THE NOVELS OF FLAUBERT

THE NOVELS OF

FLAUBERT

A STUDY OF THEMES
AND TECHNIQUES

VICTOR BROMBERT

PRINCETON, NEW JERSEY
PRINCETON UNIVERSITY PRESS
1966

Library of Congress Card No: 66-25416

Second Printing, with corrections, 1968

NOTE: A section of chapter 4 appeared in *Flaubert: A Collection of Critical Essays*, ed. Raymond Giraud, Prentice-Hall, 1964. The substance of chapter 3 appeared in *The Hudson Review*, Vol. XIX, No. 1 Spring 1966, under the title "An Epic of Immobility," and chapter 6 in *PMLA*, June 1966. For permission to reprint in a revised and enlarged form I wish to thank the respective editors.

My analysis of all texts has been based upon a reading of the originals. Translations are my own. I have, however, consulted with profit Eleanor Marx Aveling's translation of *Madame Bovary* and Robert Baldick's translation of *Trois Contes*.

Printed in the United States of America
by Princeton University Press
Princeton, New Jersey

To Beth

To Mary and Mike Keeley

Foreword

This study of Flaubert's novels grew out of a series of
Christian Gauss Seminars in Criticism which the late R. P.
Blackmur invited me to give at Princeton University in
the spring of 1964. I am deeply grateful for this challeng-
ing opportunity.

I am further indebted to the stimulating participation of
friends and colleagues present at the seminar: E. B. O.
Borgerhoff, Edward T. Cone, Claudio Guillén, Armand
Hoog, Joseph Frank, Léon-François Hoffmann, Edmund
Keeley, Jean Rousset, Edward D. Sullivan, Karl D. Uitti.
It is difficult to wish for a more acute and more demanding
audience. Discussions about Flaubert and the art of the
novel continued in R. P. Blackmur's living room, and were
often prolonged late into the night at Lowrie House. To
these spring days in Princeton I owe warm memories and
many intellectual pleasures.

But I must not forget that many years earlier, during
another memorable spring, Jean Boorsch kindled the desire
to explore Flaubert's work. His elegant lucidity was, and
still is, an inspiration.

My largest single debt is, however, to one who is too
modest to know how much I owe her.

V. B.

Yale University

Contents

THE NOVELS OF FLAUBERT

... avec la rage que l'on a pour les choses impossibles

Flaubert, *Novembre*

Flaubert's Literary Temperament

"Realist" or *"Troubadour"*?

Literary history has rendered Flaubert a poor service by indiscriminately linking his name with theories of realism and by presenting him to posterity as the founder, chief practitioner and high priest of a literary school. Flaubert himself might have applauded Paul Valéry's famous quip: one cannot indeed get drunk, nor even quench one's thirst, by staring at labels on bottles. In fact, Flaubert was prodigiously irritated by the very word and concept "realism." "Do not speak to me of realism . . .," he writes to Maupassant. "I am fed up with it. What empty nonsense." In another outburst, to Paul Alexis, he refers to the theories of realism as childish poppycock, "puérilités." A letter to George Sand is still more explicit: "I abhor what has been called realism, although they make me out to be one of its high priests."[1]

These are no doubt the biting reactions of one who did not wish to be associated with any group, least of all with writers for whom literature was not the loftiest of exercises, and whom he suspected of cultivating sensationalism. The hermit of Croisset, whose artistic and financial aloofness allowed him to view the Parisian world of journalism and of sales promotions with zestful aversion, disliked and successfully shunned all cliques and *cénacles*. Polemical

---

[1] "Ne me parlez pas du réalisme, du naturalisme ou de l'expérimental! J'en suis gorgé. Quelles vides inepties!" (Flaubert, *Corresp.*, VIII, 317); *ibid.*, VIII, 368; VII, 285. Complete citations for all notes may be found in the Bibliography.

[3]

manifestoes, whether in the form of articles or prefaces, seemed to him in about as bad taste as an actor's direct address to his public. "Why spoil one's works with prefaces and slander oneself with sign-boards?"[2] But even worse than histrionics was narrow dogma. The theoretical pronouncements of a Zola, for whose growing talent he otherwise showed much esteem, appalled him; he complained of his "narrow ideas."[3] For it was not merely the polemical noise made by the Realists and the Naturalists which he found unpalatable. It was a perspective on art with which Flaubert, out of the depths of his artistic convictions, could not possibly sympathize. If he held one consistent belief, it was indeed the priority of Art over life. Not only was he shocked by what he considered the materialism of Zola and his friends ("ce matérialisme m'indigne"), and willing to be concerned with "reality" only insofar as it was a springboard ("tremplin") to something else, but he emphatically proclaimed—and this much earlier, at a time he was planning L'Éducation sentimentale—that reality (or "vérité," as he put it) was not for him the primary condition of art.[4]

There is another, more ambiguous reason behind Flaubert's violent reactions to the word and concept of realism: his hatred of reality. The very subject of Madame Bovary, and of so many of his works, is of course drawn from everyday life. But Flaubert never ceased proclaiming his abhorrence for these subjects, his nauseous contempt for the "ignoble reality" he forced himself to depict, partly out of self-imposed therapy to cure himself of his chronic idealism, partly also out of a strange and almost morbid fascination. "J'ai la vie ordinaire en exécration," he wrote to Laurent Pichat, the director of the Revue de Paris, which was publishing Madame Bovary. His comments to Mme Roger des Genettes are even more characteristic: "People think I am in love with reality, though I hate it; for it is

2 Flaubert, Corresp., VIII, 368.
3 Flaubert, Lettres inédites à Tourgueneff, p. 118.
4 Flaubert, Corresp., VII, 359; V, 92–93.

out of hatred of realism that I undertook the writing of this novel."[5] Hatred of reality and hatred of realism are to be sure far from one and the same thing; yet Flaubert curiously equates them. Thus, while repeatedly inflicting similar subjects or projects on himself (among his unrealized projects were novels to be entitled *Sous Napoléon III* and *Les Bourgeois au XIXe siècle*), Flaubert continued with passion his denunciations of "realistic" subjects and chronically indulged in escapist reveries. The fact is that Flaubert always considered that the highest and purest pleasure of literature is its power to liberate those who practice it from the contingencies of life. Art was for him quite literally an escape. Its superiority over life was precisely its ability to transcend the conditions of living. For hatred of reality was in the case of Flaubert intimately bound up with an inherent pessimism; and pessimism in turn was one of the prime conditions of his ceaseless quest for ideal forms. "Life seems tolerable to me only if one juggles it away," he confided to George Sand.[6] The cure, according to him, was either to read a book or, better still, to write one.

Flaubert's paradoxical and almost obsessive love-hate relationship with "reality" is no doubt the chief reason for the prevailing misunderstanding concerning his "realism." The lengths to which he went in documenting himself— whether on the site of Carthage, the menu of a Parisian restaurant, the means of locomotion to Fontainebleau, or the most suitable location for the geological studies of his two pathetic clerks Bouvard and Pécuchet—only confirmed the widely held belief that he was above all a painstaking recorder and observer, a "descripteur" as Jules Barbey d'Aurevilly nastily put it, whose descriptions were a substitute for invention and imagination.[7] Not everyone, of course, has been taken in by the cliché. The "realism" of Flaubert has convinced neither Sartre, who resents what

[5] Flaubert, *Corresp.*, IV, 125, 134.
[6] Flaubert, *Corresp.*, VII, 38.
[7] Barbey d'Aurevilly, "Gustave Flaubert," in *Le Roman contemporain*, p. 99.

he calls Flaubert's "masked lyricism," nor the Marxist realist critic Georg Lukács, who denounces his distortions of reality, his decadentism and hopeless subjectivity.[8] Even if one turns to the strictly scholarly criteria of a René Wellek, according to whom realism is distinguished by its underlying didactic, moralistic and reformist intent,[9] it is obvious that Flaubert does not conform to this pattern. Harry Levin quite justly observed that the realistic alternative was always for him *malgré lui.*[10] Only in the broadest historical and cultural sense, as understood by a Levin or an Auerbach, can one indeed speak of the realism of Flaubert. For realism, definable by the author's socio-politico-economic consciousness of his own time, is marked also, in each case, by a quite peculiar and unique "transposition of reality into romance."[11] The reader and the critic may thus find labels of little use. The real task, as for all writers, still lies ahead: that of defining, as far as is possible, the particular talent or genius of an individual artist by looking closely at the texture and structure of his work, by discussing in detail the meaningful interrelation of themes and techniques. Ultimately, it is the novelist's unique temperament and vision that determine and characterize his work.

Henry James, in the wake of the critic Émile Faguet, somewhat naïvely believed that Flaubert was formed intellectually "of two quite distinct compartments"; that the divisions of his literary production, falling either into the category of the "real" or the "romantic," were as clearly marked as the sections on the back of a scarab.[12] A quick glance at Flaubert's correspondence totally invalidates such a partition. At the very time Flaubert was composing *Madame Bovary*, he confessed to Louise Colet that he was "devoured" by a need for metamorphoses, that he felt a

[8] See Jean-Paul Sartre, *Critique de la raison dialectique*, p. 94; and Georg Lukács, *The Historical Novel*, pp. 184–199.
[9] Wellek, "Realism in Literary Scholarship," in *Concepts of Criticism*, p. 253.
[10] Levin, *The Gates of Horn*, p. 285.
[11] Levin, *The Gates of Horn*, p. 55.
[12] James, "Gustave Flaubert," in *Notes on Novelists*, p. 74.

permanent desire to transmute reality. "I would like to write all that I see, not as it is, but transfigured." This alchemical urge is a permanent trait. He diagnoses his metaphoric obsession almost as a disease. "Je suis né lyrique."[13] Above all he knows that he is a poet in search of the magical, incantatory secrets of language. His struggle against words, his love of a sonorous, flexible, muscular prose, his attempt to create plastic effects that would transform words and rhythms into palpable forms, are those of an artist haunted by a compelling sense of vocation. But equally significant is his unflinching allegiance to his own Romantic heredity. His earliest works, such as *Smarh* or the autobiographical *Mémoires d'un fou* and *Novembre*, are clearly influenced by his exposure to the most extreme manifestations of Romanticism. Of this exposure Flaubert never felt ashamed. On the contrary, much like Baudelaire, he never ceased proclaiming his fidelity. "Je suis un vieux romantique enragé," he writes to Sainte-Beuve after completing *Madame Bovary*.[14] And, many years later, to his friend Turgenev, he still describes himself as a "vieux romantique," a "vieux fossile du romantisme."[15]

Troubadour was another word he cherished: he liked to think of himself as one of the last of an almost extinct race. The *troubadour*'s propensity to dream went hand in hand, in his mind, with an immense capacity for enthusiasm. Flaubert loved nothing better than to admire. He happily records his "cris d'admiration" while reading Tolstoy.[16] And his admiration, for which he had a robust capacity, went instinctively to grandiose schemes and grandiose visions. His idols were Homer, Shakespeare, Hugo. Intellectual and artistic longings, sumptuous in their extravagance, filled his mind. The subjects that haunted him were exotic, violent, stretching human passions to the very

13 Flaubert, *Corresp.*, III, 320, 375.
14 Flaubert, "Lettres inédites de Flaubert à Sainte-Beuve," presented by B. F. Bart, *Revue d'Histoire littéraire de la France*, July-September 1964, pp. 427–435.
15 Flaubert, *Lettres inédites à Tourgueneff*, pp. 6, 29.
16 Flaubert, *Lettres inédites à Tourgueneff*, p. 218.

boundaries of excess. The multiple forms of ugliness seemed to him, in true Romantic fashion, more exciting than monotonous beauty; in them he found *"moral dense-ness."*[17] The recurrent themes of his work are estrangement and the madness of desire. Love itself, he felt, was only one of the forms of madness: "une folie, une malédiction, une maladie. . . ."[18] For twenty-five years or more he lived with the obsessive image of a hermit-hero assailed by infernal temptations of the flesh and of the spirit. *La Tentation de saint Antoine*, of which there are three versions extending from 1849 to 1874, is perhaps more than any other work representative of Flaubert's permanent taste for what he himself called the lyric and metaphysical "gueulade," a term almost impossible to translate, but which binds together, in Flaubertian usage, love of extravagance, rhetorical fireworks and unquenchable longings for the inaccessible. "Let's put on the buskin," he writes after finishing the story of Emma Bovary, and "entamons les grandes gueulades."[19] The *grandes gueulades* were most conspicuous in the "Oriental" novels: *Salammbô, La Tentation, Hérodias*—but they are present everywhere: in the exotic dreams of Emma, in Frédéric Moreau's ceaseless nostalgia for the impossible, in Pécuchet's and Bouvard's formidable appetite for knowledge.

"Let's be disheveled," he cries out as he begins work on *Hérodias*[20]—and the advice seems at first glance incompatible with Flaubert's repeated call for artistic impassibility. But here precisely rests the crux of the paradox: the Flaubertian "serenity" is in the service not of impersonal mimesis, but of a higher ability to cultivate dreams. Impersonality, Flaubert explained to Louise Colet, is a sign of vitality and strength. Great works of art are, he felt, both "serene" and "incomprehensible." In other words, their supreme function is to transcend reality and to set sail for lost worlds—*"faire rêver."*[21] Did he not, even as an adoles-

---

[17] Flaubert, *Corresp.*, III, 269.   [18] Flaubert, *Corresp.*, V. 59.
[19] Flaubert, *Corresp.*, IV, 199.   [20] Flaubert, *Corresp.*, VII, 369.
[21] Flaubert, *Corresp.*, III, 322.

cent, choose to believe that he was "born elsewhere"?[22]

Thus, side by side with the so-called realist whom he most often evinces, there appears another, perhaps more authentic Flaubert endowed with an irreducible faith in the evocative witchcraft of imagination or its substitute, memory. If Flaubert the realist exists, so does Flaubert the escapist, and even Flaubert the mystic. Ecstatic reveries are for him a permanent temptation. For it is not merely love of formal or abstract beauty that makes him challenge the "scientific" approach to truth. Writers such as Sainte-Beuve and Hippolyte Taine—and he admired both—did not, he felt, take Art and Beauty (he capitalized both words) sufficiently into account.[23] As for Zola and his friends, they had altogether lost sight of the chief aim of art: "viser au beau"—perhaps an impossible task, but the only truly worthwhile one.[24] Flaubert took his own expression "culte de l'Art" quite seriously and quite literally. It was for him an almost religious vocation to "maintain the soul in a high region"[25] through a redeeming cult of Art which glorified the divorce between artistic creation and life.

Flaubert's quest, as he himself saw it, was after a higher, more general truth. And in that quest the servile reproduction of surfaces or the concern for everyday triviality was not, he knew, the most effective method. Nor could one speak of historic progression. "Henry Monnier is no more true than Racine," he tersely concludes in a letter to his young disciple Guy de Maupassant.[26] It is in this light that one must read Pellerin's vituperative remarks against reality in *L'Éducation sentimentale*. But behind Flaubert's esthetic revulsions and preferences, behind his lofty reaffirmations of the universalizing vision of all true art, one can also detect undeniable mystic velleities. One of his most symptomatic literary projects is that of *La Spirale*, which was to describe the state of permanent somnambulism of

22 Flaubert, *Corresp.*, I, 76.
23 Flaubert, *Lettres inédites à Tourgueneff*, p. 15.
24 Flaubert, *Corresp.*, VII, 351.
25 Flaubert, *Corresp.*, VII, 10.   26 Flaubert, *Corresp.*, VII, 377.

a hallucinated madman. Flaubert wanted to write an "exalting book" which would prove that happiness could be attained only in the realm of imagination or through a superior madness. The very image of the spiral suggested no doubt a liberation from the self and an ascent toward infinity. E. W. Fischer, in his suggestive analysis of the project, quite appropriately refers to Flaubert's profound interest in Balzac's *Louis Lambert* and to his enthusiastic reading of Baudelaire's *Paradis artificiels*.[27] The fact is that longings for ecstasies and aspirations toward the sublime are traits common to Emma Bovary, Salammbô, Frédéric Moreau, Félicité, and even the grotesque couple Bouvard and Pécuchet. As for hallucinations, they concerned Flaubert doubly: as a literary subject, but to begin with as a terrifying personal experience. His own crises, the result of the nervous disorder which followed the seizure of 1844, made this a very personal, but also a very uncomfortable subject. That is perhaps the reason why *La Spirale* remained unwritten.

Finally, the mystic nature of art is more than once set forth in explicit terms. In one of the letters to his mistress Louise Colet he affirms that above life and above happiness there exists something "blue," something "incandescent"—a luminosity whose distant rays still have a life-giving virtue. The splendor of genius, Flaubert feels, is but the "pale reflection of the hidden word."[28] The religious connotations of "word" point not only to the unseen regions of divine truth and inspiration (the Logos of the Scriptures, the divine Wisdom made manifest in the world of men), but more specifically to the sacred nature of literary language. Elsewhere, the mystic vocabulary is even more pointed. In the face of the "world's" hostility to art ("l'humanité nous hait"), Flaubert calls for a true communion of the martyr-saints. "Aimons-nous donc *en l'Art* comme les mys-

---

[27] Flaubert, "La Spirale," ed. E. W. Fischer, *La Table Ronde*, April 1958, pp. 96–98, followed by E. W. Fischer's extremely interesting discussion of this project, *ibid.*, pp. 99–124.
[28] Flaubert, *Corresp.*, III, 389.

tiques s'aiment *en Dieu*. . . ."[29] No wonder François Mauriac has accused Flaubert of idolatry, of having substituted art for God.[30]

Exoticism and the Orgiastic Dreams

It is clear that Flaubert's literary temperament does not correspond neatly to the stereotyped image of the impassive master craftsman, the cold-blooded manipulator of words and rhythms, the impartial verbal photographer of bourgeois life. An explosive exuberance, a permanent obsession with the formless and even the monstrous, underlie and determine the patterns of his imagination. He himself observed that what came "naturally" to him was "the extraordinary, the fantastic, the metaphysical and mythological roar." To Louis Bouilhet he confessed that what attracted him most was "exuberance."[31] This taste for profusion, this fascination with elemental forces, repeatedly impelled him to stretch his fantasy to the very limits of the human. Horror, cruelty, dreams of destruction are permanent features of his most revealing texts, and are most often related to exotic yearnings. For exoticism, with Flaubert, marks the temptation of violence and disorder. In the very same letter to Ernest Chevalier which describes his juvenile longing for "blue seas" and "balmy shores," he also refers to his "immense and insatiable desires."[32] These paroxystic yearnings are of course partly a form of escapism, a solipsistic symptom; they suggest a weary sense of the burden of self. Thus, over twenty-five years after the letter to Chevalier, Flaubert confides to George Sand that he dreams of having been a boatman on the Nile, a soldier in the Punic Wars, a pirate or a monk, perhaps even an Eastern emperor.[33] The poetry of history, so acutely felt by Flaubert, clearly manifests a desire for exotic estrangement in space as well as in time. "I carry

[29] Flaubert, *Corresp.*, III, 294.
[30] Mauriac, *Trois grands hommes devant Dieu*, p. 86.
[31] Flaubert, *Corresp.*, III, 156; IV, 76.
[32] Flaubert, *Corresp.*, I, 76.   [33] Flaubert, *Corresp.*, V, 240.

the love of antiquity in my very guts."[34] Flaubert was not the only one of his generation for whom the study of antiquity became a pretext for poetic reverie.

But above all, the exotic motifs which occur repeatedly in Flaubert's works—even when the setting is a village in Normandy—point to recurrent dreams of sexual frenzy and uninhibited orgies. Long before his actual trip to what was then called the "Orient," the adolescent yearned for regions of camels and desert wells, where women "twist and writhe" in the wildest embraces.[35] Travel, or vague notions of distant voyages, were indeed to remain associated, throughout his life and throughout his work, with erotic images. Emma, about to elope with Rodolphe, sees herself in a distant city with splendid domes, in a forest of lemon trees, surrounded by the sound of guitars and the murmur of fountains. Similarly Frédéric Moreau, in *L'Éducation sentimentale*, imagines that, together with Marie Arnoux, he rides on dromedaries or elephants through distant and prestigious lands. Often the exotic lyricism of the senses becomes more turbulent, and corresponds to imaginary orgies of violence and the most exacerbated sadism. In *Salammbô* and in the three versions of *La Tentation de saint Antoine*, Flaubert surrenders with immense relish to the goriest and most detailed visions of tortures, rapes, disembowelments, diseases and mutilations.

Flaubert's evocations of carnality and of orgiastic violence are, however, closely bound up with an unmedicable sense of sadness and futility. He himself was convinced that he carried in him the "melancholy of barbarian races," that he had inherited their *tedium vitae*.[36] He relates his immense and unquenchable desires to an "ennui atroce."[37] The continuous yawns he describes in a letter to his friend Chevalier are not unlike the monstrous yawns of Baudelaire's Ennui, ready to swallow the world or reduce it to a wasteland. This combination of sexuality and

---

[34] Flaubert, *Corresp.*, I, 171.   [35] Flaubert, *Corresp.*, I, 101.
[36] Flaubert, *Corresp.*, I, 217–218.
[37] Flaubert, *Corresp.*, I, 76.

sterility, this fusion of transcending desires and an almost metaphysical despondency finds its perfect symbolic figuration in the image of the prostitute for which the Romantics in general, but Flaubert in particular, felt an irresistible fascination. "Luxure, amertume, néant des rapports humains . . . "—Flaubert was obsessed by a very personal, almost unconscious association between lascivious and ascetic images. The silhouettes of streetwalkers in the rain are revealingly linked in his mind with fleeting evocations of monastic figures which "tickle the soul in some remote and ascetic corners."[38] Marie, the prostitute-heroine of *Novembre*, embodies simultaneously an immense appetite for life and a desperate awareness of the tragedy of human desire precisely because desire, by its very nature, implies a yearning for that which is beyond reach, for that which cannot be possessed. It is in this sense that Marie—the prostitute—can paradoxically speak of her essential virginity.

The Monastic Urge

It is only half in jest that Flaubert, in a letter to his friend Turgenev, refers to the ascetic, monklike disposition which alone made it possible to undertake as mad a task as the writing of *Bouvard et Pécuchet*.[39] In fact, the monastic image is one of the basic images in Flaubert's works. It applies to some of his most revealing characters (the hermit Saint Antoine, Bouvard and Pécuchet who end up like monks at their copying desks), as well as to his own writer-vocation. Whether this anchoretic tendency is, as Sartre asseverates, the result of a father-fixation is perhaps a point best left for psychoanalysts to debate. Flaubert himself was rather more concerned with the sacerdotal dignity of the artist, which, he was convinced, only a detachment from the world and the self-inflicted discipline and austerity of work would allow him to attain. In depth, however, the image corresponds to more than a

[38] Flaubert, *Corresp.*, III, 216.
[39] Flaubert, *Lettres inédites à Tourgueneff*, p. 200.

desire to join the ranks in a sublime martyrology of Art. The image of the monk and of the cell (and was not the study in Croisset a kind of cell?) is related to a chronic propensity to exotic and metaphysical reveries: the sense of confinement and the sense of the infinite are with him part of a dialectical scheme.

The word and concept of monk comes up insistently in his correspondence. "I live like a Carthusian friar," he writes to his mistress Louise Colet, who quite naturally showed little understanding for such eremitic tastes. "I have always locked myself up in a severe loneliness."[40] He himself was aware of the apparent contradiction between his orgiastic dreams and his almost conventual existence. "Debauches attract me, yet I live like a monk."[41] Elsewhere, he finds that he has the basic temperament of a monk precisely to the extent that he feels contempt for the follies of the human race and the vulgar satisfactions of social life. He views systematic reclusion as a "soufflet donné à la race humaine."[42] This somewhat adolescent attitude finds echoes throughout his life. To Mme Leroyer de Chantepie he proudly explains that he is what is called a "bear" ("Je vis comme un moine"); and to George Sand, many years later, pointing to the small role women played in his daily existence, he explains that he has in him "un fond d'ecclésiastique."[43]

To be sure, Flaubert experienced from childhood on an unquestionable fondness for privacy and solitude. A well-heated room, books and leisure seemed to the young Gustave the most desirable conditions for happiness. He later recalled the feeling of elation ("allégement") he felt whenever he was alone. He even wondered retrospectively at the joy he found in boyhood solitude.[44] With time, he came to understand that his claustrophilia was deeply involved with his need to protect his inner life: self-confine-

[40] Flaubert, *Corresp.*, I, 292, 320.
[41] Flaubert, *Corresp.*, II, 411-412.
[42] Flaubert, *Corresp.*, III, 397.
[43] Flaubert, *Corresp.*, IV, 247; VI, 442.
[44] Flaubert, *Corresp.*, I, 159; III, 396.

ment became the means of salvaging his dreams and his memories. Thus precisely for his most moving remembrances he liked to use metaphors of pious immurement and entombment, and evoked the "royal chamber" he has walled in.[45] To be sure, there was also a measure of pride, even a bit of a pose, in the advice he gave Louise Colet and himself to lock their doors and climb to the upper level of their ivory towers.[46] Yet the image of the locked door or the closed window cannot be attributed solely to Romantic fashion or clichés. These images, together with the monastic similes and metaphors, convey a double ascetic tendency: contempt for the "world," since the ideal is unattainable here and now ("il faut boucher toutes nos fenêtres et allumer des lustres"); but also a positive and almost maniacal devotion to the austere joys of study and work. The adolescent advises his friend Alfred Le Poittevin to "break with the outside world." The thirty-year-old writer confesses: "I love my work with the passionate and perverted love of an ascetic who loves the hairshirt which scratches his belly." At the age of fifty-five, he still proudly notes that his entire existence has been "laborious and austere."[47]

What is involved, however, is far more than an artist's pride and allegiance to his vocation. Solitude, for Flaubert, is the most potent mental aphrodisiac. True debaucheries of the imagination take shape within the confines of his self-imposed claustration. These are the "mental harems" ("harems dans la tête") he evokes in a letter of 1853.[48] A characteristic polarity is here to be noted. The monastic tendencies point to an inherent idealism; but they also imply carnal and intemperate velleities. This almost mystic voluptuousness is one of the keys to Flaubert's temperament and to his work. A very revealing passage in *Par les Champs et par les grèves* sums up this sensuous asceticism which Flaubert sees as a "superior epicureanism,"

[45] Flaubert, *Corresp.*, IV, 352.   [46] Flaubert, *Corresp.*, III, 54.
[47] Flaubert, *Corresp.*, IV, 148; I, 192; II, 394; VII, 245.
[48] Flaubert, *Corresp.*, III, 352.

a "refined gluttony."[49] His characters will repeatedly experience a strange blend of religiosity and voluptuousness. When Hilarion accuses Saint Antoine of a corrupt chastity, of a hypocritical indulgence in solitude, of a vicarious surrender to the most lascivious desires, it is almost as though Flaubert were denouncing a familiar perversity.

This extravagant asceticism must no doubt be related to his fundamental fear of life, and even—as the study of *La Tentation de saint Antoine* will reveal—to a chronic abhorrence of the flesh which recalls certain forms of Christian pessimism. Referring precisely to his monastic urges, Flaubert explained to Louise Colet (a curious statement indeed to make to one's mistress!) that there comes a moment when one needs to chastise oneself and to "hate one's flesh."[50] Thus it is the view of the old convent wall which provokes Emma Bovary's meditation on the "inadequacy" of life and the instantaneous decay of all things, and which confirms her in an almost metaphysical "dégoût" of all the pleasures of this world.

Pessimism, Pathology and Salvation through Art

Early in his life, Flaubert looked forward to a literary career almost as to a vocation of gloom. "If ever I take an active part in the world," he writes his friend Ernest Chevalier, "it will be as a thinker and *demoralizer*. I will only state the truth; but it will be horrible, cruel and naked."[51] At eighteen years, this could be attributed to an adolescent pose. But at twenty-five, similar remarks begin to betray a congenital disposition. "I was strangely born with little faith in happiness," he confides to Maxime Du Camp. "I have had, in my childhood, a total foreboding of life."[52] In fact, one is repeatedly struck by how *old* Flaubert sounds in his letters, though he is still in his youth or middle years. At times this precocious aging is

49 Flaubert, *Par les Champs et par les grèves*, p. 156.
50 Flaubert, *Corresp.*, III, 77.
51 Flaubert, *Corresp.*, I, 41. Italics mine.
52 Flaubert, *Corresp.*, I, 201.

explicitly stated, almost as a matter of sad pride. "I feel as though I were forty years old, or fifty, or sixty,"[53] he writes in 1852, when he has barely turned thirty! And it is not so much a question of explicit statement as of a prevailing tone. Ideas of death, decomposition and nothingness literally haunt him. The view of a child almost automatically conjures up images of senility and decrepitude. "The contemplation of a naked woman makes me think of her skeleton." Despair, he writes elsewhere, is his "normal state," a despair which is indubitably provoked by the permanent obsession with physical corruption and death. "Comme le néant nous envahit!" Flaubert is painfully aware, almost to a pathological degree, not only of death around him, but of the "necropolis" he carries within himself.[54] Flaubert's pessimism, comparable in intensity to that of a Pascal, a Leopardi or a Schopenhauer, constitutes in itself a powerful poetic inspiration. In its extreme form, however, it can lead to dreams of self-annihilation. Edmond de Goncourt recalls an intimate conversation during which Flaubert, without any attempt to strike a pose, expressed his total discouragement and his yearning for nonbeing.[55]

This permanent confrontation with undoing, Flaubert himself attributes to early exposure to the dissection room of the Hôtel-Dieu hospital in Rouen, where his father was chief surgeon. From the garden where he and his sister played, he could see the corpses on the table; he recalls that the flies attracted by the smell of decay were the same flies that hovered around the flowers and his own face. It is most likely that Flaubert exaggerates; what might have been a rare occurrence he transformed retrospectively into a habitual scene. But this macabre sensitivity is nonetheless an important feature of his temperament, and it is bound up with a medical inquisitiveness. "How many dramas I have set in the Morgue. . . . "[56] He

53 Flaubert, *Corresp.*, II, 364.
54 Flaubert, *Corresp.*, I, 221; III, 145; IV, 215; V, 247.
55 Goncourt, *Journal*, X, 99.   56 Flaubert, *Corresp.*, III, 270.

refers, of course, largely to unwritten works; yet his imagination repeatedly flirts with death motifs. His novels are filled with funereal images and with scenes of disease and destruction. Throughout his life he remained fascinated by medical lore, especially by descriptions of horrible maladies and infirmities. Even his interest in the marquis de Sade can be interpreted as a mixed fascination and revulsion for the realities of the flesh. According to the Goncourt brothers, he viewed the divine marquis as the incarnation of the *Antiphysis*.[57] It is "nature" itself which Flaubert the pessimist abhorred.

His is, however, not a negative, but a resilient pessimism. Flaubert finds inspiration in his very obsession with decay. He views the artist as an alchemist who creates beauty out of the very impurity of life. An extended metaphor, in one of his letters, develops, with somewhat dubious taste, the image of the latrine as artistic fertilizer. He advises Louise Colet not to neglect the "décompositions fécondantes," and states that the writer is a sewage cleaner ("vidangeur") and a gardener who extracts delectations from putrefaction.[58] Ultimately, the form-giving powers of the artificer were to distill crude reality, transmuting it into ideal essences rising from the creative spirit toward the absolute and the ideal. No passage suggests more clearly Flaubert's notion of an artistic redemption. None brings into sharper focus the relation between his "realism" and his mystical yearnings. The dilemma of Flaubert is to be found largely in this apparent contradiction. The demoralizer who wants to reveal the naked truth also believes that beauty, like a star, "cannot be detached from heaven."[59]

The Correspondance *and the Writer's Vocation*

The footnotes to this chapter clearly indicate the importance of the *Correspondance*. Some readers—André Gide among them—were almost willing to trade the novels

[57] Goncourt, *Journal*, IV, 178.
[58] Flaubert, *Corresp.*, III, 407.   [59] Flaubert, *Corresp.*, I, 285.

for the letters. In their intrinsic human and artistic interest, these letters provide indeed invaluable insights into Flaubert's literary temperament. Often preserving the rough vigor of the spoken sentence, they are at the same time familiar and yet elevated in spirit. They reflect a double Flaubertian requirement: friendships and intellectual contacts, but also the satisfactions of distance, independence and the dignity of isolation. Writing from his study in Croisset, Flaubert could at the same time feel very close and even intimate, and still protect his inner resources and the loftiness of his artistic dreams. There is much to commend these letters on the strictly human level: spontaneity, movement, a grouchy vivaciousness, pride and tenderness, and always a touching allegiance to his friends and to his ideals. But there is also far more.

The *Correspondance* is in fact one of the most moving documents concerning the anguish and problems of the literary artist. Flaubert is no doubt the first writer in France to display a systematic concern for the possibilities, technical difficulties, challenges and criteria of the novel as a dignified and important artistic genre. This was a new concern. Although the French novel was to assume in the nineteenth century an unprecedented prestige, usurping, as it were, the traditional preëminence of dramatic and epic poetry, although it was to become the artistic medium through which some of the greatest artists were to attempt their summas, fictional literature was on the whole not taken seriously. Boileau had refused outright to consider it as an honorable genre; and all through the eighteenth century, despite Marivaux, Lesage, Rousseau, Laclos and Diderot, the novel was still relegated, even by its very practitioners, to the level of a minor and generally frivolous literary activity. Even Stendhal, who at first, like so many writers of his time, dreamed of glory as a playwright, never submitted his efforts as novelist to any close scrutiny. His most acute observations are to be found in marginal comments; they are sporadic and almost accidental.

Flaubert was convinced that the novel had its laws which remained to be discovered, propounded and applied. He was convinced that steady meditation on the subject had endowed him with a clearer vision than anyone had ever had of the potentialities and of the limits of fiction. Repeatedly he expresses pride in his "esthetic progress": "I know how it should be done" ("Je sais comment il faut faire").[60] The verb *savoir* must here be taken with its full etymological implications. Flaubert staunchly believes that literature can (and should) be as precise as a science; that it does not copy truth, but that it becomes truth through disciplined invention. While composing *Madame Bovary*, he searches for what he calls "a rigorous method" ("méthode impitoyable") which would enable him to transcend his private emotions and bestow upon his art "the precision of the physical sciences."[61] One may smile at some of the more naïve claims in favor of a scientifically precise prose. The fact remains that Flaubert submits to an exacting apprenticeship, and that he imposes on himself a truly ascetic discipline. Did he not compare himself once to a pianist who practices with lead weights on every finger?[62] As for his capacity to observe himself in the very act of composing, it reveals an almost clinical self-control.

It is Flaubert's originality, in discussing the novelist's *métier*, to have centered his attention on the complex question of style. Flaubert knew that it was not the subject that mattered; that a novel, just as a poem, has its inner validity and logic, and that only the appropriate use of language and rhythm can provide the texture and the structure which alone make up literary beauty. Hence the corollary that "there do not exist in literature any beautiful artistic subjects"[63] and the paradoxical belief that

[60] Flaubert, *Corresp.*, II, 343.
[61] Flaubert, *Corresp.*, III, 291; IV, 164.
[62] Flaubert, *Corresp.*, III, 3.   [63] Flaubert, *Corresp.*, III, 249.

"beautiful" subjects could even be dangerous since they did not force upon the artist the realization that beauty in art can come only from his own *artistic* efforts. Style is thus more than a technical device or virtuosity; it represents the very vision of the novelist. Flaubert here anticipates some of the most cherished modern notions: ". . . le style étant à lui tout seul une manière absolue de voir les choses. . . . "[64] The statement is bold and far-reaching.

Style, for Flaubert, obviously involved far more than vocabulary and syntax. It was the very spirit of a work. "Style is as much *beneath* the words as *in* the words," he explains to his friend Ernest Feydeau.[65] Yet even at the level of sheer rhythm and musicality, Flaubert had dreams of a new kind of prose, as subtly cadenced as the best poetry, as precise as the language of sciences—a style which would "penetrate the idea like a stiletto. . . ."[66] Elsewhere he speaks of the musical justness of the well-chosen word. Verbal denseness was for him as vital a matter as the correct conception ("*tout dépend du plan*"); he ceaselessly reminded himself of the importance of finding the irreplaceable expression as well as of the necessity of a clear design, a "dessin prémédité."[67] This concern for balance, gradations, modulations and delicate nuances appears most clearly in his subtle observations on the art of the dialogue. He himself, particularly in *Madame Bovary* and *L'Éducation sentimentale*, was to display his mastery of the *demi-teinte* and of the various forms of indirect discourse.

The most resounding esthetic pronouncements in the *Correspondance* are unquestionably those concerning the cult of impersonality. They are also the pronouncements that have lent themselves to the greatest amount of misunderstanding and distortion. Statements concerning the God-like stance of the artist ("The author in his work must be like God in the universe, present everywhere and

[64] Flaubert, *Corresp.*, II, 346.   [65] Flaubert, *Corresp.*, IV, 315.
[66] Flaubert, *Corresp.*, II, 399.
[67] Flaubert, *Corresp.*, II, 362; IV, 239–240.

visible nowhere")[68] have created the image of a writer whose aim was an Olympian impassibility, a proud, almost cruel indifference to human woes. The truth is altogether different. Flaubert's dogma of impassibility is not a sign of arrogance but of artistic integrity and humility. He was convinced that the poet must not sing about himself, that he should never be the subject of his lyric expansiveness. The truly great artist's "superhuman impersonality" is part of his attempt to lose himself in a reality larger than the self. His life matters not at all. "Arrière la guenille."[69] The artist thus must almost attempt to convince posterity that he did not exist!

Other reasons impelled Flaubert to suspect subjectivity. He was convinced that private passions hampered, limited and falsified artistic creativity. Personal "emotions" were too close to nature, too unrefined, too despotic. The flesh is perishable, he admonished Louise Colet; sensitivity does not make the artist, just as passion does not make poetry.[70] But there is also a serious dose of pessimism in this lesson of impersonality. The God-like perspective may well be a form of escapism. It implies a human condition for which there exists no adequate human compassion. It is no doubt such a tragic discrepancy between the absurdity of man's suffering and the futility of any subjective justification which Flaubert had in mind when he aspired to describe events "from the point of view of a superior joke" ("blague supérieure")—that is, "as God sees them."[71]

Impersonality did moreover not at all exclude understanding and compassion. In a letter to George Sand in which he denied himself as novelist the right to hate or love his characters, he proclaimed unequivocally the importance of *sympathie*, for that was another matter: "One never has enough of that."[72] Elsewhere he explains

[68] Flaubert, *Corresp.*, III, 61–62.
[69] Flaubert, *Corresp.*, IV, 326.
[70] Flaubert, *Corresp.*, II, 460–461.
[71] Flaubert, *Corresp.*, III, 37.   [72] Flaubert, *Corresp.*, V, 397.

that impersonality and objectivity, while preventing the writer from egotistically imposing himself, allow him—and this is the height of art—to absorb the outside reality and make it part of his own substance. "Our heart must serve only to feel those of others."[73] During one of his more exalted moments while writing *Madame Bovary*—the *Correspondance* is also a novelist's logbook—he experiences ecstatic delights at "no longer being himself," at circulating freely in his own creation: " . . . J'étais les chevaux, les feuilles, le vent. . . . "[74] Curiously, the dogma of impassibility is here clearly related to Flaubert's fervid pantheistic longings.

We are thus far indeed from the artificer's supposed coldness and arrogance. Flaubert's ideal of impersonality is really one of a majestic and quasi-universal mimesis: the artist's mind must, he feels, be as vast as the ocean, and the shores should be well out of sight. Flaubert's yearning for total experiences, his passionate dreams of the inaccessible are at the very heart of his theoretical pronouncements. It is significant that in the passage describing the artist's joy in assuming all the dimensions of his creation, as well as in many others of theoretical importance, Flaubert makes use of spatial imagery.

The writer's vocation as it appears in the *Correspondance*, even in passages more specifically concerned with problems of technique, thus repeatedly implies a passionate transcending of reality. It also implies an experience in enthusiasm and anguish. Nowhere does Flaubert's inveterate idealism appear more spontaneously than in the many pages inspired by love for artistic beauty. The mystique of Art is for him a true religion whose values he places far above the vulgar notion of human happiness. For it, all sacrifices are justified. No passages in the *Correspondance* are more moving than those which evoke the joys of his own creation, joys which brought him into an almost "holy" communion with the artists he

[73] Flaubert, *Corresp.*, III, 383-384.
[74] Flaubert, *Corresp.*, III, 405.

revered. He reminded Louise Colet to love her art with an "exclusive, ardent and devoted love."[75] But he also knew that it was a bitter joy, that inspiration was at the same time happy and funereal, that it was like a defiant challenge to life itself.

Flaubert's notion of the artist as tragic hero is closely bound up with the Romantic belief that the artist's vocation is a divine curse or malady. Thus, in moments of despondency—and they are not rare—Flaubert refers to his love of literature as a "vérole constitutionnelle"—a hereditary syphilis—and complains of his incurable sore. At times, the writer's anguish leads to almost suicidal yearnings. The "supplice" of struggling with words exhausts him, and he thinks of death with real longing ("Je pense à la mort avec avidité").[76] But the worst tortures are perhaps those of impotence. Flaubert is painfully aware of sterility and silence. Despite his stubborn struggle with words and forms, he is at bottom convinced of the impossibility of language. "I suffer from the infirmity of having been born with a special language whose key I alone possess."[77] The drama of incommunicability, which was destined to become one of the major literary themes of our time, is at the heart of Flaubert's creation.

Yet, despite a latent despondency, Flaubert never loses faith in the sacerdotal function of the artist. Not only does he call for the reign of the mandarins, but in the face of universal corruption and vulgarity he can see salvation nowhere else but in the "small group of minds" who, through the ages, succeed in passing on the torch. This notion of a spiritual aristocracy implies, of course, an experience in *communion*. "Let us love each other *in Art* as the mystics love each other *in God* . . . ," he exhorts Louise Colet, who probably had other ideas of love.[78] The divinity of art as well as the notion of an atemporal collegium of artists once again points to Flaubert's mystic

[75] Flaubert, *Corresp.*, I, 232.
[76] Flaubert, *Corresp.*, IV, 215–216, 230–231, 348.
[77] Flaubert, *Corresp.*, I, 239.   [78] Flaubert, *Corresp.*, III, 294.

velleities. Sartre somewhat unfairly accuses him of seeking such abstract solidarity with the chosen few only to hide from himself, and juggle away, his own unalienable liberty.[79] But it is unquestionably true that Flaubert viewed his artistic life as a *destiny,* that he conceived of the artist's vocation much as Baudelaire does in "Les Phares":

C'est un cri répété par mille sentinelles

Adolescent Exercises: Themes and Prefigurations

No survey of Flaubert's literary temperament as it reveals itself outside of his major novels can afford to neglect the rich mine of early texts, many of which have been collected under the title *Oeuvres de jeunesse inédites.* Flaubert was indeed very proud of his good sense in not publishing his juvenilia. The precocious perfectionist was in no hurry to appear in print. Yet the impressive list of writings which preceded *Madame Bovary* contains many pages of extreme importance in casting light on the artistic development of Flaubert, many also of high intrinsic merit. The literary production of Flaubert between 1831, when the ten-year-old boy dedicated to his mother a short résumé of the reign of Louis XIII, and 1845, when he completed the first version of *L'Éducation sentimentale*, indicates indeed a highly active and fecund literary imagination. Over forty titles, including several scenarios, make up the complete list. Only two of these—*Bibliomanie* and *Une Leçon d'histoire naturelle, genre commis*—were published by Flaubert himself.[80]

The variety of genres, techniques and themes is equally impressive. Philosophical tales, historical studies, supernatural stories, projects for plays, autobiographical works,

---

[79] Sartre, "Introduction," in *Écrits Intimes de Baudelaire,* pp. CXVI-CXVIII.

[80] Jean Bruneau, in an exhaustive study of these early texts—some of which go back to Flaubert's school years—has recently provided their patient inventory, classified them, and discussed in full detail Flaubert's technical apprenticeship. *Les Débuts littéraires de Gustave Flaubert 1831–1845* is thus an invaluable contribution to our understanding of the writer's formative years.

satirical and mystic writings: Flaubert seems to reënact and sum up in his own juvenile activities all the literary fashions of Romanticism. *Un Parfum à sentir* (1836), a story of misery and suicide, insists on the theme of fatality and poses a moral and social problem; *La Peste à Florence* (1836) deals with fraternal jealousy and hatred; *Rage et impuissance* (1836) is a horror tale describing the burial alive of a country doctor; *Rêve d'enfer* (1837) is about divine creation, the fallen angel, and the eternal problem of evil; *Quidquid volueris* (1837) is a story of a monstrous man-ape who commits rape and murder; *Une Leçon d'histoire naturelle, genre commis* (1837) is a "physiologie" in the taste of the period, and one of the early sources of *Bouvard et Pécuchet; Passion et vertu* (1837) tells the tragedy of an adulteress who kills her husband and her children; *Agonies* (1838) is an attempt at a spiritual autobiography; *La Danse des morts* (1838) is a mystic-philosophic venture whose protagonist is Satan; *Mémoires d'un fou* (1838–1839), a more "personal" work, marks a clear evolution toward autobiography; *Smarh* (1839) is a half dramatic, half narrative "diablerie" (the figure of the Devil fascinated the young reader of Goethe and Byron); finally *Novembre* (1842), a pungent and poetic account of adolescent dreams, with the central figure of the prostitute Marie, is already a small summa of Flaubertian obsessions and themes. Even in literary terms it is quite a remarkable text. In many ways, these early exercises reflect the influence of writers Flaubert read and admired (Rousseau, Scott, Sade, Quinet, Nodier, Dumas, Balzac, Hugo—in addition, of course, to Goethe and Byron), but they also permit him to exorcise their very influence. Above all, he experiments with techniques and slowly acquires the novelist's skills: the art of a dialogue more subtly integrated in the narration; the art of dramatic and thematic descriptions; the even more difficult art of controlling and modulating the author's own voice.

As for the *Éducation sentimentale* of 1845, which

Flaubert also refused to publish, and which has scarcely anything in common with the great novel of 1869 bearing the same title, it belongs to the transitional period during which Flaubert's vocation as novelist takes a more definite form. It represents indeed the author's first attempt at full-length fiction, and in its development, structural denseness and contrapuntal effects it already constitutes a significant achievement. Reacting against a univalent transcription of private experiences and motifs, Flaubert here creates the more complex situation of two characters who dramatically and thematically embody his own dreams, tensions, disillusionments and new insights. Henry and Jules, two childhood friends with many common hopes and aspirations, turn out to have totally dissimilar destinies. Henry, a Balzacian *arriviste*, is set on conquering the capital. His first "success" is an adulterous affair which brings him all the way to America. But he soon experiences the death of love, and in losing his illusions he also loses his ideals. The world of money and power will be his domain. Jules, on the other hand, grows in spiritual and intellectual stature. Suffering develops his inner life and he devotes himself to the intense pursuit of Art and Beauty.

The defects of this first novel are evident: the style is at times declamatory; the metaphors are often strained; there are needless pages of violence and adolescent prurience. The texture of the book becomes particularly thin after Henry's departure for New York with his mistress; clearly Flaubert was not at his best developing a story of consummated love. Also the satiric nature of the dialogue, as well as the frequent moralizing, tends to be tedious. But the *Éducation sentimentale* of 1845 marks an unquestionable technical development. Not only does Flaubert deal here with larger units and a larger scope (even the chapters become longer), but he has learned to utilize dialogue in a new manner, and he no longer needs to rely so much on his own interventions, explanations and analyses.[81] More important still, the 1845 version of the *Éducation sentimentale* integrates into one single poetic structure a number of central themes: the priority of dreams, the erosion of ideals, the tragedy of the imagination, the unalterable conflict between life and creation, the death of love, the divorce between thought and matter. Even pantheistic meditations are fused into the substance of the novel. Jules experiences for Nature an "intelligence aimante."[82] His philosophical musings display a characteristic fascination with the monstrous harmonies of creation as he toys with dreams of infinity.

If one looks closely at Flaubert's earliest works, those conceived between his fifteenth and his twenty-first years, one is struck indeed by a continuity of motifs and a recurrence of themes which help to understand the underlying unity of novels as dissimilar in appearance as *Madame Bovary*, *Salammbô* and *Bouvard et Pécuchet*. The patterns of his early fictional imagination, though influenced no doubt by current literary fashions, closely parallel the more permanent traits revealed in his correspondence: a taste for violent eroticism, an obsession with death, a metaphysical pessimism, an almost pathological attraction to decay and to the notion of nothingness, a blasphemous posture in the face of the very conditions of existence.

The erotic strains may at first seem like typical manifestations of adolescent ardor. Thus, in *Un Parfum à sentir*, the young Gustave composes dithyrambic lines in praise of women's breasts ("Oh! la gorge d'une femme . . ."). His voluptuous daydreams further find their habitual expression in exotic longings. M. Ohmlin, in *Rage et impuissance*, evokes the sensuous climate of the "Orient," and in particular the "brown, olive-colored skin of Asiatic women." Similarly, in the largely autobiographic *Mémoires*

[81] Jean Bruneau puts it well: "The dialogues of the first *Éducation sentimentale* possess already one of the essential characteristics of the great novels: they have a satirical tendency" (*Les Débuts littéraires de Gustave Flaubert*, p. 431).
[82] Flaubert, *Oeuvres de jeunesse inédites*, III, 164.

d'un fou, the seventeen-year-old author yearns for "quelque femme à la peau brune, au regard ardent. . . . " But sensuality and exoticism soon take on a more somber note. The very same passage leads to a vision of Roman debauches and to collective wallowings in orgies. Neronic images thus haunt Flaubert long before *La Tentation de saint Antoine*, *Salammbô* and *Hérodias*. In *La Danse des morts*, written the same year, Nero appears as Satan's "favorite son"; he calls for unheard-of suffering and convulsions, for a blending of carnal savagery and amorous delight. These sadistic tones are even more pronounced in *Quidquid volueris*. The monstrous Djalioh rapes lovely Adèle in a scene of almost hysterical brutality: claws penetrate the flesh, blood flows on the girl's alabaster breasts, "ferocious cries" are heard, and the entire passage ends in the victim's and in the assaulter's gory death. The direct influence of the marquis de Sade, whom Flaubert discovered during that very period, appears quite unambiguously in the private notebook which has been posthumously entitled *Souvenirs, notes et pensées intimes*. One extremely revealing passage, quoted by Jean Bruneau, is given over to a sketchy pastiche of a typical "Sadian" scene: sobbing women, all dressed in black, are brought into a room equipped with sofas, while fierce claws are heard scratching at the doors.[83]

Flaubert was of course familiar with Pétrus Borel's charnel house literature. The *Contes immoraux* had appeared only a few years earlier, and there are many indications in Flaubert's juvenile texts that he had read the "Lycanthrope" 's macabre tales with care. The profanation of a tomb, the exhuming of a corpse, the nauseous details of decomposition told in *Agonies*, present analogies with stories such as *Champavert*. As for the bacchic death struggle of the two drunkards in *Ivre et mort*, it brings to mind the savage duel between two Negroes in Borel's story *Jaquez Barraou*. But the macabre and pathological are

[83] The passage, which appeared in the *Catalogue de la succession Franklin-Grout*, is quoted in Bruneau, *Les Débuts littéraires de Gustave Flaubert*, p. 277.

not merely literary fads for Flaubert; they correspond to deeply rooted needs and obsessions. Suggestions of disease, as well as the use of "clinical" images, are recurrent features in his mature work. This "medical" imagination appears, for instance, in *Quidquid volueris*. The young girl's pale complexion is attributed to a "congenital gastritis," and Djalioh's passion is revealed through physical symptoms such as fever, cracked lips and skin eruptions. As for the description of his blinking eyelids and of the wild movement of his eyeballs, it might have come straight out of a medical textbook on his father's shelves.

What is specifically Flaubertian, and not merely to be attributed to literary influences, is the steady preoccupation with the erosive power of life and with death as a physical reality. The sight of an alluring décolleté is spoiled for Flaubert by thoughts of the malignant disease which lurks behind that breast. Death itself is repeatedly presented in its most unsavory reality. The fly-ridden corpse which, in *Un Parfum à sentir*, is exposed in the morgue, is characteristic of the kind of images that besiege Flaubert's imagination. More specifically, however, he seems to be haunted by the recurrent nightmare of being buried alive. Not only is the fantastic and sepulchral tale *Rage et impuissance* concerned with a horrible death-in-the-tomb, but even the personally revealing *Novembre* more than once expresses the specific horror of such a death. "But I would not have wanted to be buried; the coffin terrifies me," explains the narrator. And the very last sentence of this key text refers once again to his fear of being buried alive: "Il recommanda qu'on l'ouvrît de peur d'être enterré vif. . . . " Lethal confinement, needless to add, will be a central theme, in one form or another, in several of his major works.

The staring into the face of "reality" remains a somewhat theoretical and derivative exercise in these adolescent works. But it is an already characteristically Flaubertian stare, composed of terror but also of exaltation. Reality thus proposes to Flaubert its own transcendence.

Hence the recurring flirtation with the notion of nothing-ness—on the one hand, the narrator of *Novembre,* who explains that he was "born with a desire to die"; on the other, the Satan of *Smarh* proclaiming the beatitude of nonbeing. The distance between gloom and ecstasy is peculiarly short with Flaubert. A curious bond—affective and dialectical—exists between his brand of pessimism and his pantheistic reveries. The perspective is often both blasphemous and transcendental. The voice from the underground, in *Rêve d'enfer,* proclaims the ineptness of divine creation and derides any future efforts at creating new worlds. The cynical conclusion or "moralité" in *Rage et impuissance* spurns the so-called goodness of God, denounces the "stupidities" of the Eternal Father, and exhorts all men to rebel against the conditions of human existence. Yet the very tone of revolt implies a craving for significance, a frustrated inquiry into realms of the unknowable. Life is thus envisaged simultaneously as a condemnation to live (Satan, in *Rêve d'enfer,* is unable to commit suicide) and as an initiation, through the very "néant" of existence, into the area of absolutes. Flaubert's juvenilia may propose, in a somewhat profuse and still unassimilated manner, various stereotyped extremes of the Romantic sensibility, but this very incoherence contains in germ the Flaubertian paradox: a pessimism which steadily nourishes the nostalgia for the Ideal. In the negation of life, Flaubert finds his most potent source of inspiration.

The text most suggestive of the Romantic heredity, but also most personally revealing, is *Novembre* (1842). Flaubert himself felt that this work marked the end of his youth; he hinted that it provided a key to his personality, that anyone who read it carefully could guess a "thousand untold things" ("mille choses *indisables*") which might cast light on his further development.[84] No task is easier than to enumerate the most obvious literary influences

---

[84] Flaubert, *Corresp.,* I, 410.

(some of them are explicitly evoked in the text: René, Werther, Don Juan) and to establish the inventory of Romantic clichés. Like Emma Bovary, young Gustave has read many books, and the books he has read inflamed his imagination. *Novembre* is a true repertory of Romantic motifs: the antitheses of cynicism and tenderness, of enthusiasm and despondency; the cult of memories; the usual dose of algolagnia; hackneyed elegiac and lyric images (autumnal leaves, empty barrels, the echo of lost chords, evocative ruins, proud eagles); rhetorical questions on the meaning of life; a sense of ennui and tragic dissatisfaction; the suicidal urge coupled with a yearning for escape; the solipsistic veneration for one's own suffering. But it is also an intense, spiritual self-portrait of an adolescent, and as such it is a remarkably powerful text.

The pages devoted to the sexual tensions of adolescence are particularly successful. Eroticism, to be sure, is the pretext for many a gaudy passage. But from behind the ostentatious prose there emerges a proleptic pattern. Sexuality, in this early work, is already very profoundly linked to the dream of the impossible. Love thus assumes a dual value, symbolized by the dual reality of Marie (prostitute and idealized creature) as well as by the inner scission or *dédoublement* of the narrator: "me dédoubler moi-même" is one of his most voluptuous desires. This disjunction is further expressed by a permanent tendency to translate carnal velleities into imaginary debauches, into "voluptés de la pensée." Eros, for the young Flaubert, is a deeply narcissistic experience; but this narcissism only accentuates the inner rift. "I would have liked to be a woman . . . so as to be able to admire myself, undress myself . . . and look at my reflection in the stream." The narrator's words would seem to lend support to Sartre's contention that Flaubert, in *Madame Bovary*, sought an esthetic metamorphosis into femininity.[85] Such longings, together with clearly onanistic traits, stress a fundamental theme of solitude and incommunicability.

[85] Sartre, *Critique de la raison dialectique*, p. 90.

Sex and the modes of failure bear an intimate association in the Flaubertian vision. *Novembre* stresses a sense of premature fatigue which carries the incipient threat of paralysis. An inconsolable sadness accompanies the first manifestations of sensuality, finding its logical expression in the funereal embraces of Marie, and later in the "lugubrious" love-making of Emma Bovary. *Novembre* already provides the two key themes by means of which Flaubert transmutes eroticism into an ideal, impossible and absolute quest. The first is the theme of adultery. "From that point on there existed for me one truly beautiful word in the human language: adultery." This magic word, largely because of his own desire for the unattainable Mme Schlésinger, was to be linked forever in his imagination with the very notion of the forbidden and the unrealizable. The other theme is that of the double image of Marie, lascivious whore and pure virgin: "je suis restéc comme j'étais à dix ans, vierge. . . . " The paradox points to the lasting dream of lost innocence, which, in *L'Éducation sentimentale*, is so powerfully linked to defeat and degradation by means of a complex series of "prostitution" images.

For the collector of prefigurative thematic elements, *Novembre* is a fertile terrain. A close analysis of this text tends, in fact, to discredit some of the source hunting so assiduously undertaken by the exegetes of *Madame Bovary* and other later novels. The narrator himself alludes to the persistence of certain thoughts and concerns: ideas with which one has lived intimately do "flow inside you like life itself." Thus even petty details seem to rehearse patterns and situations which later find a more substantial development. Marie's childhood, like Emma's, takes place on a farm, in the proximity of fields and cows; she too undergoes an early apprenticeship in isolation. The parallel is almost an ironic commentary, for Emma's secret vocation will also be that of a courtesan. But there are other similarities: dreams of physical ecstasies ("des nuits pleines de luxure"); a characteristic mixture of sensuality and mysticism (Marie in church longingly looks at the naked figure of Christ, just as Emma's erotic imagination is stimulated by the conventual atmosphere and the comparisons of the betrothed and the celestial lover that occur in sermons); a feverish exaltation achieved through books (Marie has read *Paul et Virginie* at least a hundred times!); elaborate and violent desires (the heroine of *Novembre* yearns for the amorous intertwining of snakes, for the destructive embraces of wild animals); the growing conviction that nobody can satisfy her thirst for absolute experiences, that she is doomed to the frustration of remaining forever deprived of an ideal fulfillment.

Even elements of *L'Éducation sentimentale*, written over twenty-five years later, are prefigured in *Novembre*. Marie, the available whore, is also the elusive shadow of the woman found, lost and forever sought. In that respect, she is an early version of Mme Arnoux, whose first name is also Marie. Inversely, in her meritricious and voluptuary function, she turns out to be the very ersatz-consolation for an unattainable ideal—much as la Maréchale, in *L'Éducation sentimentale,* who receives the embraces meant for another woman. Marie thus embodies the two interlocked roles later played out in contrapuntal fashion by Mme Arnoux and Rosanette Bron. These similarities are further stressed by some rather striking details. The cutting of the hair inevitably brings to mind the last encounter between Frédéric and Mme Arnoux; and even the words describing this supremely moving scene echo the earlier texts. "There comes a moment during farewells when the beloved person is no longer with us." The same sentence appears almost word for word at the end of the prostitute episode in *Novembre*.

Novembre is, however, not the only text which can be linked directly to the more mature works. At least two early literary efforts must be considered extremely important in the genesis of *La Tentation de saint Antoine*, that strange book which was to occupy Flaubert's imagination until he finally published the third version in 1874.

La Danse des morts (1838) presents, together with the prestigious figure of a Satan in the guise of a voluptuous "Oriental" despot, the explicit theme of temptation ("Oh! que de tentations!"), as well as a series of techniques and themes which were to characterize the different versions of Saint Antoine's visions of anguish: dramatic dialogues, historical panoramas, epic and allegoric effects, the omnipresence of destruction and death.

Smarh (1839) is even more clearly an Ur-*Tentation*. In addition to the obvious influence of Byron's "Mysteries" and to echoes of *Faust* (did Flaubert not ironically, in a brief epilogue, call himself "un petit Goethe"?), the adolescent text contains many specific elements which point forward to the very tone and texture of the *Tentation*: a complex rhythmic prose, the figure of the hermit near his cabin in Asia Minor, surrealistic effects, an emphasis on the grotesque. As for Smarh's "temptations," more elaborate than those in *La Danse des morts*, they are physical (Yuk's erotic teasing of the Woman), but above all intellectual in nature. Flaubert develops the theme of the *libido sciendi*, which will haunt him until his death brings to a halt the writing of his epic of intellectual voracity, *Bouvard et Pécuchet*. In *Smarh*, composed at the age of eighteen years, Flaubert couples the Faustian thirst for knowledge and dreams of the ungraspable with a pervasive fear of nihility. Satan notes that Smarh yearns for total knowledge ("Il faut donc que tu connaisses tout!"). But he also warns him. What if he succeeds only in discovering "un vaste néant"? It is in the light of this desire and this fear that one must interpret the Icarian flight through space: after exaltation come terror and despondency. An infinite fatigue oppresses Smarh as he asks to be returned to earth. Satan teaches him to fear that bitter knowledge of nothingness. But he also communicates to him a suicidal fervor. "O béatitude de la mort." The basic dialectics of Flaubert's vision are outlined in these early texts.

Finally, even the dramatic situations and moral dilemmas of the later novels are foreshadowed in Flaubert's youthful literary exercises. Thus *Passion et vertu* (1837), which treats with sympathy the criminal actions of an adulteress, raises some of the key issues later developed with infinite nuances in *Madame Bovary*. The literary temperament of Flaubert colors the original *fait divers*. The adulterous woman is endowed by him with what might be called congenital desire—not that of the flesh alone, but of the spirit which longs for "immense spaces and boundless horizons." Her frustration is of a metaphysical nature: the awareness of the Impossible.

The lesson of the *Oeuvres de jeunesse* is clear. The continuity of motifs and continuity of preoccupations which mark these diversified early texts, and which provide the link with the major books to follow, do indeed suggest a fundamental unity of themes and of vision underlying works as apparently dissonant in technique and dramatic setting as *Madame Bovary* and *La Tentation de saint Antoine*. The time has come to look more closely at Flaubert's story of his great sinner, and at the deep family bonds that exist between her and Flaubert's great saint.

Madame Bovary:

THE TRAGEDY OF DREAMS

Ah! que notre verre est petit, mon
Dieu! que notre soif est grande!
Par les Champs et par les grèves

The Myth of the "Pensum"

Several myths continue to distort our perspective on *Madame Bovary*. Flaubert set so much store by technical perfection, he so vociferously denied the intrinsic merits of a "subject" and proclaimed instead the supreme importance of style, he complained so bitterly of the tortures of composition and of the desperate baseness of his Norman setting, that it is only too easy to believe that the novel was for him primarily an exercise in self-discipline, perhaps even a much needed therapy to rid himself of his disheveled romanticism. The subject had supposedly been suggested to Flaubert ("Why don't you write the story of Delaunay?") to help him achieve literary sanity, after Louis Bouilhet and Maxime Du Camp, summoned for a solemn consultation, advised him to throw the manuscript of *La Tentation de saint Antoine* into the fire.[1]

---

[1] It is Maxime Du Camp, in *Souvenirs littéraires*, who tells of the episode. But Du Camp's reminiscences, often marred by a desire to belittle Flaubert, cannot always be trusted. Delamare (or Delaunay, as Du Camp calls him, thinly disguising the real name) was a mediocre *officier de santé*, a former student of Dr. Flaubert whose wife had lovers, made debts and committed suicide like Emma. See Francis Steegmuller's lively account of the novel's genesis in *Flaubert and Madame Bovary*, and Claudine Gothot-Mersch's extremely useful and intelligent study, *La Genèse de Madame Bovary*. Complete citations for all notes may be found in the Bibliography.

Many comments in Flaubert's *Correspondance* seem to substantiate these views. His ideal, as he confided it to Louise Colet, was to write a "livre sur rien," a book "about nothing at all," with almost no subject—a book, in short, which would exist by virtue of the "inner strength of its style."[2] In thus posing as an axiom the nonexistence of intrinsically "beautiful" or "ugly" subjects, and in affirming his conviction that style, all by itself, is "an absolute way of seeing things," Flaubert heralded significant modern notions, and seemed to point the way to some of the truly original achievements of later fiction. His own technical prowess, his supreme dedication to his art, his exigent standards all explain why he has assumed an almost exemplary stature. *Madame Bovary* came indeed to be considered a paragon of the genre. Writers admired it as one admires a lesson. For Henry James, Flaubert was the "novelist's novelist." For Zola, *Madame Bovary* represented the *roman type*.[3]

To be considered a "novelist's novelist" is of course an enviable reputation. But the very expression seems to imply a somewhat theoretical, overly deliberate and even "cold" or lifeless creation. Henry James was filled with professional admiration for Flaubert, but he also found *Madame Bovary* morally shallow. This indeed seems to have been the slowly acquired fame of the novel: it was considered an astonishing feat of literary organization, displaying an unusual mastery of structure and texture, but a work that did not spring from the author's heart, whose subject even ran counter to the author's temperament—in short, a self-imposed task! And here again, numerous remarks in Flaubert's letters seemed to confirm these feelings. "One must write more coldly," he explains to Louise Colet, who was herself rather given to effusive writing. "Let us beware of this kind of over-excitement which is called inspiration. . . . " His cult of impassibility led him

---

[2] Flaubert, *Corresp.*, II, 345.
[3] Henry James, "Gustave Flaubert," in *Notes on Novelists*, pp. 85 and 108; Zola, "Gustave Flaubert," in *Les Romanciers Naturalistes*, p. 125.

to paradoxes: "The less one feels a thing, the better one is able to express it." And still while writing *Madame Bovary*: "I am truly tired of this work; it is a real *pensum* for me now."[4] This feeling of self-inflicted, yet stubbornly continued punishment is one of the strongest impressions left by Flaubert's letters. Thus it can be said that the *Correspondance*, admirable though it is, ultimately rendered the author a disservice. Not taking into account that most of these letters which evoke the drudgery of his work were written late at night, when Flaubert was exhausted by the unending battle with words, readers have all too easily adopted the stereotyped view of a stubborn and masochistic novelist engaged in an impressive but sterile literary exercise.

The truth is somewhat different. Not only are there sources other than the Delamare story (the *Mémoires de Madame Ludovica*,[5] for instance, which tell of the adulteries and financial difficulties of Mme Pradier, whom Flaubert frequented long before the unfavorable verdict against *La Tentation de saint Antoine*), but the theme of *Madame Bovary*, and in particular the central motif of adultery, had been a major obsession of Flaubert ever since his adolescence. *Passion et vertu*, written at the age of sixteen years, is indeed a striking miniature version of *Madame Bovary*. Based on an actual case history reported in the *Gazette des Tribunaux*,[6] this short "conte philosophique" tells of the adulterous Mazza and of her seducer Ernest, who is clearly a first version of Emma Bovary's lover Rodolphe. Mazza surrenders to her passion with such a

[4] Flaubert, *Corresp.*, III, 104; II, 462; IV, 91.

[5] Gabrielle Leleu uncovered this curious document in the volume entitled "Recueil de documents divers réunis par Flaubert pour la préparation de *Bouvard et Pécuchet*" which Mme Franklin-Grout had given to the Bibliothèque de Rouen. In addition to many details which parallel the events in *Madame Bovary*, there are also striking similarities of expression. ("Du nouveau sur 'Madame Bovary,'" *Revue d'Histoire littéraire de la France*, July-September, 1947, pp. 210–244.)

[6] The account appeared in the issue of October 4, 1837, p. 1,183. It is reproduced in Jean Bruneau, *Les Débuts littéraires de Gustave Flaubert, 1831-1845*, pp. 132-135.

total frenzy that Ernest, almost afraid (in this he announces Léon) decides to abandon her. Desperate, Mazza
kills her husband and her children, and finally takes her
own life by poison. The story was written in 1837, some
fifteen years before Flaubert set to work on *Madame Bovary*.
The subject can therefore hardly be called new or alien to
the author's more permanent preoccupations.

But it is not so much the subject as it is the themes and
the psychological drama which sharply prefigure the later
novel. In *Passion et vertu*, literature also serves as a pur-
veyor of illusions. The lover also plans his seduction coldbloodedly, and almost cruelly. As for the adulterous Mazza, her "immense desires" obviously transcend the mere
gratification of the senses. A metaphysical malaise is at
the root of her yearning for excess. The flesh and its
pleasures turn out to be an immense disappointment. The
ennui she experiences stems from a hunger which can
never be satisfied. Flaubert in fact compares Mazza to
those "starved people who are unable to nourish themselves." Her longing for the inaccessible ultimately leads
to dehumanization ("Elle n'avait plus rien d'une femme
. . . "), to madness and to an inescapable attraction to the
ultimate absolute, death.[7]

The significance of a text such as this can scarcely be
stressed too much. Not only were some of the key themes
of *Madame Bovary* (sterile but frenetic eroticism, sensuous
longing for the absolute, flirtation with death) already
fully sketched out in Flaubert's mind in 1837, but this
long gestation should encourage critics to subordinate considerations of sheer technical accomplishments to the
deeper meanings of the work. *Madame Bovary* is hardly
an artificial or arbitrary exercise—even though Flaubert
himself claimed that the subject was unpalatable to him.
It corresponds in fact to some of the basic patterns of
his imagination.

[7] Flaubert, *Oeuvres de jeunesse inédites*, I, 241–275.

First Impressions

The opening chapter describes Charles Bovary's first day at school. The young boy is so clumsy, his attire so ludicrous, that he almost automatically provokes the cruel hilarity of the other students. The author stresses the boy's pathetic inelegance, his timidity, his ineffectual good will, his trancelike docility and resignation. All the physical details of the scene serve to bring out Charles' ineptness as he enters into the somnolent classroom atmosphere. He at first remains in the corner behind the door, almost invisible: the first impression is one of unredeemed insignificance and self-effacement. His hair cut short on his forehead suggests obtuseness. His jacket, which seems too tight around the armholes, suggests constriction and limitations. His stout, unshined hob-nailed shoes express the boy's dullness and awkwardness. His stiff countenance—he does not dare to cross his legs or lean on his elbows, and he listens "attentive as if at a sermon"—conveys an almost servile submissiveness to authority. But it is above all the boy's headgear, a pitiful, unsightly combination of shako, bearskin, billycock hat and cotton nightcap, which sums up, in its tiers and superstructure, the layers and monumentality of the wearer's unintelligence. The scene ends when Charles, as a punishment for having innocently provoked mirth and class disorder, is told to conjugate twenty times "*ridiculus sum.*"

Readers have often wondered why Flaubert began his novel as though Charles Bovary were the central character. The opening scene seems to have no bearing on Emma's tragedy, and Emma herself, of course, does not yet exist on Charles' horizon. Moreover, the very point of view of this first scene remains puzzling. The collective personal pronoun *nous* ("We were in class when . . . ") evidently communicates the proper tone of childhood reminiscences. But this point of view is not sustained, and very soon an anonymous author's perspective replaces this more personal voice. It seems hardly conceivable that so careful a craftsman as Flaubert should not have noticed the discrepancy, and that the curiously oblique approach should be the result of inadvertence.

The mere fact that the novel does not end with Emma's death, and that once again, in the final pages, Charles comes to stand out in the foreground, should be sufficient indication that he is not a peripheral character. He is not only the permanent victim of a fate he cannot control any more than he can control the cruel laughter which greets his first appearance at school, he also serves to bring out the basic themes of blindness and incommunicability. For Charles "sees" Emma (the structure of the novel ensures that our first glimpse of Emma passes through Charles' consciousness), but he is constitutionally unable to *understand* her. Flaubert denies himself the facile prerogatives of the omniscient author. We are gradually led to the unique perspective of Emma. But this is achieved progressively: Charles serves as a transition. The mysterious "nous" can thus be considered part of those subtle modulations whereby Flaubert guides our vision to the very center of tragedy, while exploiting all the possibilities of an ironic distance.[8]

It would be a mistake, however, to reduce Charles to a purely functional role. A careful reading of the text, as well as of the available scenarios, reveals an intrinsic interest in the character. His early courtship of Emma, at the Bertaux farm, is treated with obvious warmth. His nascent sensations of love—associated with the sights and smells of country life—are almost touchingly presented. The various drafts, moreover, insist on human traits which are far from ludicrous. Young Charles is a "gentle nature, sensitive as a young man should be. . . . " His love for his wife is deep and tragic, and it bestows upon him an undeniable stature: "ADORES his wife, and of the

---

[8] Jean Rousset has admirably shown how the novel, precisely by such transitional devices, progresses according to a movement "which proceeds from the outside to the inside . . ." ("*Madame Bovary* ou 'le livre sur rien,' " in *Forme et signification*, pp. 109–133).

three men who sleep with her, he is certainly the one who loves her most [—This is what has to be stressed]."[9] Remarks such as these clearly indicate that the very conception of the character justified his central position in the opening chapter.

More important, however, than either the technical function (transitional perspective) or the human interest of Charles Bovary, is the thematic value of his initial appearance in the schoolroom. The systematic use of character in the service of themes is indeed one of the salient traits of Flaubert's work. And not only characters, but objects also assume a primary thematic importance. Charles' cap is thus not merely an absurd personal appendage, but its heteroclite aspect, its senseless accumulation and confusion of styles, symbolize an abdication of the human spirit in the face of pure phenomena. The cap, in its very multiplication of shapes, represents the essence of meaninglessness and incongruity. Such an extension of meaning to objects is clearly one of Flaubert's conscious methods. In the description of the cap which appears in one of the earliest drafts, Flaubert states that it was a "synthesis" of all the ugly and uncomfortable headgears in existence, that it was one of those pitiful things "in which matter itself seems sad."[10] And the cap is far from an isolated example. The *pièce montée* served as a dessert at the wedding (with its porticoes, colonnades, nutshell boats, lakes of jam, and its cupid balancing itself in a chocolate swing) or the improvised therapeutic apparatus for curing club feet (with its eight pounds of iron, wood, leather, nuts and screws) fulfill similar functions.

The opening scene of the novel is thus not so much an introduction into a given character's private world, as an indirect statement of motifs and themes. The pathos of incommunicability (the teacher at first cannot even

9 Flaubert, *Madame Bovary—Nouvelle version précédée des scénarios inédits*, pp. 7, 21.
10 Flaubert, *Madame Bovary—Nouvelle version précédée des scénarios inédits*, p. 135.

understand Charles' name), the constriction of a narrow world here symbolized by school routines, the loneliness of the individual in the face of a harassing group, and above all, the themes of inadequacy and failure, are all set forth in these first pages. The entire beginning is under the triple sign of inadequacy, drowsiness and a passively accepted necessity. The work which ends with Charles' lamentable thought, "It is the fault of fatality!" appropriately begins on a note of resignation.

Rhythm and Symbolic Details

Two Flaubertian characteristics stand out immediately: the importance of significant details and a blocklike composition involving a double rhythm. The first chapter typically provides a *scene* (the arrival of Charles in school), and then immerges the reader into a continuum of time: Charles' youth, his adolescence, his education, his career, his first marriage. This double perspective, dramatic and narrative, constitutes the basic Flaubertian unit, and these units, in turn, provide the permanent tension between temporal immediacy and the denseness and elasticity of time. Flaubert may not have thought in terms of chapter units (the chapter divisions appear only in the final manuscript sent to the printer), but he did plan his novel around a series of key scenes and episodes: the agricultural show; the first seduction scene or *baisade*, as he crudely puts it in his outlines; the visit to the priest. The staggering number of outlines, the infinite patience with which Flaubert copied and elaborated them, is clear testimony to the importance of careful plotting in *Madame Bovary*. "*All depends on the outline*," he asserts to Louise Colet. And, even more significantly, he has this advice to give to his friend Ernest Feydeau: ". . . books are not made like babies, but like pyramids, with a premeditated plan, by placing huge blocks one above the other. . . . "[11]

Thus each chapter centers on one major subject and could

[11] Flaubert, *Corresp.*, II, 362; IV, 239–240.

easily be given a relevant title: chapter 1: the childhood and studious youth of Charles; chapter 2: the meeting with Emma; chapter 3: the marriage proposal; chapter 4: the wedding; chapter 5: the Bovary house in Tostes; chapter 6: the education of Emma; chapter 7: the routine of married life; chapter 8: the Vaubyessard ball; chapter 9: Emma's nervous illness. And the same double rhythm of narration and description is maintained throughout. Almost every chapter contains a central scene or tableau: the visit to the sick farmer, the first impression of Emma, the wedding feast, the famous ball scene, the description of the daily meals. The unique act is thus juxtaposed with the daily routine, until the two seem to merge in a pattern of repetition and uniformity. Percy Lubbock's distinction between "scenic" and "panoramic" elements in *Madame Bovary* conveniently points to the author's binocular vision[12]; but it is a simplification, for it fails to take into account the more profound rhythmic patterns which are concerned not only with spatial, but with temporal perspectives. Georges Poulet's phenomenological approach, stressing alternating movements of contraction and expansion, brings us closer to the fundamental movements of the novel.[13]

As for Flaubert's love of descriptive detail, it is probably the one element in his work that has met with the most misunderstanding. Barbey d'Aurevilly summed up many contemporary reactions when he termed Flaubert an "enragé descripteur."[14] The brothers Goncourt similarly were disturbed by the importance of "props" which, they felt, choked his characters and were largely responsible for the soulless quality of the novel.[15] Such reactions cannot be attributed merely to professional jealousy or critical nearsightedness. Many readers continue to be

[12] Lubbock, *The Craft of Fiction*, pp. 69ff.
[13] Poulet, "Flaubert," in *Les Métamorphoses du cercle*, pp. 371–396.
[14] Barbey d'Aurevilly, "Gustave Flaubert," in *Le Roman contemporain*, p. 99.
[15] Goncourt, *Journal*, IV, 124, 144.

disturbed by Flaubert's apparently gratuitous fascination with material realities, and particularly with the life of objects.

The functional nature of the Flaubertian "detail" is perhaps best illustrated, early in the novel, in the pages which provide our first glimpses of Emma. During Charles' first visit she pricks her fingers while sewing, and repeatedly puts them to her mouth to suck them. In another characteristic pose, she stands motionless, with her forehead against the window, looking into the garden. The two basic traits of her character are clearly brought out: sensuousness and the propensity to dream. (The act of sucking a bleeding finger obviously had strong erotic associations for Flaubert: in his scenarios, he has Emma suck Léon's slightly wounded finger, and this gesture supposedly characterizes her increasing sexual frenzy.)[16] Thus a number of details, during Charles' first encounters with her, betray Emma's temperament: her full, fleshy lips that she has a habit of biting when silent (the French verb *mordillonner* is far more suggestive); the soft down on the back of her neck which the wind seems to caress; the small beads of perspiration on her bare shoulders; her particular way of throwing her head back in order to drink the almost empty glass of curaçao, her lips pouting, her neck straining, while with the tip of her tongue she attempts to lick in feline fashion the few remaining drops.

Even her languorous manner of speaking, the modulations of her voice which seem to lead to a murmur, her half-closed eyelids as her thoughts appear to wander—all these suggest a strong erotic potential which finds its first symbolic awakening during the dance ritual at the Vaubyessard ball. The waltz (considered immoral by the Imperial prosecutor) sweeps Emma into a whirlwind of sensations, as she surrenders to the promiscuity of the dance. Here too, the details are all chosen with care: the

[16] Flaubert, *Madame Bovary—Nouvelle version précédée des scénarios inédits*, p. 106.

dance begins slowly, but soon the tempo increases; Emma's dress catches against the trousers of her partner as their feet "commingled"; a torpor seizes her, and the movement becomes increasingly accelerated, until Emma, panting, almost faints, and has to lean back against the wall "covering her eyes with her hand" (I.8). The obvious sexual symbolism is proof not only of the purposefulness with which Flaubert selects his detail, but reveals the extremely powerful sexual undertones of the novel which—if one is to judge by the outlines and scenarios—Flaubert prudently toned down in his final draft. For in his scenarios, he stresses almost obsessively, and with considerable crudeness of thought and of language, the increasingly morbid sensuality of Emma. This sensuality extends beyond her character, it invades the entire world of *Madame Bovary*. According to Flaubert's sketches, Charles—after Emma's death—was to suffer from an "unhealthy love," whipped on by retrospective sexual jealousy: "amour malsain—excité par celui des autres—d'actrice—envie de la baiser."[17]

The significant, carefully plotted detail is, however, not limited to character analysis. Indeed, this is one of its lesser functions. From the very outset, it serves as a "relative" symbol. The flat fields around the Bertaux farm, stretching their great surfaces until they fade into the gloom of the sky, represent the very monotony of experience to which Emma seems condemned. The horse's movement of fright as Charles reaches the farm almost assumes the value of a warning. One may prefer to call these "relative" symbols, because symbolism as practiced by Flaubert is rarely absolute in kind (pointing to a system of universal correspondences), but almost always of a strictly literary nature, fulfilling a dramatic or thematic role. Its function can be premonitory or proleptic,

17 Flaubert, *Madame Bovary—Nouvelle version précédée des scénarios inédits*, p. 123. See also p. 127. Flaubert's "sexual" imagination played insistently with the seduction scene in the forest, and even more so with the hotel encounters in Rouen. Even in her first affair, with Rodolphe, Emma becomes a real sex addict: "manière dont elle l'aimait profondément cochonne" (p. 97).

as when Emma, watching the dark clouds from her window, sees them gather and roll ominously in the direction of Rouen. Similarly, when Charles carries his former wife's bridal bouquet up to the attic, Emma wonders what would happen to her own after she died. (Later she herself destroys her bouquet.) An entire moral climate can be evoked by means of such details. The street organ brings to Emma airs played "elsewhere" (in elegant theaters and salons), but transposed to the constricted atmosphere of Tostes. The unglamorous contrast is further stressed by the coarseness of the man who turns the handle, by his well-aimed long squirts of brown saliva.

The exploitation of details for ironic contrasts seems almost a perverse pleasure with Flaubert; he sometimes carries it to cruel extremes. Thus Homais, when a proper tomb for Emma is discussed, suggests a temple of Vesta or a "mass of ruins." Charles finally opts in favor of a mausoleum which on the two main sides is to have "a spirit bearing an extinguished torch." It is easy to see, however, how close the use of such contrasts comes to a moral commentary. When Flaubert refers to the mud on Emma's boots as the "crotte des rendez-vous" (the "mud of the rendezvous" II.12); when he has the beadle, in the cathedral, point out to the lovers a piece of statuary which is supposedly "a perfect representation of nothingness" and exhort them to look at the "Last Judgment" and the "condemned" in Hell-flames—one can hardly speak of the author's lack of intervention, of his impassibility! At times, the symbolic detail serves as an ironic punctuation, as it almost graphically plots the stages of a moral evolution. The plaster statue of a priest which adorns the Bovary garden in Tostes soon loses its right foot; later, white scabs appear on its face where the plaster has scaled off; and during the moving to their new home in Yonville, the plaster priest falls from the cart and is dashed into a thousand fragments. The gradual destruction of the ecclesiastical figure parallels the gradual disintegration of their marriage. Finally, the apparently gratuitous detail can have both a prophetic and a seductive value: on her trip to the convent, young Emma eats from painted plates that tell the story of Mademoiselle de La Vallière, the famous favorite of Louis XIV. Even the seemingly insignificant fact that the explanatory legends of this glamorous destiny are chipped by the scratches of knives (how many travelers have stopped at the same inn and eaten from the same plates!) tends to orient the reader's mind toward a "moral" interpretation.

"One eats a great deal in Flaubert's novels," observes Jean-Pierre Richard in his brilliant essay.[18] It would seem indeed that Flaubert had an alimentary obsession. In an amusing letter to his friend Louis Bouilhet, he himself comments on this gastronomic imagination. "It is a strange thing how the spectacle of nature, far from elevating my soul toward the Creator, excites my stomach. The ocean makes me dream of oysters, and last time I crossed the Alps, a certain leg of chamois [antelope] I had eaten four years earlier at the Simplon, gave me hallucinations."[19] Food plays an extraordinary role in his novels: feasts, orgies, bourgeois meals, peasant revels. This concern for appetite and digestion corresponds unquestionably, as Richard suggests, to the larger themes of his work: the "appetite" for the inaccessible, the voracious desire to *possess* experience, the preoccupation with metamorphoses, the tragedy of indigestion, and ultimately the almost metaphysical sense of nausea as the mind becomes aware that not to know everything is to know nothing. The very essence of *bovarysme* seems involved in this frustrated gluttony.

In *Madame Bovary*, food, the ritual of meals, deglutition and rumination play a particularly important role. One would almost be tempted to explicate the entire novel in terms of its gastronomic and digestive imagery. Sensuousness (old Rouault's taste for rare legs of lamb),

[18] Richard, "La Création de la forme chez Flaubert," in *Littérature et sensation*, p. 119.
[19] Flaubert, *Corresp.*, IV, 114.

a penchant for debauched sexuality (Emma licking the drops of curaçao, the drops of sauce dripping from the senile lips of the lecherous old duc de Laverdière), but above all a certain quality of vulgarity are conveyed. The Rabelaisian wedding feast—sixteen hours of eating and drinking, coarse jests and bawdy songs—is a true festival of rustic rowdiness and bad taste, the crowning symbol of which is the pretentious and utterly grotesque wedding cake. Similarly, the feast of the agricultural show, with its dirty plates and animal-like promiscuity, serves primarily to describe an atmosphere of chaos and gross inelegance.

In contrast to these plebeian *ripailles* stands the gastronomic supper at the Vaubyessard ball, with its delicately blended emanations of truffles, aromatic viands, rare flowers and fine linen. The silver dish-covers, the cut crystal, the champagne—all contributes here to the impression of urbane refinement, and sets up in Emma, through whose consciousness the entire scene is viewed, the basic tension of the novel. Her background and her lofty dreams come into such evident clash that she is almost compelled to *negate* the one or the other. Emma's choice is typical: ". . . in the refulgence of the present moment, her entire past life, so distinct until then, faded away completely, and she almost doubted having lived it" (I.8). The entire episode at the Vaubyessard ball has—we are told—made "a hole" in her life. And it is revealing that the awareness of this sudden disappearance of a given reality coincides with the degustation of a maraschino ice which voluptuously melts in her mouth.

The common onion soup which awaits her upon her return to Tostes is an ironic reminder of a reality which refuses to be thus negated. After merging with, and even symbolizing, Emma's growing dreams of luxury and passion, alimentary images point again to the vulgarity and triteness of her environment. And it is not only a specific ugliness, but the odious quality of existence itself which is brought out through images of rumination. Flaubert—

witness the names of *Bov*ary and *Bouv*ard—is haunted by the bovine image. Repeatedly, Emma is repelled by her husband's eating habits, by the gurgling noises he makes when taking soup, or by his way of cleaning his teeth with his tongue. Just as his mastication seems to make impossible any contact between his love and her needs, so Bournisien's laborious digestion stresses his inadequacy as a priest when he fails to intuit her desperate condition.

Meals and digestive processes thus punctuate a monotonous existence which condemns Emma to an imprisonment in the self. The very rhythm of mediocrity is conveyed by cycles of alimentation, until finally the process of eating becomes a symbol of habit: "It was a habit among other habits, like a predictable dessert after the monotony of dinner" (I.7). The act of setting the table is the drab ritual of life itself, with its eternal repetition and sameness. And, as if to emphasize the meaninglessness of this routine, Homais interrupts the Bovary meals regularly every evening, at 6:30, with his pompous presence and preposterous chatter.

Ultimately, the mealtimes come to symbolize Emma's utter dejection, as all the "bitterness of existence" seems served up on her plate. The smell of the boiled beef mixes with the whiffs of sickliness that arise from her soul. The image of the plate combines, in this context, the finite and the infinite: "toute l'amertume de l'existence"—but reduced to, and confined within the petty circle of her own monotonous life.[20] All living becomes an endless erosive consumption. Food and waste (or disease) are indeed repeatedly brought into juxtaposition: the kitchen smells penetrate into the consulting room, and the coughing of the patients can be heard in the kitchen. The alimentary metaphor conveys the reality of life itself:

[20] Erich Auerbach, in *Mimesis*, takes this scene (I.9) as a point of departure for his discussion of Flaubert's particular type of realism. Georges Poulet, in *Les Métamorphoses du cercle,* has brilliant pages on "contracted space" in *Madame Bovary.*

puisque la portion vécue avait été mauvaise, sans
doute ce qui restait à *consommer* serait meilleur. (II.2)

Il connaissait l'existence humaine tout du long, et
il s'y *attablait* sur les deux coudes avec sérénité. (II.3)

The verb *consommer* has, of course, a double meaning:
beyond the alimentary image there is also the idea of
waste and destruction. Ironically, Emma's very death is
provoked by *swallowing* poison, and the first symptoms of
her agony are those of major indigestion.

Even more ironic is the victory of Existence over Tragedy itself: life simply continues, mediocre and indifferent.
Flaubert exploits alimentary images with the same bitterness that makes him grant Homais the Legion of Honor
at the end of the novel. After Emma almost throws herself out the attic window following Rodolphe's desertion,
she is caught again by the sickening routine of life: " . . .
she had to go down to sit at the table." She tries to eat,
but the food chokes her. "Et il fallut descendre . . . "—
the very dreariness of life's continuity is conveyed by
this call to join her husband at the dinner table. So also,
life continues during her very agony: Homais, who cannot let slip by an occasion to entertain a celebrity, invites Doctor Larivière for lunch. (The very pedantry of
Homais manifests itself earlier through his love for all
manners of "recipes.") And at the end of the wake, Homais and Bournisien enjoy cheese, a large roll and a bot-
tle of brandy in the very presence of the corpse (" . . .
puis ils mangèrent et trinquèrent, tout en ricanant un
peu . . . "). The novel ends with old Rouault's reassurance
that, despite Emma's death, Charles will continue to receive his yearly turkey!

*Patterns of Imagery: Her Dreams Too High, Her House
Too Narrow*

Flaubert takes cruel satisfaction in ironic contrasts.
Many of them are set up in a somewhat obvious fashion:
the Bovary dog-cart and the elegant carriages of the

guests at the Vaubyessard ball; Charles' smugness and Emma's frustration; her exaltations and her moments of torpor; the alternations of ardor and frigidity; Emma's vibrating body still tingling from the caresses, while her lover, a cigar between his lips, is mending a broken bridle! At times, the antithesis tends to be more subtle: the knotty articulations of a peasant hand appear on the very page where the lovers' fingers intertwine.

These planned juxtapositions do, however, point to the heart of the subject. They emphasize the basic theme of incompatibility. Their implicit tensions stress a fundamental state of *divorce* at all levels of experience. But they also fulfill a dramatic function. If Charles' father happens to be a squanderer and an almost professional seducer, if Charles himself, while still married to his first wife, is drawn to Emma because she represents a forbidden and inaccessible love, these ironies are part of an effective technique of "preparation." And these very anticipatory devices—whether prophetic in a straightforward or an ironic fashion—are in turn related to the theme of "fate" which Flaubert propounds with characteristic ambiguity. "C'est la faute de la fatalité!" is Charles' pathetic, yet moving final comment. But the notion of "fatality" is of course one of the most belabored Romantic clichés; Charles' exclamation carries its own condemnation, at the same time that it implies a debunking of the tragic ending of the novel. Rodolphe, writing his cowardly letter of rupture to Emma, hits upon the expression: ". . . accuse only fate"—and he congratulates himself on his skillful use of a word "which is always effective"! The expression coincides with the very devaluation of love. Similarly, Charles blames the pitiful outcome of the club-foot operation on a malevolent destiny ("La fatalité s'en était mêlée"), when in reality only his hopeless incompetence is at fault. Yet who is to deny that, in addition to elements of pathos, the novel constantly suggests an all-pervasive determinism: Emma's temperament, the character of Charles, the effects of heredity, the erosive quality of small-town life, the noxious influence of books, the structure of the novel itself?

Flaubert significantly devotes an entire chapter to Emma's education in the convent. Her private symbolism of love, mysticism and death is determined by this experience. The "mystic languor" provoked by the incense, the whisperings of the priest, the very metaphors comparing Christ to a celestial lover, predispose her to confuse sensuous delights and spiritual longings. The convent is Emma's earliest claustration, and the solicitations from the outside world, whether in the form of books which are smuggled in, or through the distant sound of a belated carriage rolling down the boulevards, are powerful allurements. As for Emma's reactions to the books she reads, the image of a female Quixote comes to mind.[21] She too transmutes reality into fiction. Here, as in Cervantes' novel, literature itself becomes one of the strongest determinants.

Yet there is, in *Madame Bovary*, a necessity stronger even than the temperamental, social and intellectual pressures to which the protagonist is subjected. It is a necessity inherent in the inner logic and progression of Flaubert's own images. The very chapter on Emma's education (I.6) reveals a characteristic pattern. The primary images are those of confinement and immobility: the atmosphere of the convent is protective and soporific (" . . . elle s'assoupit doucement . . . "); the reading is done on the sly; the girls are assembled in the study, the chapel or the dormitory. Very soon, however, images of escape begin to dominate. These images are at first strictly visual: ladies in castles (typically also claustrated, and dreamily expecting in front of a window the cavalier with a white plume); madonnas, lagoons, gondoliers and angels with golden wings; illustrations in books depicting English ladies kissing doves through the bars of a Gothic cage (still

<hr />

[21] Harry Levin, in *The Gates of Horn* (p. 246), quotes a prophetic passage from Kierkegaard's *Either/Or*: "It is remarkable that the whole of European literature lacks a feminine counterpart to *Don Quixote*. May not the time for this be coming, may not the continent of sentimentality yet be discovered?"

the prison theme). Soon, however, the images become less precise, giving way to vaporous dreams ("pale landscapes of dithyrambic lands"), and to an increasingly disheveled exoticism: sultans with long pipes, Djiaours, Bayadères, Greek caps and Turkish sabres. The suggested confusion of these images rapidly degenerates into indifferentiation and ultimately even chaos, as palm trees and pine trees, Tartar minarets and Roman ruins, crouching camels and swimming swans are brought into senseless juxtaposition. Escape seems inevitably to lead to a manner of disintegration, even to images of death (perhaps even a suggested death-wish), as the swans are transformed into dying swans, singing to the accompaniment of funereal harps, and Emma, infinitely bored by it all, but unwilling to admit it to herself, continuing her dreams by habit or by vanity, finally withdraws into herself, "appeased."

The chapter on Emma's education is revealing, not merely because it proposes a parable of the entire novel, but because the progression of images corresponds to a pattern repeated throughout the book: from ennui to expectation, to escape, to confusion, back to ennui and to a yearning for nothingness. But whereas the symbolic detail is often, with Flaubert, part of a deliberate technique, this logic of imagery associations, these recurrent patterns depend on the spontaneous life of images, on their mutual attractions and irremediable conflicts, on a causality which operates at an unconscious, *poetic* level. The novel as a whole is thus constructed around recurrent clusters of images, all of which are part of definable, yet interrelated cycles. These cycles, or cyclic themes, do parallel on a massive canvas the inevitable movement, from boredom to self-destruction, which characterizes *Madame Bovary* in its overall conception as well as in its detailed execution.

First the patterns of ennui. This begins early in the novel. The eternal sameness of experience is already suggested by the weekly letters to his mother which the boy Charles writes regularly every Thursday evening with the same red ink, and which he seals with the same three wafers. Charles' working habits are moreover compared to those of a mill-horse. The primary means for suggesting an anesthetizing routine are temporal. Emma gets into the habit of taking strolls in order to avoid the "eternal" garden. The days resemble each other (". . . the same series of days began all over"); the future seems like an endlessly dark corridor. And repeatedly, the mournful church bell punctuates the return of the monotonous hours and days with its characterless lament. The repeated use of the imperfect tense, with its suggestions of habitual action, further stresses the temporal reality of Flaubertian boredom. Even comic effects contribute to an impression of sameness (Flaubert's sense of comedy constantly exploits repetitions): on the day of the agricultural show, the local national guardsmen and the corps of firemen are being drilled endlessly up and down the Yonville square. "Cela ne finissait pas et toujours recommençait."

The underlying sense of hopelessness and monotony is also conveyed by means of liquid images. There is a great deal of oozing, dripping and melting in Flaubert's fictional world. During Charles' early courtship of Emma, the snow is melting, the bark of the trees is oozing, one can hear drops of water falling one by one. Later, when the bitterness of her married existence seems to be served up to her nauseatingly during their daily meals, Emma is aware that the walls are "sweating." These liquid images, suggesting erosion and deterioration, are of course bound up with a sense of the emptiness of Time. A steady *écoulement*, or flow, corresponds to feelings of hopeless waste and vacuity. These liquid images of an annihilating temporality will be even more pervasive in *L'Éducation sentimentale*. But *Madame Bovary* also brings out this immense sadness of time's undoing. Old Rouault explains that, after his wife died, grief itself dissolved (". . . ça a coulé brin à brin . . ." I.3). The steady flow becomes the very symbol of a chronic despair. After Léon's departure, Emma is plunged again into a life of spiritual numbness: "The river still flowed on, and slowly pushed its ripples along the slippery banks" (II.7). Finally, the monotony of existence is conveyed through a series of spatial images. The Norman landscape near Yonville is "flat," the meadow "stretches," the plain broadens out and extends to the very horizon—"à perte de vue." This colorless landscape is in harmony with the lazy borough sprawling along the river banks. Emma, throughout the novel, scans the horizon. But nothing appears which would relieve the deathlike evenness.

This spatial imagery clearly constitutes the bridge between the theme of ennui and the theme of escape. Once again, the series of images can be traced back to the early pages of the novel which deal exclusively with Charles. Repeatedly, he opens his window, either to stare at the muddy little river which in his mind becomes a wretched "little Venice" and to dream of a yearned-for elsewhere, or to indulge in love reveries as he leans in the direction of the Bertaux farm. The window becomes indeed in *Madame Bovary* the symbol of all expectation: it is an opening onto space through which the confined heroine can dream of escape. But it is also—for windows can be closed and exist only where space is, as it were, restricted—a symbol of frustration, enclosure and asphyxia. Flaubert himself, aware that Emma is often leaning out the window, explains that "the window in the provinces replaces the theater and the promenade" (II.7). More, however, is involved than a simple taste for spectacle. Jean Rousset, in a brilliant essay, quite rightly suggests that the open window unleashes "mystical velleities."[22] In fact, the symbolic uses of the window reveal not only a permanent dialectic of constriction and spatial-

[22] Rousset, "*Madame Bovary* ou 'le livre sur rien,'" in *Forme et signification*, pp. 109–133. Rousset sees the window in Flaubert as a symbol of the "limitless within the confined."

THE NOVELS OF FLAUBERT

ity, but an implicit range of emotions embracing the major themes of the novel.

Emma's characteristic pose is at, or near, a window. This is indeed one of the first impressions Charles has of her: ". . . il la trouva debout, le front contre la fenêtre." Windows which are "ajar" are part of her literary reveries in the convent. The image, from the very outset, suggests some manner of imprisonment as well as a longing for a liberation. After her marriage, her daily routine brings her to the window every morning. When she goes through one of her nervous crises, she locks herself up in her room, but then, "stifling," throws open the windows. Exasperated by a sense of shame and contempt for her husband, she again resorts to the typical gesture: "She went to open the window . . . and breathed in the fresh air to calm herself" (I.9). The sense of oppression and immurement is further stressed after Rodolphe abandons her: the shutter of the window overlooking the garden remains permanently closed. But the imprisonment in her own boundless desire is intolerable. Emma's sexual frenzy, which reaches climactic proportions during her affair with Léon, is probably the most physical manifestation of her need to "liberate" herself. The window, as symbol, offers an image of this release. It is revealing that she first glimpses her future lover, Rodolphe, from her window. Similarly, she watches Léon cross the Yonville square. And it is characteristic also that, upon Léon's departure from Yonville, Emma's first gesture is to open her window and watch the clouds. The space-reverie at first corresponds to a sense of hope: either the surge toward emancipation, as after the Vaubyessard ball (Emma "opened the window and leant out"); or the process of convalescence (Emma, recovering from her nervous depression, is wheeled to the window in her armchair). But the space-hope is even more fundamentally a space-despair. From the garret where she reads Rodolphe's letter and almost commits suicide, all the surrounding plain is visible. The garret-window offers the broadest panorama. But it is a dreary view; the endless flat expanse provides a hopeless perspective.

Chronic expectation turns to chronic futility, as Emma's élans toward the elsewhere disintegrate in the grayness of undifferentiated space. Daydreams of movement and flight only carry her back to a more intolerable confinement within her petty existence and her unfulfilled self. But expectation there is. Just as the chatelaines in her beloved Gothic romances wait for the dashing cavalier on his black horse, so Emma lives in perpetual anticipation. "At the bottom of her heart . . . she was waiting for something to happen" (I.9). Flaubert insists, somewhat heavily at times, on this compulsive expectance of the conclusive event. The frustrated local barber, dreaming of a shop in the theater district of some big town, thus walks up and down "like a sentinel on duty" waiting for customers. And Emma, casting despairing glances upon her life's solitude, interrogates the empty horizon. Each morning, as she wakes up, she hopes that this day will bring a three-decker, laden with passion to the portholes. Every evening, disappointed, she again longs for the morrow.

Images of movement reinforce the theme of escapism. Emma enjoys taking lonely walks with her greyhound and watching the leaps and dashes of the graceful animal. Restlessness and taste for aimless motion point to the allurement of a mythical *elsewhere.* Once again, the theme is ironically broached early in the novel, in pages concerned with Charles. "He had an aimless hope. . . . " Images of space and motion—the two are frequently combined —serve, throughout the novel, to bring out the vagrant quality of Emma's thoughts. Departure, travel and access to privileged regions are recurring motifs. The "immense land of joys and passions" exists somewhere beyond her immediate surroundings: the more accessible things are, the more Emma's thoughts turn away from them. Happiness, by definition, can never be *here.* "Anywhere out of the World"—the title of Baudelaire's prose poem—could sum up Emma's chronic yearning for the exotic. "It seemed to her that certain places on earth must yield happiness, just as some plants are peculiar to certain places and grow poorly anywhere else" (I.7). By a skillful, and certainly far from gratuitous touch, Flaubert concludes Emma's initiatory stay at the Vaubyessard residence with a visit to the hothouses, where the strangest plants, rising in pyramids under hanging vases, evoke a climate of pure sensuality. The exotic setting becomes the very symbol of a yearned-for bliss. The "coming joys" are compared to tropical shores so distant that they cannot be seen, but from where soft winds carry back an intoxicating sweetness.

Travel and estrangement come to symbolize salvation from the immurement of ennui. Emma believes that change of abode alone is almost a guarantee of happiness. "She did not believe that things could be the same in different places . . . " (II.2). The unseen country is obviously also the richest in promises of felicity. Paris remains sublimely alluring precisely because—contrary to his original intentions—Flaubert does not grant Emma access to this promised land. Her first conversation with Léon typically exploits the Romantic cliché of the "limitless" expanse of the ocean, which "elevates the soul" through suggestions of the ideal and of infinity. And Léon's blue eyes seem beautiful to Emma because they appear more limpid than "those mountain-lakes where the sky is mirrored." The culmination of the travel imagery coincides with plans for Emma's elopement with Rodolphe (" . . . il fera bon voyager . . . " II.12) and with her visions of life in gondolas or under palm trees, to the accompaniment of guitars, in far-off countries with splendent domes and women dressed in red bodices. The very concept of emancipation is bound up with the notion of voyage. During her pregnancy Emma hopes to have a son, because a man is free: "he can travel over passions and over countries, cross obstacles, taste of the most far-away pleasures." And part of Rodolphe's prestige when she meets him is that he appears to her like a "traveler who has voyaged over strange lands." As early as her disappointing honeymoon (which, she feels, ought to have led to "those lands with sonorous names"), she knows that Charles did not, and could not, live up to her ideal of man as initiator to remote mysteries. She yearns for the inaccessible with a naïve but pungent lyricism: " . . . she was filled with desires, with rage, with hate" (II.5). Her desperate escapism, which ultimately alarms and alienates both her lovers, is of an almost sacrilegious nature. It is significant that sex is repeatedly associated with mystico-religious images (the remarkable death scene pushes the association to its logical conclusion), and that the assignation with Léon takes place in the Rouen cathedral, which Emma's distorted sensibility views as a "gigantic boudoir." Emma's tragedy is that she cannot escape her own immanence. "Everything, including herself, was unbearable to her" (III.6). But just as her walks always lead back to the detested house, so Emma feels thrown back into herself, left stranded on her own shore. The lyrical thrust toward the inaccessible leads back to an anesthetizing confinement.[23]

The cycles of ennui and spatial monotony, the images of escape (window perspectives, motion, insatiable desire for the elsewhere), are thus brought into contrapuntal tension with an underlying metaphoric structure suggesting limits, restriction, contraction and immobility. The basic tragic paradox of *Madame Bovary* is unwittingly summed up during Emma's first conversation with Léon. They discuss the pleasures of reading: "One thinks of nothing . . . the hours slip by. One *moves motionless* through countries one imagines one sees. . . . "[24] As for the sense of limitation, the very site of Yonville (the diminutive conglomeration in the midst of a characterless, undifferentiated landscape) suggests a circumscribed and hopelessly hedged-in existence. As soon as one enters the small market town,

[23] Georges Poulet, in *Les Métamorphoses du cercle*, points to the alternating rhythm of contracting and expanding movements in *Madame Bovary*.

[24] Italics mine. The French reads: "On se promène immobile . . ." (II.2).

"the courtyards grow narrower, the houses closer together, and the fences disappear. . . ." The entire first chapter of Part II, which introduces the reader to Yonville, plays on this contrast between expanse and delimitation. The very life of Yonville suggests constriction. Viewed from a distance—for instance during Emma's promenade on horseback with Rodolphe—the small community appears even more jammed in. "Emma half closed her eyes to recognize her house, and never had this poor village where she lived seemed so small to her." The same feeling of constriction is experienced inside her house, as Emma bewails "her too exalted dreams, her narrow home" (II.5). The entire tragic tension of the novel seems to be summed up in this experience of spiritual claustrophobia. The sitting-room where Emma, in her armchair, spends hours near the window, is distinguished by its particularly "low ceiling." The predominant impression is one of entrapment or encirclement. In a somewhat labored but telling simile, Flaubert compares Emma's married life to a complex strap which "buckles her in" on all sides (II.5).

This imagery of restriction and contraction is intimately related to the disintegrating experiences of sameness, interfusion and confusion of feelings, indiscrimination, abdication of will and lethal torpor. Space is lacking even in the Yonville cemetery, which is so full of graves that the old stones, completely level with the ground, form a "continuous pavement." This absence of a hiatus has its stylistic counterparts in the tight verbal and dramatic juxtapositions. There is no solution of continuity between the platitudinous official speeches, the lowing of the cattle and Rodolphe's talk of elective affinities. The seduction scene at the *comices agricoles*—a chapter of which Flaubert was particularly proud—is almost a continuous exercise in telescoping of levels of reality. Everything tends to merge and become alike. Even the villagers and the peasants present a comical and distressing uniformity. "Tous ces gens-là se ressemblaient."

Confusion, whether due to oppressive monotony, moral

drowsiness or spiritual anesthesia, is one of the leitmotifs in *Madame Bovary*. Once more, the opening pages are revealing. When Charles reads the list of course offerings at the medical school, he experiences a spell of "dizziness." Riding toward the Bertaux farm, he falls into a characteristic doze wherein his most recent sensations "blend" with old memories: the warm odor of poultices "mingled" in his brain with the fresh smell of dew. *Confondre, se mêler* are among Flaubert's favorite words. "Et peu à peu, les physionomies se confondirent dans sa mémoire" (I.8). As the Vaubyessard ball recedes into the past, the sharp outlines dissolve and all the figures begin to merge. Emma's ability to distinguish between levels of values dwindles as the novel progresses. "She confused in her desire the sensualities of luxury with the delights of the heart" (I.9). Later, this commingling of sensations becomes increasingly habitual, until no clear notions at all can be distinguished.

Emma's lust, her longing for money and her sentimental aspirations all become "confused" in one single, vague and oppressive sense of suffering. While listening to Rodolphe's seductive speeches, she conjures up other images: the viscount with whom she waltzed at Vaubyessard, his delicately scented hair, Léon who is now far away. The characteristic faintness ("mollesse") which comes over her induces an overlapping and a blurring of sensations which is not unlike a cinematographic fade-out. (". . . Puis tout se confondit . . ." II.8.) But this psychological strabismus is not here a technique whereby the author creates suspense or modestly veils the action. It corresponds to an abdication of choice and will, and points to the very principle of disintegration. As she is about to seek solace from the priest, Emma longingly recalls her sheltered life in the convent where she was "lost" ("confondue") in the long line of white veils. The memory makes her feel faint ("molle"); and she yearns for anything which would submerge and absorb her existence (II.6). The latent yearning for annihilation or nothingness is probably the most fundamental tragic impulse of Flaubertian protagonists. Not only does Emma dream of dissolving herself in an all-absorbing whole, but approaching death is described as a "confusion de crépuscule." Ultimately, not only all desire but all pain is absorbed in an all-embracing and all-negating woe. Thus Charles' retrospective jealousy, when he discovers Emma's infidelities, becomes "lost in the immensity of his grief." The frustration of all desire and of all hope is so great that nothing short of total sorrow and total surrender to nonbeing can bring relief.

A state of numbness or even dormancy is one of the chronic symptoms of *bovarysme*. *Mollesse, assoupissement* and *torpeur* are other favorite words of Flaubert. They refer most generally to a vague sensuous well-being, to a condition of nonresistance and even surrender. When Emma hears Rodolphe's flattering, if not original love declaration (he compares her to an angel), her pride "like one who relaxes in a bath, expanded softly" ("mollement"). The almost untranslatable *mollement* appears again, a few pages later, when Rodolphe puts his arm around Emma's waist and she tries "feebly" to disengage herself. Numbness and drowsiness occur almost regularly in a sexual context. During the nocturnal trysts in the garden, Emma, her eyes half closed, feels her emotion rise with the softness ("mollesse") of the perfume of the syringas. Her physical submissiveness to Rodolphe is termed "a beatitude that benumbed her" ("une béatitude qui l'engourdissait" II.12). And when she meets Léon again at the opera in Rouen, she is assailed by the "torpor" of her memories.

The pathological nature of such torpid states is strongly suggested. Early in the novel, her torpor follows moments of "feverish" chatter, and corresponds to periods when Emma suffers from heart palpitations. But the real pathology is of the spirit, not of the body. Just as the somnolence of the listeners at the agricultural show reflects the dullness of the speeches and the intellectual indolence of the townspeople, so Charles' congenital yawning symbolizes his inadequacy. When the coach arrives in Yonville, Charles is still asleep. During the evening at the Homais, he regularly falls asleep after playing dominoes. Such drowsiness seems contagious. Only Emma's takes on a more symbolic aspect. She suffers from an "assoupissement de sa conscience" (II.7): her very conscience is made numb. And in this numbness there is not only the principle of despair, but of death. All desire, like Baudelaire's *ennui*, leads to an omnivorous yawn. After Léon leaves Yonville, Emma's sensuous and sentimental frustration expresses itself through an infinite lassitude, a "numb despair." Her blinds are now kept closed (recurrence of the window motif), while she herself spends her days stretched out on her sofa, reading a book. The very atmosphere of Emma's burial will be one of monotony and sickening tedium. As Charles leads the funeral procession, he feels himself growing faint at this unending repetition of prayers and torches, surrounded by the insipid, almost nauseating smell of wax and of cassocks. A liturgical torpor invests him, and reduces all pain to a blurred feeling of weariness.

The very movement of the imagery in *Madame Bovary* thus leads from desire to frustration and failure, and ultimately to death and total undoing. Images of liquefaction and flow, which will be central to *L'Éducation sentimentale*, here also serve to convey the processes of dissolution. Emma almost perversely savors the slow disintegration of her being. The maraschino ice melting in her mouth corresponds to an entire past she wishes to negate. But the present, no matter how much one counts on it to beget change, never really disrupts the hopeless continuity of life. The tiny river near Yonville symbolizes a "time" which knows neither alteration nor respite ("La rivière coulait toujours . . . ," II.7). This temporal symbolism is bound up with the experience of loss and erosion: the great love with Rodolphe is like "the water of a river absorbed into its bed" until Emma begins to see the mud

(II.10). During her convalescence, the falling rain is the background to the sick woman's daily anticipation of the "inevitable return" of the same petty events. But it is above all morbidity of spirit or body which is suggested through fluid or soluble metaphors. From the empty and bloody orbits of the Blind Man flow "liquids" which congeal into green scales. Similarly, a "black liquid" oozes from the blisters on Hippolyte's leg. And after Emma dies, a "rush of black liquid" issues from her mouth, as though she were still vomiting. Even the soil thrown up at the side of her grave seems to be "flowing" down at the corners. This fluent quality of life points not only to mortality, but to decomposition. "Whence came this insufficiency in life, this instantaneous rotting of everything on which she leant?" (III,6). Emma's question goes to the very heart of the book. For life, in the Flaubertian context, is a steady process of decay.

This relentless deterioration of everything is very different from the Balzacian wear and tear which is most often the price man pays for his tragic energy. Flaubert's heroes not only have a vocation for failure, but they fail independently of any investment of fervor. Charles' early fiasco at his examination foreshadows his entire career. Paradoxically, it could be said that unsuccess precedes the act of living. In Flaubert's world, life is not fought out and lost, but *spent*. It is only appropriate that Emma should be congenitally improvident. For she is a squanderer not only of money. In a strained but revealing simile, Flaubert compares her loss of illusions to a steady act of "spending." "Elle en avait dépensé à toutes les aventures de son âme . . . " (II, 10). But it is, in reality, her own self that she is dissipating, as though urged on by the desire to fade or melt away. Flaubert elsewhere speaks of death as a "continuous swooning away" (an "évanouissement continu").[25] The death-wish is a permanent reality

---

[25] Flaubert, *Bouvard et Pécuchet*, Chapter 8. On the subject of this expression, J. P. Richard writes: " . . . ever since his birth, the Flaubertian being has not ceased dying. He has lived through

in the fictional world of Flaubert; it most often reveals itself through an almost mystical desire to vanish or be absorbed by a larger whole. On her way to Father Bournisien, Emma dreams of the "disappearance" of her entire existence. The longing for nothingness is often linked to religious or pseudo-religious images. In Emma's mind, it is most often associated with memories of the convent, with a desire to return to it, as one might to a maternal womb. The desire to stop living ("She would have liked not to be alive, or to be always asleep," III.6) corresponds to a quasi-metaphysical fatigue, to the immedicable pain of having been betrayed by life itself. In the face of universal abandon, the Flaubertian heroine is driven to dissipation. She becomes the willing accomplice of all the forces of disbandment.

Structure, Irony and Point of View

The convoluted fabric of images, often circuitous and apparently bound by an uncontrolled necessity, amply suggests that Flaubert is not indulging in a mere virtuoso exercise. The imagery, in *Madame Bovary*, appears almost self-generated: a determinism seems to preside over its pattern, and this pattern itself corresponds to the forms of the author's imagination, thus testifying to the all-importance of themes in his work.

This is not to deny the willed construction of the novel. Though he claimed that he hated plans and outlines, Flaubert was an inveterate planner and plotter. Sainte-Beuve, who enjoyed paying left-handed compliments, observed that in *Madame Bovary* "nothing is left to chance."[26] The sketches and scenarios, as well as the astonishing *journal de bord* which is his correspondence, are ample proof of this. Flaubert's hesitations and ultimate decisions all bespeak an unrelenting concern for structure. The very strategy of Emma's adultery is revealing. In one of

successive swoonings" ("La Création de la forme chez Flaubert," in *Littérature et sensation*, p. 147).

[26] Sainte-Beuve, *Causeries du lundi*, XIII, 346–366.

the earlier scenarios, Léon becomes her lover before Ro-dolphe.[27] But very soon, Flaubert introduces a significant change: the love for Léon is to remain repressed. The reason for this repression is clear, and Flaubert himself has commented on it: Emma's "fall" with Rodolphe will become that much more *necessary*. Her successful defense against Léon fills her with the sadness of her own "sacri-fice," increases her resentment of her husband, and makes her an eager victim of any aggressive seducer.

Clearly, also, Flaubert took immense pains preparing and articulating his episodes. "Ils arrivèrent, en effet, ces fameux Comices!" Opening sentences often impose the very rhythm of Time. "Ils recommencèrent à s'aimer"—the beginning of chapter 12 of Part II is a good example of the Flaubertian change of gears by means of which the unique act slips into a dreary continuum, and hope is transmuted into an unheroic despair. As for the almost unbearable acceleration toward the end of the novel, nota-bly in chapter 7 of Part III, when, after the delirium of the senses, Emma frantically attempts to ward off finan-cial disaster, it is brilliantly executed.

Yet the very care with which Flaubert proceeded result-ed in a certain laboriousness: the novel, at times, seems a bit too "constructed," the symbols appear perhaps just a trifle too obvious. With even a mild dose of ill will, one could easily magnify some characteristics of Flaubert's technique into significant defects. The exposition is indeed very slow, and occupies a good third of the novel. Not until chapter 9 of Part II does the dramatic action begin. Flaubert himself was aware of it. Having reached this part of the novel, he writes: "Now I am about to start the action, and the passions will become effective." He was, in fact, worried about the absence of action ("I thus have a stretch of fifty pages without a single event. . . . ") as well as about the blocklike composition and the excessive preparations: "I believe that this book will

27 Flaubert, *Madame Bovary—Nouvelle version précédée des scénarios inédits*, p. 4.

have one great defect, namely the lack of *material* proportion. I have already two hundred and sixty pages, but which contain nothing but preparations for action. . . ."[28]

But Flaubert was unfair to himself. For if the construction of the novel is indeed laborious and could be compared, as Flaubert himself might well have done, to the patient stacking of solid masses one on top of the other, this blocklike composition is also responsible for the admirable "scenes" which constitute the very anatomy of *Madame Bovary*. These scenes are themselves at times mere expository devices, such as, for instance, the beginning of Part II—the scene at Mme Lefrançois' inn—whose function it is to present a number of new characters (Binet, Léon, Homais, Bournisien, Hivert, Lheureux) and to introduce the reader to the atmosphere of Yonville. But most often the "scene" in Flaubert corresponds to a particular vision. The ambulant love scene in the cab (III.1), where all the reader is granted is the view of the cab with its blinds drawn, now trotting quietly and then galloping furiously, driven by a puzzled and exasperated coachman, conveys— in its disordered movement as well as in its picturesque details—the very nature of Emma's erotic experience. The changes of speed, the dizzying crescendi, the torn letter scattered to the wind by an ungloved hand and falling on a field of red clover (an obvious reminder of the burning of her wedding bouquet), acquire a symbolic value. Indeed, all of Emma's life is a race ending in death (the cab is "shut more closely than a tomb"), and the lumbering machine into which Emma agrees to step because "it is done in Paris" is a grotesque but also malefic vehicle.

To be sure, the episode comes very close to being a tour de force. A relish for bravura similarly appears at the very conception of the famous *comices* chapter. The idea of having Rodolphe court Emma while prize cattle low and official speeches are declaimed, appealed to Flaubert

[28] Flaubert, *Corresp.*, III, 423; II, 351; III, 247.

because he was fond, in advance, of the "symphonic" effect he might achieve.[29] As craftsman, he valued the challenge to create an animated triptych. The scene, ultimately, is far more than a clever display of technique: the comical juxtaposition and contrasts, the insistence on animality, as well as the general flow of meaningless words, not only bring out the vulgarity and stupidity of Emma's world, but constitute a parody, or rather a mockery of love. The central meaning of the novel is somehow conveyed in this chapter of futility and degradation.

But to enjoy Flaubert's art at its purest, that is where least tainted by the display of technical prowess, one should turn to another famous scene, though perhaps less spectacular than the *comices* chapter: Emma's visit to Father Bournisien (II.6). Flaubert explained his intentions in a letter to Louise Colet: Emma, almost undergoing a religious crisis, seeks help from the inept and utterly pedestrian priest who, unable to intuit her anguish and aware only of physical suffering, remains totally deaf to her secret hope, and thus helps close the door to spiritual salvation.[30] In the novel, however, analysis and commentary are totally absent. Language here carries the entire burden, and primarily the dialogue, which is the more effective for being used so sparingly in Flaubert's work. Emma's frustrating conversation with Bournisien rests almost entirely on a basic misunderstanding: she speaks of moral suffering, seeks solace and needs "no earthly remedy"; his mind turns exclusively to the discomforts of the flesh: the summer heat and the distress of indigestion. The very interruption of her sentences by Bournisien's irrelevant remarks stresses the fundamental lack of communication between them.

On one level, the scene is painfully comic. Flaubert almost indulges in caricature. The grease and tobacco stains on Bournisien's cossack, his noisy breathing, the shower of cuffs he distributes among his pupils, his thick

[29] Flaubert, *Corresp.*, III, 335, 365.
[30] Flaubert, *Corresp.*, III, 166–167.

laughter and cheap puns, all stress his coarseness and peasant mentality. He answers Emma's complaint that she is "unwell," with the admirable *mot de comédie*: "Well, and so am I." But there is a deeper irony in this passage. For the priest, reminding Emma that her husband is the "doctor of the body" (while he, Bournisien, is the "doctor of the soul"), is astonished that Charles Bovary did not prescribe something for her. After advising her to take some tea (always good for the digestion), he ends the conversation with a "Good health to you, madame" which is doubly ironic since he not only sends her back empty to an unbearable life, but specifically to a cohabitation with an incompetent husband-doctor. The very drama of incommunicability is summed up by this exchange:

"But you were asking me something. What was it? I really can't remember."
"I? Nothing . . . ! nothing . . . !"

A scene such as this involves the very nature of Flaubertian comedy. The intimacy between laughter, cruelty and tragic absurdity is indeed characteristic of Flaubert. Comedy, in *Madame Bovary*, appears on one level as a Molièresque farce. The ludicrous accoutrements (Charles' cap, Homais' costumes) are excellent illustrations of Bergson's theory of laughter: "le mécanique plaqué sur le vivant." Rigidity is here in conflict with life itself. Binet, the captain of the corps of firemen, wears a collar so high and stiff, a tunic so tightly buttoned, that his entire body, above his legs, seems paralyzed. The visor of his helmet, covering his face down to his nose, totally blinds him. This rigidity of attire and of body is paralleled by an equal stubbornness of mind which condemns the Flaubertian comic figures to an imprisonment within their ridicules, just as the Flaubertian "hero" becomes the quixotic victim of a perilous illusion. *Idées fixes*, misunderstandings, pedantry, boors and bores, the absurdities of medical practice and the humiliations of the flesh—all these are part of the tradition of comedy. What distinguishes

Flaubert is the unusual stress laid on language itself, both as symptom and as an instrument of denunciation. This dual role of style is best exemplified in Flaubert's systematic exploitation of clichés. Homais' "opinions" (on weather, on hygiene, on women), his articles to the Rouen newspaper, are fundamentally as inane and as exasperating as Flaubert's lifelong entries into his *Dictionnaire des idées reçues*, which, one suspects, he consulted repeatedly while writing *Madame Bovary*. The same almost perverse satisfaction occurs whenever he can weigh down a character under the load of his own unalterable ineptness.

Stylistic caricature and parody are among Flaubert's more obvious talents. But they correspond not merely to the author's desire to mock the mental foibles and the vulgarity of bourgeois society: too much has been made of Flaubert the *bourgeoisophobus*! This comedy of language reaches out to the very heart of the novel. When, for instance, Rodolphe writes his hypocritical, and fundamentally caddish farewell letter to Emma, and Flaubert studs this masterful missive with the most hackneyed Romantic thoughts and mannerisms, the author's attitude is critical, to be sure: Rodolphe is fully conscious of his own lies. But the irony of the passage reaches beyond the victim of seduction and the egoism of the seducer. It involves indirectly the very meaning of the novel: the tragicomedy of lies, ersatz and illusion. And it is characteristic of Flaubert that comedy is for him simultaneously an instrument of "meaning," an expression of his indignation and a technique of oblique intervention.

This raises the question of Flaubert's passionate "presence" in his own novel. The myth of the author's impassibility indeed crumbles as soon as the reader attunes his mind to the peculiar vehemence of Flaubert—a vehemence which most often, at least in his fictional work, takes the form of a contained wrath. A permanent, and to some extent artificially cultivated ire seems to be one of Flaubert's most fecund sources of inspiration. To the brothers Goncourt he once explained: "Indignation alone keeps me going. . . . When I will no longer be indignant, I will fall down flat."[31] This propensity for anger reveals itself in the peculiar Flaubertian irony *at the expense* of his characters. We are here far from the tender, protective and lyrical smile of a Stendhal. Flaubert proceeds with an apparent absence of charity. Thus he has Charles almost push Emma into the arms of Rodolphe. This type of devastating irony is the common note. When Emma is about to ride off with Rodolphe, Homais' exhortation is like an invitation for trouble: "An accident happens so easily! Be careful! Your horses perhaps are impetuous!" (II.9).

This kind of irony is tragic by nature. It makes of the reader an accomplice of "destiny." Charles is the privileged victim of this cruel game. When Rodolphe invites Emma to go horseback riding with him, it is Charles who encourages her not to worry about public opinion: "Health before everything!" It is again he who thanks her for making a trip to Rouen to consult Léon on a business matter: "How good you are!" (III.2). The entire episode of the club-foot operation is conceived and executed in order to humiliate Charles. One almost has the impression that Flaubert enjoyed destroying Charles professionally. (Is there a hint here of a secret animosity toward his father?)[32] But others are not spared. Hippolyte first is congratulated by Father Bournisien on his gangrenous leg because this is an excellent opportunity to reconcile himself with Heaven, and later hears the surgeon explain that it is indifferent to him "to carve a Christian or the first fowl that turns up" (II.11). And Emma herself, after her lover's treason, is exposed to her husband's jovial approval of Rodolphe's "free life": "He absents himself like that from time to time to have fun, and I must say that he's right when one has money and is a

[31] Goncourt, *Journal*, X, 123.

[32] Did not the medical textbook consulted by Flaubert refer to the case of a ten-year-old girl unsuccessfully treated by Doctor Flaubert? (Jean Pommier, "Noms et prénoms dans 'Madame Bovary,'" *Mercure de France*, June 1949, pp. 244–264.)

bachelor!" (II.13). This turning of the knife culminates, toward the end of the novel, in Charles' almost morbid curiosity as he lifts the veil to see Emma's already decomposing face.

The author's presence is felt not only in such ironies of detail. Irony in the structure of the novel also points to the author's chronic "intrusion," and constitutes, so to speak, a built-in commentary. The most flagrant examples—though perhaps they show Flaubert at his most arbitrary—are the episodes with the Blind Man. The relationship between irony, the tragic spirit, and even a certain allegorical mood is nowhere more tightly drawn than in these passages. The Blind Man himself is a semigrotesque and semilugubrious figure, whose creation corresponds to Flaubert's taste for the pathological, and possibly also to memories of his trip to the Near East. A beggar afflicted with a horrible skin disease and with two huge, oozing empty eye-sockets, he appears at critical moments during the latter stages of Emma's life, like an embodiment of corruption and meaningless death. The first time Emma sees him is after one of the hotel-room meetings with Léon, and the ghastly contrasts between the innocent love ditty he sings and the leprous horror of his face is like a macabre emblem of all physical love. And it is significant that this first encounter takes place in the very chapter (III.5) which insists on Emma's moral corruption: her gluttony, her taste for lies, her walks through the red-light district, the voluptuousness and sadness of the hotel room with its faded elegance that reeks of decomposition.

The second meeting with the Blind Man (III.7) provides no less of a commentary on the action and moral situation. Emma is returning from a rendezvous with Léon during which she tried, with lascivious provocation, to convince her lover to steal money for her. This second scene with the Blind Man conveys an even more pungent and more terrifying symbolism. The ideas of Law and Society are invoked by Homais, who would like to see such intrusive beggars locked up. The pariah-like existence of the Blind Man is of course related to Emma's subjective feeling—particularly strong in this chapter—of being herself an outcast. Similarly, Homais' allusions to crime and penology are meant to resound in Emma's mind. But it is the Blind Man's revolting pantomime which most profoundly affects Emma: his head thrown back, his tongue sticking out, his hands rubbing his belly, his guttural cry are a repellent burlesque of all appetite and gratification, and more specifically a hideous mockery of the sex act. The scene ends with Emma's flinging to the beggar her last five-franc piece, as though money had exorcising virtues—an additional irony given the context of the novel.

The third appearance of the Blind Man—even more melodramatic than the others—coincides with the exact moment of Emma's death. The ditty he sings this time combines erotic and macabre motifs. The tragic elements of the scene are almost theatrical in a classical sense: the blind beggar is like an ancient chorus, present as an observer and as a mourner. His very blindness seems to endow him with supernatural vision, at the same time that it symbolizes a hopeless impasse in the face of the Absolute. His appearance, which interrupts the priest's prayers ("the muffled murmur of the Latin syllables"), did provoke the ire of the Imperial prosecutor. But it could be easily argued —as did Flaubert's lawyer, Maître Sénard—that far from representing a profanatory intrusion, the Blind Man is the living "reminder of her fault, remorse in all its horror and poignancy." Indeed, the arrival of the beggar not only coincides with her death, but seems to provoke it. The passage nonetheless remains characteristically ambiguous. The sinister laughter of Emma—a laughter which is described as "atrocious," "frenetic" and "desperate"—certainly does not bespeak the peace of a soul about to be released from human bondage. The laughter sounds much rather like a satanic expression of scorn in the face of life's ultimate absurdity, death.

The exact nature of the author's perspective remains

one of the most puzzling questions in *Madame Bovary*. Traditional interpretations insist either on frigid impassibility (the myth of objectivity) or on mordant satire (the double myth of the bourgeois-hater and the anti-Romantic). The truth is both more elusive and more interesting. For there is ambiguity not only in Flaubert's implicit commentary, but in the very method by which this commentary is textured into the fiction. Flaubert's almost exclusive instrument of intervention is style itself; it is this precisely which disconcerts the reader used to more formal, and more obvious techniques of intrusion. But this reliance on the resources of syntax enables Flaubert to be both "in" and "out" at the same time. This double perspective is nowhere better illustrated than in the countless examples of *style indirect libre*, of which Flaubert is a pioneer in French letters as well as the masterful practitioner, and which he utilizes not only as an elliptic abstract of conversation and as a subtle way of underlining clichés, but as an equivalent for interior monologue. Yet it is only an equivalent, for it allows him to formulate clearly that which, in the character's mind, remains unformulated or only half-formulated, and thus establishes a gap between what the characters feel and what the author understands. It is this somewhat elastic gap which represents the area of the author's personal commitment.

Some examples may clarify these remarks. First a rather simple illustration. When Emma lies naked in the sumptuous hotel-room bed, and Flaubert writes that "nothing in the world was so lovely as her brown head and white skin standing out against this purple color, when, with a movement of modesty, she crossed her bare arms, hiding her face in her hands" (III.5), this lovely pose is obviously appreciated both by Léon and by the author. But when Flaubert's style penetrates into the very consciousness of the protagonist, the focus becomes less clear: "But she— her life was cold as a garret whose dormer-window looks northward, and ennui, the silent spider, was weaving its web in the dark, in every corner of her heart" (I.7). Who

is thinking this? Is it a series of clichés to be attributed
to the character, or is it the character's vague sensation
that the author translates and elaborates into images? The
same fundamental ambiguity presides over many comparisons and metaphors. "The future was a dark corridor,
with its door at the end shut tightly" (I.9). We are no
doubt "inside" the character: it is Emma's sense of frustration and gloom that the metaphor conveys. But the
metaphor also carries an "objective" value: it corresponds
to the theme of claustration that Flaubert develops
throughout the novel. This duplicity of the *style indirect
libre* is perhaps most clearly illustrated in a passage where
Emma dreams of an "impossible" love, while aware of the
very principle of disintegration in her life:

> No matter! She was not happy—she had never been.
> Whence came this insufficiency in life—this instantane-
> ous turning to decay of everything on which she leant?
> . . . But if there were somewhere a being strong and
> beautiful, a generous nature, full at once of exultation
> and refinement, a poet's heart in the form of an angel,
> a lyre with sounding chords ringing out elegiac epithala-
> mia to heaven, why, perchance, should she not find him?
> Ah! how impossible! Nothing, anyhow, was worth the
> trouble of seeking it! Everything was a lie! Every smile
> hid a yawn of boredom, every joy a curse, all pleasure
> surfeit, and the sweetest kisses left upon your lips noth-
> ing but the unattainable desire for a greater delight.
> (III.6)

Clearly the passage fuses the character's interior monologue with the author's point of view. But even that point
of view is not clear: Flaubert's pity blends with his caricature of Romantic dreams, and nothing would be more
difficult than to draw a line separating the two. Finally,
even the caricature of the Romantic clichés remains ambiguous. On the one hand, the cliché—both as an intellectual and a stylistic *fausse monnaie*—is the permanent object
of Flaubert's scorn; but clichés are also, no matter how

ludicrous and objectionable, the surprising and touching conveyors of the characters' "innocence." This is what neither the literal-minded reader nor a callous seducer such as Rodolphe is likely to understand. In one of the most curious passages of the novel, commenting on Rodolphe's insensibility to Emma's genuine emotion (he has heard the same expressions of love so often!), Flaubert explains that it is a grave mistake not to seek candor behind worn-out language, "as though the fullness of the soul did not at times overflow in the emptiest metaphors" (II.12). And Flaubert, in what may appear like an *apologia pro domo*, suggests that nobody can ever give the exact measure of his needs and of his sorrows, that human speech is "like a cracked tin kettle on which we strike tunes fit to make bears dance, when we long to move the stars." This feeling that human speech cannot possibly cope with our dreams and our grief goes a long way toward explaining why so often, in the work of Flaubert, the reader has the disconcerting impression that the language of banality is caricatured and at the same time transmuted into poetry.

We are perhaps touching here on the very secret of Flaubert's lyrical achievement within a realistic framework. But the framework, or setting, should not blind us to the fact that Flaubert's temperament and practice, despite all the noise made around the substantive "realism," has little in common with the products of a Champfleury, a Duranty, or even a Daumier. "One need only read *Madame Bovary* with intelligence," writes Guy de Maupassant, "to understand that nothing is further removed from realism." And Maupassant goes on to explain that Flaubert's sentences soar above the subject they express, that in order to convey the stupidities of Homais or the silliness of Emma, his language assumes majesty and brilliance, "as though it were translating poetic motifs. . . ."[33] One of the most striking features of Flaubert's art is indeed his

[33] See Maupassant's study for the edition of Flaubert's works published by Quentin. Reprinted in the Conard edition of *Madame Bovary*, Flaubert, *Oeuvres complètes*, p. 544.

ability to shift, without transition, from the trivial to the lyrical—or rather, to transmute the one into the other. This alchemy is not the result of chance: Flaubert was fully lucid about the dangers of a double "tone," and determined to bring about a poetic fusion. "The entire value of my book . . . will have been the ability to walk straight on a hair, suspended between the double abyss of lyricism and vulgarity (which I want to fuse in a narrative analysis)."[34]

Critics—in the wake of Baudelaire, who saw *Madame Bovary* as an artist's bold "wager"—have been aware that the novel's originality stems in large part from the interplay of the author's point of view with that of the heroine, that these two points of view alternate, clash and at times overlap.[35] Erich Auerbach, who has probably provided the clearest formulation, explains that Flaubert bestows "the power of mature expression" on the material which the heroine affords in its complete subjectivity; that consequently Emma not only "sees," but is herself "seen as one seeing."[36]

The tension between style and that which it describes, the superiority of the former over the latter, point to the fundamental paradox of Realism.[37] For Realism, far from providing a harmony between style and subject—the kind of harmony that would make one forget the very presence of a "style"—accentuates the gap between "unpoetic" reality and the poetic attempt to transcend it in the very act of describing it. Far from defeating art, as naïve minds might

[34] Flaubert, *Corresp.*, II, 372. According to Harry Levin, one of Flaubert's achievements is precisely "eloquent banality" (*The Gates of Horn*, p. 258). Alison Fairlie puts it as follows: "This is a book which combines parody, representation and poetry in a particularly original way" (*Flaubert: Madame Bovary*, p. 13).

[35] Baudelaire, "Madame Bovary," in *L'Art Romantique, Oeuvres complètes*, pp. 444–450. See in particular Jean Rousset, "Madame Bovary ou 'le livre sur rien,'" in *Forme et signification*, pp. 109–133; and Percy Lubbock, *The Craft of Fiction*, p. 87.

[36] Auerbach, *Mimesis*, p. 427.

[37] Anthony Thorlby writes about the new function of description in Flaubert: "To describe this illusion in realistic prose, and yet to make his style superior to all that he reckoned prosaic or illusory, meant that description was intended to carry a new (and seemingly self-defeating) significance" (*Gustave Flaubert and the Art of Realism*, p. 35).

have feared, the practitioners of "Realism" have contributed powerfully toward a very cult of art. The examples of the Goncourt brothers and of Huysmans are revealing. This cult of art, or rather of style, can be dangerous: contempt for the very "reality" evoked goes hand in hand with coquetries of style and ultimately leads to forms of preciosity. Paul Valéry, who was altogether suspicious of the novel as a genre (perhaps in part for this very reason), pointed to the contradictions of a method which consisted in describing banality while the language used to describe it was to be beautiful in itself. "Realism curiously led to giving the impression of the most contrived artifice."[38] This indeed seems to be the basic dilemma: precisely to the extent that the artist (call him a "realist" or not) wanted to deal with the very triteness of life, style tended to develop into an all-important and self-containing value. A style in a vacuum is, however, not only the expression of a fundamental disdain; it also points to an awareness or fear of sterility. Psychologically or historically, the gap is never great between realism and decadentism.

These considerations may point to the impasse of Flaubert's art. A certain duplicity vis-à-vis his characters, a basic lack of solidarity with the world in which they move and suffer, and the insistence on the self-redeeming qualities of style, have made Flaubert vulnerable to the charge of having dehumanized the novel. The rift between the author's artistic, sophisticated vision and the insufficient, confused vision of the protagonist is probably responsible, as much if not more so than the Parnassian aspects of Flaubert's prosody, for a certain rigid, inanimate quality. One misses, in Flaubert's work, those approximations and hesitations, those imperceptible human tremors, thrusts and recoils which convey artistically the very drama of existence in the works of a Stendhal, a Dostoevsky or, in our own day, a Nathalie Sarraute. Yet it is precisely this

[38] Valéry, "La Tentation de (saint) Flaubert," in *Variété V*, p. 614.

rift, or rather the telescoping of two unrelated perspectives, which bestows upon the novel a unique beauty. A stereoscopic vision accounts in large part for the peculiar poetry and complexity of *Madame Bovary.*

This stereopsis is particularly evident in the beautiful landscape descriptions. When, at the beginning of April, the primroses are in bloom and a soft wind blows over the flowerbeds, when the gardens look festive (like women getting all dressed up, explains Flaubert) and the evening vapors between the leafless poplars seem like a subtle gauze caught in the branches (II.6)—it is quite clear that it is Flaubert the artist who is speaking directly to us. Yet it is true that the quality of the description—in particular the very coquettishness of Nature—coincides, on another level, with the mood of the heroine. The overlap necessitates a double reading of the passage. There is, on the one hand, Flaubert the landscape painter, sensitive to the melancholy beauty of Normandy and fond of misty seasons; but there is also Emma the dreamer—and the vision of the former corrects, enhances and transcends that of the latter.

The same is true of the two other outstanding landscape passages. During their "honeymoon" in Rouen, Léon and Emma take a boat to have dinner on one of the islands (III.3). In approximately ten splendid lines, Flaubert evokes the dockyard, the caulking mallets resounding against the hulls of the vessels, the smoke of tar, the large spots of oil undulating in the purple color of the sun—the very poetry of a river port. As they row toward the island, the city noises gradually grow distant. But the entire passage corresponds not merely to Flaubert's own attachment to the river—the permanent spectacle from his windows at Croisset; it also suggests Emma's transformation of the commercial port into a grandiose and lyrical image of departure, and her landing on the little island into an arrival in an exotic country of bliss. Similarly, the distant view of Rouen, in chapter 5 of Part III, involves double optics: the character's subjective, vague, unformu·

lated feelings as the town appears "like an amphitheater," and the author's ability to see and to render the tableau. The personal poetry of the author and the reaction of Emma do not, of course, coincide. But the thematic validity of the passage depends almost exclusively on this very discrepancy which, once again, stresses the divorce between a reality perceived by the author (and by his accomplice, the reader) and the illusions of his heroine. The author describes the monotonous landscape, "motionless as a picture," the anchored ships, the meanders of the river, the factory chimneys. But this apparently gratuitous description acquires its full significance once we become aware that Emma, looking at exactly the same panorama, experiences a giddiness, an inebriating sensation of space and infinite possibility, as she is about to enter the rather dull provincial town which for her is an "enormous capital" and even a true Babylon!

This ability to be simultaneously "inside" and "outside" his characters leads to even greater complexities if one considers the poetry of adultery. Indeed Emma views adultery as a privileged condition. "I have a lover! a lover!" she keeps repeating to herself with a sense of wonder. It seems to her like a long-awaited initiation to a mystery: "She was entering into a world of marvels. . . ." She feels surrounded by an azure infinity (the adjective "bleuâtre" occurs repeatedly in the novel) as she joins the "lyric legion" of the adulterous fictional heroines she so admires (II.9). But Flaubert's attitude is by no means one of clinical detachment. It would be a misreading not only of the novel, but of Flaubert's entire work, to consider *Madame Bovary* a moral denunciation of conjugal infidelity! For the author also, adultery was a magic word. Ever since his adolescence the notion of adultery was endowed with a poetic and a tragic meaning. His own life-long dream of an adulterous relation with Elisa Schlésinger had much to do, no doubt, with this poetization of illegitimate love. But there are other reasons, in addition to the obvious autobiographical echoes. To the entire generation reared on Romanticism—and Flaubert is as much a "victim" as Emma—adultery, because of its officially immoral and asocial status, acquired a symbolic value: it was a sign of unconventionality, rebellion and authenticity. But more important still—and here Flaubert the *troubadour* reworks one of the main themes of Western poetry—adultery holds out the promise of beauty precisely because it is the forbidden happiness, the inaccessible dream, that which always eludes: the Ideal. It is in this light that one should reread the juvenile works of Flaubert: *Mémoires d'un fou, Novembre*, the first *Éducation sentimentale*—where adultery is viewed as a "supreme poetry" made up of a mixture of voluptuousness and malediction.

The famous exclamation "Madame Bovary, c'est moi . . ." is thus not merely the sally of a writer irritated by seekers of sources and models. A curious symbiotic relationship exists between Flaubert and his heroine. The novelist, despite his practice of a double perspective, draws his fictional creature toward himself, and discovers himself in Emma even more than he projects himself into her. This complex relationship, in which the writer is to some extent playing hide-and-seek with himself, in which he punishes himself while granting himself a perspective that transcends the limits of his own temperament, makes it extremely difficult to assess the exact measure of personal involvement and to come to grips with the nature of this tragic experience. Emma's death exists, on the one hand, as a pathological fact, inevitable as the effects of the arsenic she swallows. But as she strains to kiss the crucifix, and as the priest gives the extreme unction to all those parts of her body that have lived, loved and suffered, an immense pity, an immense sadness and an immense fraternal understanding seem to emanate from Flaubert's text which will forever baffle those readers who view the novel principally as an anti-Romantic and antibourgeois satire.

Tragedy of Reality or Tragedy of Dreams?

Nothing is in fact more elusive, more subject to contradictory and frustrating interpretations, than the meaning of Emma's tragedy. Allan Tate described her as a "silly, sad and hysterical woman."[39] Summary though this judgment may be, it represents what one might call the clinical approach. On one level, the disease is social, and can be diagnosed as a form of *déclassement*: Emma's education and tastes are above her class. This social pathology has been denounced by Paul Bourget, who was altogether concerned with the moral and psychological dangers of a steady democratization.[40] The mobility of classes led, in his opinion, not only to the tragic maladjustment of the individual, but to a national disaster.

On another level, the clinical approach deals exclusively with Emma as an individual case history, studies the anatomy of her aberrations and admires in Flaubert the master dissector. Sainte-Beuve set the tone. In his article for the *Moniteur Universel*, he praised in Flaubert the deft surgeon: "The son and the brother of distinguished doctors, M. Gustave Flaubert holds the pen as others hold the scalpel."[41] Emma's moral corruption is indeed progressive, like the steady deterioration of an organism undergoing the stages of a fatal disease. Especially in Part III of the novel, Flaubert insists on her imbalance and morbid excesses: the neglect of house and child, the taste for orgiastic books, the loss of *pudeur*, the rapacious desire for money, the aggressive sensuality. "She became irritable, greedy, voluptuous. . . ." One vice leads to another: she develops a talent and a taste for lying; it becomes "a need, a mania, a pleasure" (III.5). Finally her very senses seem affected: her behavior becomes "odd," she assumes lascivious poses and a look of "infernal boldness," goes to a popular ball in debauched company, tries to goad her lover

[39] Tate, "Techniques of Fiction," in *Collected Essays*, p. 132.
[40] Bourget, "Gustave Flaubert," in *Essais de psychologie contemporaine*, p. 179. Emile Zola also observed that Emma has received "an education above her class." She reads novels, plays the piano and suffers from "the terrible ennui of déclassé women" (*Les Romanciers Naturalistes*, p. 140).
[41] May 4, 1857. Reprinted in Sainte-Beuve, *Causeries du lundi*, XIII, 346–363.

into stealing, and at the end quite literally prostitutes herself to her first lover. Even her sexual behavior with Léon,
after a while, takes on a distinctly morbid quality: when
they meet in the hotel room, she undresses "brutally," tearing off the thin lace of her corset, which swishes around
her hips "like a gliding snake" (III.6). The simile leaves
something to be desired; but it does convey a feeling of perversity and even of agony—the latter being further developed in the almost medical description of Emma's physical ecstasy, which Flaubert presents as a deathlike trance:
her forehead is covered with cold drops of perspiration, her
lips are quivering, her eyes are wild, her embrace feels
lugubrious. The love act is like a caricature of death, pointing to the very vanity of Emma's existence.

A somewhat loftier interpretation of Emma's tragedy
must stress that which unquestionably is at the center of
the book: the drama of Reality. Repeatedly, Emma "wakes
up" to the realization that her capacity to dream is powerless to change the world. To be sure, some of these awakenings—as when she suddenly discovers that her child has
dirty ears—only confirm her slovenliness and her withdrawal to a selfish world of illusions. Her ability to create
for herself a world of make-believe is so powerful that it
becomes contagious: she corrupts her husband from beyond the grave. But the awakenings are no less a form of
tragic lucidity—a lucidity that bestows additional beauty
on her refusal to be satisfied with what is. Stretching the
point somewhat, Paul Bourget saw Emma Bovary as a victim of the nefarious and corrosive force of "Thought."[42]
But Emma's forte is certainly not thinking! Like Don
Quixote, she has read too many books, and the books she
has read are those most likely to inflame her imagination.
It is not her intellect, but her capacity to dream and to wish
to transform the world to fit her dreams, which sets her
apart. The parallel with Don Quixote almost imposes itself.
Like Don Quixote's friends who decide to burn his books,

[42] Bourget, "Gustave Flaubert," in *Essais de psychologie contemporaine*, p. 155.

Emma's mother-in-law suggests that reading be prohibited and that what she needs in order to be cured are "chores" and above all "manual work." Flaubert's and Cervantes' novels have further in common a certain autocritical tendency which makes of both works outstanding examples of ambiguity, literary subversion and yet latent idealism. Emma, like the sad knight, is a victim of her Romanticism: but she also transcends her own foolishness. Hers is a true mania for believing in the impossible—a mania, moreover, that Flaubert knew only too well. Seen in this light, Emma's shortcoming is not that she has had illusions, but that she was unable to make her dream-vision victorious over the "reality" represented by the Homais of this world![43] It is a strange book indeed that permits one to interpret the same traits as symptoms either of a self-destructive disease or of an insufficient virtue!

In defense of Emma!—much of the novel does indeed seem to have been written in this spirit. Sympathy, warmth and compassion emerge at every point from behind the apparently detached diagnosis. "At this very hour, my poor Bovary no doubt suffers and cries in twenty villages of France . . . ," Flaubert wrote to his mistress Louise Colet.[44] "Ma pauvre Bovary . . ." But one need not go to the *Correspondance*: the text of the novel amply echoes these feelings. When Emma, having decided to borrow money from her former lover, enters the domain of La Huchette, "her poor oppressed heart" opens out amorously at the memories of past happiness. Again, after she takes the poison, and as the dimness of agony is settling upon her thoughts, Flaubert sorrows for this "poor heart" which continues to sing out its intermittent lament. And if Flaubert has imprisoned Emma in an inept and hostile world, if even religion is shown to be ignorant and pedestrian, this is not

[43] Jean-Pierre Richard brilliantly sums up such a view: " . . . il faudrait peut-être voir en *Madame Bovary* bien moins le procès de l'illusion romanesque que le procès d'un romanesque incapable de soutenir jusqu'au bout ses illusions" ("La Création de la forme chez Flaubert," in *Littérature et sensation*, p. 202).
[44] Flaubert, *Corresp.*, III, 291.

so much out of a personal vengeance against a world he abhors, but to bring out Emma's tragic solitude.

For Emma's rebellion, distorted though her values may be, is the only attitude that even remotely comes close to being whole-souled. And though it can be attributed largely to selfishness and to plain irresponsibility, it is not devoid of a measure of courage and even of dignity. Despite her vanity (it is the riding habit that decides her to accompany Rodolphe), her emotions have an unquestionable authenticity. There is candor in her desires. Flaubert repeatedly insists on the genuine and even delicate nature of her sentiments, blaming Léon, for instance, for dozing to the music of a love whose "delicacies he no longer noted" (III.6). Albert Thibaudet, pointing to the conniving lyricism of the author, suggests that Emma's very sensuality is of a delicate and almost religious nature.[45] Indeed, there is a curious blending of honest appetite and deeply felt longing for spirituality in Emma's very eroticism. The genesis of the novel confirms this fusion of sensuality and mystical yearnings. Flaubert's original intention, at the time he was still traveling in the East, had been to write the story of a mystical virgin, living in the provinces, and tormented by her erotico-religious imagination (". . . une vieille fille dévote et ne baisant pas," according to his own crude words).[46]

What has remained of these original intentions is Emma's terrible sense of isolation, and her unquenchable aspiration for some unattainable ideal. Hers are dreams that destroy. But this destructive power is also their beauty, just as Emma's greatness (the word is inappropriate only for literal-minded readers) is her ability to generate such dreams. Despite all her pretentious and hysterical behavior, Emma grows in stature; and toward the end of the novel, at the moment of her complete defeat in the face of reality, she acquires dignity and even majesty. When she comes for the arsenic, she appears to Justin as "extraor-

[45] Thibaudet, *Gustave Flaubert*, p. 94.
[46] Goncourt, *Journal*, IV, 166–167.

dinarily beautiful, and majestic as a phantom." Her fulfilled death-wish now also brings about a tragic serenity.
After taking the poison, she returns home "suddenly
calmed, and almost with the serenity of an accomplished
duty." But even earlier, she displays a sense of dignity acquired in suffering. Indignant when Monsieur Guillaumin
tries to take shameless advantage of her desperate situation, she rebukes him with a terrible look: "I'm to be
pitied—not to be sold!"

It is Baudelaire who unquestionably carried the image
of a tragic and idealized Emma Bovary to its extreme. In
an article studded with paradoxes, and which deserves a
privileged place among the most spirited pages written on
Madame Bovary, Baudelaire insists that despite his zeal
as a "comedian," Flaubert, being unable to divest himself
of his sex and to turn himself into a woman, infused his
own "virile blood" into the veins of his fictional creature,
and thus raised Emma to the rank of a superwoman em-
bodying all the qualities of "ideal man": energy, ambition
and above all that "supreme and tyrannical faculty," imagination.[47] Emma's so-called defects are transformed into
qualities. Even her taste for deception and talent for lies
bespeak dandyish virtues, and a virile, "exclusive love for
domination." For dandyism, as Baudelaire understood it,
was an aristocratic, stoical and decadent manifestation,
and Emma, because of her androgynous nature, was not
unfit to be one of its fictional representatives.

This elevation of Emma above the ordinary condition
of woman (the "animal pur"), corresponds to Baudelaire's
deep-seated misogyny. But some such transcendence of
the strictly feminine element can be detected in the very
genesis of the novel. Mazza, the adulterous heroine of the
juvenile *Passion et vertu*, is filled with contempt for all
other women: "Oh! women! women! she hated them deep
in her heart. . . ."[48] As for Emma, it is clear that Flaubert

[47] Baudelaire, "Madame Bovary," in *L'Art Romantique, Oeuvres
complètes*, pp. 440–450.
[48] Flaubert, *Oeuvres de jeunesse inédites*, I, 263.

repeatedly alternates attitudes of languor with masculine poses and moments of almost manly behavior. The physical descriptions are revealing. "She wore, *like a man*, thrust between two buttons of her bodice a tortoise-shell eyeglass." This is how she appears during Charles' first visit to the farm. Later, when Rodolphe enters her life, she still displays an almost provocative masculinity: she parts her hair on one side and rolls it under "like a man" (II.7). The repeated expression "comme un homme" is not gratuitous. A strange reversal of roles takes place—not only with her husband (it is he who, after the wedding night, looks like a deflowered virgin), but with her lover Léon, who plays the submissive part: "It was he who was becoming her mistress rather than she his" (III. 5).

It would be a mistake, however, to limit the meaning of the novel to the complexities of Emma's character or to her own tragic destiny. Even structurally, both at the beginning and at the end, the novel extends beyond its protagonist. Between Emma's death and the last line of the book, which tells of Homais' decoration, there are three full chapters. The significance of this lengthy epilogue is clear, and it is stressed by the bitter concluding line: "He has just received the cross of the Legion of Honor." The temporal perspective of this sentence, with its stress on the present, suggests the permanence of the Homais of this world.

The epilogue indeed marks the victory of Homais. His already bustling and intrusive temperament is as though galvanized by Emma's death. He becomes ubiquitous ("on ne voyait que lui sur la place, depuis deux jours"), lavishes advice, succeeds in having his enemy the blind beggar locked up for good, and, no longer satisfied with his contributions to the Rouen newspaper, begins to entertain sociological and literary ambitions. The tone of caricature prevails until the very end; but this caricature acquires a universal resonance. The pharmacist's success is not merely the triumph of an individual: it is the apotheosis of mediocrity, the worldly glorification of a wingless humanity. Baseness wins out, and this victory only reaffirms the purity and even greatness—no matter how relative—of Emma's doomed aspirations. And beyond the victory of mediocrity, the epilogue confirms the victory of life itself— a life which continues, unmoved by the suffering it dispenses, denying its own significance through a refusal to bestow value on any individual destiny. Life simply *is* and *continues*: a bit of holy water and of chlorine water take care of the dead. As for the living—except for Emma, and therein lies her uniqueness—they never seriously quarrel with life. The priest, in the very presence of Emma's corpse, calmly enjoys cheese and brandy. And Emma's father, after the burial, calmly lights his pipe.

It is easy to see why so many readers have felt that the novelist's outlook was essentially nihilistic. "Son roman manque de coeur," commented the brothers Goncourt. As for Zola, he considered Flaubert the "greatest negator" in French literature.[49] Even our contemporary critics, though used to much inhumanity in letters, continue to read into the novel a message of negation and untragic despair. Flaubert's esthetics of impassibility seem to confirm this notion of a basic nihilism. The highest aim of art, Flaubert maintained in one of his letters, was neither to provoke laughter, nor to provoke tears, but to be serene and hermetic.[50] This apparent negation of tragic values corresponds in fact to a new form of tragedy: a period which discovers the pathos of the unheroic hero also discovers the tragedy of the very absence of Tragedy. For tragedy means consolation: the tragic spirit corresponds to man's unceasing need to justify apparently unjustifiable suffering. Thus the chorus, in *Oedipus Rex*, though sympathetic with the king, hopes that the oracle will be vindicated: pure contingency seems more atrocious than the cruelest of fates. *Madame Bovary*, despite the implicit hatred of an

[49] Goncourt, *Journal*, IV, 144; Zola, "Gustave Flaubert," in *Les Romanciers Naturalistes*, p. 194.
[50] Flaubert, *Corresp.*, III, 322.

untragic world, poses the problem of the very possibility of a tragic work in a contemporary context.

Ultimately, it does not matter whether we believe with Baudelaire that Flaubert infused his virile spirit into the veins of Emma, or whether we are convinced by Sartre's less flattering notion that in *Madame Bovary* Flaubert disguised himself as a woman[51]—the result is a masked confession. Only the masking of the confession is further complicated by Flaubert's effort not to write a confession at all, and by the unwitting duplicity such an inner tension created. For disguise can be a method of self-discovery and honesty, but it can also be an instrument for self-deception. Sartre, in typical fashion, is somewhat unfair when he insists on Flaubert's bad faith, which he attributes to his awareness and alienation as bourgeois. But there is unquestionably much in Flaubert's own emotional make-up, and even more in the novel itself, to suggest that the drama of Emma Bovary—psychological as well as social—was not merely an intuitive and objective account of an external reality. Much of Flaubert's work centers indeed on the theme of "temptation": far from being the antidote to the first *Tentation de saint Antoine, Madame Bovary* assimilates some of its basic substance. The suffering of which Flaubert complained so insistently during the writing of the novel cannot be attributed solely to stylistic anguish, to the "affres du style"; it betrays permanent wounds, the sorest of which are self-inflicted. Only the cult of Art might provide some relief.

[51] Sartre, *Critique de la raison dialectique*, p. 89.

Salammbô:

THE EPIC OF IMMOBILITY

La plastique est la
qualité première de l'art
Flaubert

The Debauches of the Imagination

The opening chapter of *Salammbô*, with its orgiastic barbarian feast and the ethereal appearance of the patrician virgin, plunges the reader into an acrid and dreamlike world. This combination of brutality and almost mystic disincarnation is characteristic of Flaubert's poetic imagination. The African dream had long haunted Flaubert. Already in *La Tentation de saint Antoine*, which he temporarily set aside, but which continued to take new shapes in his mind, Flaubert had exploited the metaphorical potential of his African image. The exotic dream goes back to his early adolescence. It was not merely literary—although literary fashions, and in particular Victor Hugo's *Les Orientales*, did much to inflame his imagination—but deeply felt and psychologically explosive. The long voyage through Egypt, Syria and Palestine in 1850 only confirmed Flaubert in his view of this continent as the theater of the elemental mysteries of life, where sex was related to infinity and death, where a permanent original creation was also close to permanent undoing and nothingness, and the dawn of religions announced the twilight of the gods.

It is not surprising that a work founded on such an excessive, almost delirious appetite for the forgotten and the unknown, should have met with incomprehension.

Since it was not a traditional "novel," it soon became fashionable to treat it as a piece of historical research, and to condemn it on those grounds. A pedantic archeologist, Wilhelm Froehner, set out to prove that Flaubert's archeological reconstructions were sheer invention.[1] As though these reconstructions were not merely a pretext, a safe-conduct to the regions of dream! Readers still tend to view the novel as a museum of dead objects. Critics who believe that authentic documentation is irrelevant in a work of fiction are appalled by the pedantic pretense at historical veracity. In his attempt to capture the poetry of History, Flaubert had—it was felt—sterilized his own imagination. He was thus accused of betraying history for fancy, and at the same time of allowing pedantry to crush his imagination.

Contradictions such as these made it convenient simply to dismiss the work as a "historical novel," blaming Flaubert for his choice of a period—the world of Carthage—about which we know almost nothing. For there exists no "contact" in *Salammbô*: the enigmatic nature of the characters seems only to underscore our basic indifference to the ruthless struggle between Carthage and its Mercenaries, as well as our almost total lack of knowledge of the society Flaubert set out to resuscitate. Georg Lukács believes that *Salammbô* illustrates the decline of the historical novel: dehumanizing monumentality, emphasis on objects and on the picturesque rather than on human situations, irrelevant social and historical context.[2] The gap between the human action and the political tragedy does indeed suggest a double tendency of decadentism: the attraction to soulless facts as well as a "making private" of history. Flaubert's taste for the trivial and the brutal can thus, in Marxist terms, be interpreted as an inability to transcend historically his own subjectivism.

[1] Froehner, *Revue contemporaine*, December 31, 1862; February 15, 1863. Flaubert wrote a spirited point-by-point rebuttal which revealed the extraordinary range of his historical research. Complete citations for all notes may be found in the Bibliography.
[2] Lukács, *The Historical Novel*, p. 199.

These accusations are not altogether unjustified. Yet even a prejudiced reading of the novel reveals an extraordinary control over the literary material. Flaubert is not only a fine painter of crowds—the most remarkable before Zola—but a superb painter of landscapes. The vaporous sunsets and dawns so typical of Mediterranean cities; the immensity of a land, harsh and voluptuous, swept by heavy breezes, bathed and refreshed by moonlight and soon after scorched by the desert sun; the glaring light distorting or even abolishing all sense of distance, and transforming the sea into molten lead—these images, as well as those of the terraced and undulating city of stone and ivory offering itself to the glance like an opulent cornucopia, make up the very texture of the book. And they are not gratuitous. If the forms of the hills are compared to the swollen breasts of women, it is because this vision corresponds to the sexual languor and sexual obsessions of the Barbarians, who themselves, just like the landscape, surrender alternately to hedonistic indolence and to uncontrollable crises of savagery.

Equally impressive is the dreamlike atmosphere which suffuses some of the key scenes, and which bestows upon them an almost surrealistic logic and necessity. "Tanit," the chapter devoted to the nocturnal theft of the sacred veil (the "Zaïmph"), is an initiation into the inner chambers of the temple as well as into the secret recesses of the author's imagination. The furtive theft somehow corresponds to a deep compulsion. The oneiric imagery is at times quite explicit. In a suffocating atmosphere, Mâtho walks between two parallel galleries where heavily tattooed women sleep on mats like reclining idols. Later, as he rushes up the large stairs toward Salammbô's room, Mâtho experiences that "strange ease which one feels in dreams" (chapter 5).

But the most overwhelming impression left by *Salammbô* is one of nightmarish brutality for which, because of the clearly erotic associations, there is no better word than sadism. Prisoners into whose faces pebbles are thrown to make them cry out in pain; writhing bodies whipped to death to the accompaniment of the lions' roar; panting women tearing the flesh and piercing the eyes of captives —these are familiar scenes in *Salammbô*. Were the brothers Goncourt really unfair when they remarked in their *Journal* that Flaubert, whose mind was haunted by the marquis de Sade, had an undue appetite for turpitude?[3] The observation which perhaps most upset Flaubert in Sainte-Beuve's series of three articles devoted to *Salammbô* was the critic's hint at the sadistic tendency of his imagination.[4] Flaubert, in his letter to Sainte-Beuve, protested: considering his subject and his sources, he had been "sober and very tame."[5] But the protestation does not sound altogether convincing.

Flaubert was obviously not too eager to repeat his experiences with Imperial justice; yet from his correspondence, especially during the period of the novel's composition, it is quite clear that he enjoyed immensely the idea of his "truculente facétie" shocking the bourgeois reader. "Let's be ferocious . . . . Let's pour brandy on this century of sugar water. Let's drown the bourgeois in a grog eleven thousand degrees strong, and may his mouth burn! . . ." Almost triumphantly, he announces to his friend Ernest Feydeau that he is now tackling the gorier passages, that his protagonists begin to walk through disemboweled guts. "Baudelaire will be happy! and the shades of Pétrus Borel, white and innocent like the face of Pierrot, will perhaps be jealous."[6] The reference to Baudelaire is revealing: the two writers share a taste for the horrible and the pathological. As for Pétrus Borel, the "Lycanthrope," whose frenetic charnel house tales make him a specialist of the gruesome, his name occurs on several occasions in Flaubert's correspondence during the period that he is working on his Carthaginian novel. And clearly, the writing of *Sa-*

3 Goncourt, *Journal*, III, 72–73.
4 Sainte-Beuve, *Nouveaux lundis*, IV, 71.
5 Flaubert, *Corresp.*, V, 65.
6 Flaubert, *Corresp.*, IV, 432, 455.

lammbô did not exorcise the demon of cruelty. In June 1862, while correcting final proofs, Flaubert muses about *"dark and terrible* books."[7]

Salammbô reads indeed like a compendium of atrocities. Mutilation is almost the key image of the novel. The ferocious battle elephants of Carthage, with torn-out bowels hanging from their tusks, seem to symbolize the prevailing brutality. Even vampirism and cannibalism find their way into the book. But the most characteristic mode is one of lascivious cruelty which inflames the mind and the senses of both sides in this relentless war, and which shows up, in its most acute form, when Mâtho's living body, at the end of the novel, is being slowly torn to shreds by an entire population. Women let their nails grow especially for this occasion. An "infamous curiosity" compels them when Mâtho appears: the desire to "know" him utterly. The author himself refers to the "mystic lewdness" which prevails that day in Carthage.

The horror becomes at times so intense, so oppressive, that Flaubert suggests an immense nausea. Thus the starving Barbarians, trapped in the pass of the Battle-Axe, soon give up feeding on the rotting corpses of their dead comrades. The horror has been too great. The stench of decomposition stings the nostrils, troubles the eyes, penetrates into the very skin. "An immense disgust overwhelmed them. They would have no more of it. They wanted to die" (14).

The death-dream is paralleled by an obsession with disease. Hanno's leprosy—his unsightly ulcers and crusts, his greenish flesh all in shreds, his stench camouflaged by precious perfumes—corresponds to a deep-rooted obsession with pathology already evident in Flaubert's earliest writings, as well as in *Madame Bovary.* "I feel a need to dissect," he confesses to a friend. And he explains: "It is strange how attracted I am to medical studies."[8] Just as later, when writing *L'Éducation sentimentale,* he was to

---

[7] Flaubert, *Corresp. Supplément,* I, 288.
[8] Flaubert, *Corresp.,* IV, 349.

visit the Sainte-Eugénie Hospital to observe children suffering from croup, so during the composition of *Salammbô* he undertook research on various afflictions, particularly on the ravages of thirst and hunger. Perhaps this dedication to the pathological represents an effort to rid himself of his obsessions and to expel the evil spirit of Sade. "I disembowel men with prodigality, I spill blood, I write in a cannibalistic style. . . ."[9] There is something compulsive in the very tone of Flaubert. The goriness and carnage of the novel may well betray a yearning to transcend animality.

But whether Flaubert's poetry of horror represents a permanent trait of his psychology to which he here surrenders with relish, or whether the stress on the sanguinary is symptomatic of a redeeming struggle with his own demons, the result is one of sensationalism. The Romantic tirade and the taste for the spectacular are the two traits which most sharply distinguish *Salammbô* from *Madame Bovary*. There is something histrionic, and even operatic, about the entire work. The feast of the Mercenaries during which Salammbô emerges on the upper terrace, the return of Hamilcar and the crowds thronging the steps of the Acropolis, the brazen colossus appearing like a prop out of *Aïda*, the hierarchical cortèges proceeding to the rhythm of cymbals, castanets and tambourines—all these scenes of movement and monumentality seem to unfold on an outsized stage to the accompaniment of trumpets and choral effects. *Salammbô* has unquestionably the makings of a Hollywood extravaganza.[10]

Is it fair, however, to dismiss *Salammbô* as a dazzling display of images by a writer endowed with a talent and propensity for debauches of the imagination? Is dazzlement all that is sought and achieved?

[9] Flaubert, *Corresp.*, IV, 337.
[10] The novel did inspire a number of opera composers, among them Moussorgsky, who set to work on it immediately after the novel's publication, but who abandoned his project a few years later.

The Death-Feast and the Thirst for the Unattainable

The shimmer and hardness of precious stones introduces the reader into a world of plastic forms. The novel begins in an almost artificial light, as the moon and the campfires are reflected on hard, glittering surfaces. The entire first chapter suggests alternately the chiseled, polished forms of the goldsmith, and those others, heavy, solid and immobilizing, of the sculptor and the architect. The bronzelike massiveness only helps bring out the delicacy of gems. The metaphorical unity of tone is obvious. The entire description of the orgy in Hamilcar's gardens stresses artifact. It also stresses a mixture of animalism and of a dehumanized plasticity of "pure" forms. The captains wear bronze cothurnes; the monkeys on the trees are terrified by wavering lights, burning in porphyry vases; oblong flames tremble in brazen cuirasses; in their drunkenness the soldiers toss to each other ivory stools and gold spatulas. When Salammbô appears on top of the marble palace with its ebony staircase, the lapidary images become more graceful: from her temples fall strands of pearls; on her bosom she wears a collection of luminous gems and, connecting her ankles, a delicate gold chainlet. Even the sound effects in this opening chapter are tinkling or metallic. The clinking of cups, the crash of Campanian vases, the limpid ring of large silver plates mingle with the crunching sound of the soldiers' jaws.

Nature itself, in this first scene, appears transmuted into a work of art, indeed *petrified*. Not only is the black sand mixed with powdered coral, and the sunlight described as a "rain of gold," but an avenue of cypress trees is metamorphosed into a double colonnade of green obelisks. If objects have a life of their own, life in turn is here made inert and immutable. This death principle is illustrated by Salammbô's song, telling of Masisabal's decapitated head, attached to the prow of a ship, and which the combined action of the sun and the sea water embalmed and made "harder than gold" (1).

The taste for the tableau further contributes to the sense of immobilization. And so does the imperfect tense, which seems to imprison the action in an eternal present. "C'était à Mégara, faubourg de Carthage, dans les jardins d'Hamilcar." This carefully balanced first sentence of the novel imposes its weight and seems to offer no issue. The lion pit, as well as the audible presence of the *ergastulum*, with its imprisoned slaves and clattering chains, further conveys a feeling of claustration. This immobilization extends to vegetation (the trunks of trees become "bloodstained columns") as well as to human beings. Mâtho, at the end of the chapter, stands motionless, having assumed an almost statuesque pose. Indeed throughout these opening pages, as well as later in the novel, men assume sculptural traits or stances. The Barbarians, who have daubed themselves with vermilion, look like "coral statues"; the clean-shaven Greeks look "whiter than marble"; the Elders, on the platform of the towers, stand "motionless as the stones" (2); the priestesses of Tanit lean on their elbows, with their chins in the palms of their hands, "more immobile than sphinxes"; Hanno's bloodless face seems powdered with "marble dust" and he looks like a "gross idol roughly hewn out of a block of stone"—almost an "inert object" (2). The entire panorama unrolling before our eyes takes on vague forms, "like the gigantic billows of a black, petrified ocean" (1). Even the sea appears immobilized and solidified, "figée" (congealed). Nature itself —just like the sacred fish with precious stones in their gills— is thus denatured. Behind the entire opening passage, one senses an attempt to translate living and unstable forces into the arrested patterns of art.

This immobilization of life is paralleled by an inverse tendency, but whose effect is paradoxically similar: movement bestowed upon the motionless and even the lifeless. Thus verbs of action are made to serve as verbs of description. The fig trees on the first page "surround" the kitchens, the sycamore trees "extend" to masses of verdure, vines "climb" up the branches of pine trees. The landscape seems to act out a geometric ballet: the conical roofs of heptagonal temples "stand out" in the early dawn, houses "climb up" the slopes, "mass together" like a herd of black goats "descending" the mountains, the streets "stretch out," the palm trees "jut out" beyond the walls. At times, the entire setting seems to propel itself into motion.[11] At others, inanimate objects seem to palpitate with life: glass bowls reflecting the light of the torches become "enormous throbbing eyeballs" (1).

As a result of this double tendency (immobilization of life and animation of the inanimate) the distinction between the organic and the inorganic almost vanishes, and *being* and *becoming* tend to merge. The very techniques exploited by Flaubert in the first chapter of *Salammbô* point to some permanent and important features of his work: Nature transformed into Art; a dehumanization and bestialization of man (at the orgy, the soldiers imitate the cries and leaps of ferocious animals); the permanence of death as suggested by the petrifaction of life; a predilection for the statuesque and the lapidary which corresponds to a horror of the amorphous and to an inner struggle between the stable and the unstable; a fusion of movement and immobility symbolizing a cosmic rhythm and necessity.

Some of Flaubert's central themes and obsessions thus emerge in the very first pages of *Salammbô*. The exotic repast is not merely sensational or decorative. As is so often the case with Flaubert, food and appetite, which mean life and nourishment, also point to death. Discontent, violence and destruction are intimately associated with carnivorous greed and the processes of digestion. The Mercenaries eat, "leaning on their elbows, in the tranquil pose of lions devouring their prey." Indeed, animals of prey constitute a permanent presence, and a permanent metaphor, in *Salammbô*. On the flags, in the temple of

[11] Benjamin Bart sees an intimate relationship between this mobility of Flaubert's landscapes and his "pantheism" (*Flaubert's Landscape Descriptions*, p. 44).

Moloch, enormous lions, the living symbols of the Sun-Devourer, crouch like sphinxes. (Once more, we witness the metamorphosis of the animated into the statuesque.) And, as though to underscore the relationship between food, animalism and death, Flaubert has the carcasses of half-burned apes tumble down from the charred branches among the dishes of the feast.

Food and destruction do not represent an arbitrary association. The "cupidité des estomacs," as Jean-Pierre Richard suggests, does point to a thirst for the absolute.[12] The multiple dishes representing every possible culture and an almost infinite variety of mores are indeed like invitations to a global voracity. But soon the relative and the absolute clash, as the appetite proves far larger than the capacity to digest. The drunken eyes of the soldiers seek to "devour with their glances" all those things which they lack the power to seize and carry away. Impotence leads to exasperation. And just as sexual excess is bound up with a secret yearning to dissolve, consume and ravage, so here the orgy of food and drink leads up to a "vertigo of destruction" which whirls over this drunken army and impels them to strike, break and kill at random.

From the very beginning, "total" forces seem to be at play. The first chapter, in its very structure, opposes the feminine softness and mystical lasciviousness of the Moon and the hardness and fierceness of the Sun. The dialectic of the eternal couple, Tanit and Moloch, is indeed at the core of the novel. The scene opens as night falls. When Salammbô appears, she is, in her softness and pallor, like an incarnation of the lunar principle. Her pallor is in fact attributed to the moon. And her movements as well as her effect on the assembled men derive from lunar influences: her languorous poses and glances, the undulations of her body, her song which tells of the female monster whose tail "undulated like a rivulet of silver over the dead leaves,"

[12] Richard, "La Création de la forme chez Flaubert," in *Littérature et sensation*, pp. 117–219. According to Richard, the Flaubertian "voracity" is basically tragic.

her sensuous savoring of the excitement she provokes. This voluptuous and provocative Moon-Tanit is met by the aggressive and destructive male force of the Sun-Moloch. At the end of the nocturnal first chapter, the Sun appears: the god, as if rending himself, fecundates Carthage with a "rain of gold."

The death-feast, the vertigo of destruction and the omnipresence of absolute forces locked in fierce battle remain permanent realities in *Salammbô*. The opening chapter, so high in color and movement, is thus not merely of dramatic, but of proleptic interest. It also points to some of the most fundamental Flaubertian themes: the theme of sacrilege and the theme of inaccessibility. Boiling alive the sacred fish of the Barca family is not just a sadistic pastime; it corresponds to an irresistible desire to desecrate. The Mercenaries' impulse to "devour with their glances" what they cannot seize and possess corresponds to the Flaubertian nostalgia for the unattainable. Its keenest manifestations, in these opening pages, occur when Mâtho, transfixed, looks up longingly at the distant Salammbô. And this separation not only represents the distance—political and social—which separates them ("She is remote and inaccessible!" 2), but prefigures the final scene of the novel, when Mâtho, inexorably drawn to his hated love, dies at the foot of the terrace, staring at the figure of Salammbô above the balustrade.

A Parnassian Epic

Inordinate dreams (or nightmares) assume plastic concreteness in *Salammbô*. The book must ultimately be judged as a poem. But not in the flippant terms of André Gide, who speaks of the "disarming childishness of the poet."[13] The poetry of *Salammbô* goes beyond a mere quality of the imagination. It echoes a pressing inner music, and expresses itself through complex rhythms, by means of a language in which words themselves become palpable, sensuous realities. Flaubert moreover clearly set

[13] Gide, *Journal*, p. 266.

out to explore the poetic potential of French prose, which he felt could achieve a hitherto unsuspected beauty.[14] To Louise Colet, at a time when he was still busy writing *Madame Bovary*, he confided his dreams concerning a new prose style which, without ceasing to be "prose," would combine the virtues of artful rhythms and an almost scientific precision.[15] Zola recalls how Flaubert used to asseverate that a beautiful page of prose was twice as difficult to write as a page of beautiful verse. His ideal was to create out of an ordinary language, amorphous and devoid of sharp outlines, a prose "hard as bronze, glittering like gold."[16] The jewel-studded paragraphs of *Salammbô*, with their calculated varieties of meter and skillful contrapuntal effects, seem to answer this ideal.

The words "poem" and "poetry" indeed found their way repeatedly—and quite naturally, it would seem—into the critical opinions of those contemporaries who were able to appreciate *Salammbô*. Leconte de Lisle praised it as a "beautiful poem." Hector Berlioz referred to it as "an invention of the highest poetry." And J. M. de Hérédia, perhaps the most representative poet of the school known as the "Parnasse," hailed Flaubert as the "schalischim of poets," and compared the novel to a "temple of granite, covered with precious marble . . . , blending all its ornaments into a general magnificence. . . ."[17] The very terms of Hérédia's comparison seem to place Flaubert's work squarely among the Parnassian poets.

The practice and ideals of this group—as illustrated by writers such as Théophile Gautier, Leconte de Lisle, Théodore de Banville and Hérédia—marked a reaction against the highly personal and sentimental effusions of the first wave of Romantic poets. Lamartine's lachrymose, mellifluous and vaporous reveries, but even more so the his-

---

[14] Flaubert, *Lettres inédites à Tourgueneff*, p. 106.
[15] Flaubert, *Corresp.*, II, 399; III, 142–143.
[16] Zola, "Gustave Flaubert," in *Les Romanciers naturalistes*, pp. 134–135.
[17] Quoted in the Conard edition of *Salammbô*, Flaubert, *Oeuvres complètes*, pp. 504ff.

trionic and self-pitying playfulness of Alfred de Musset, were the favorite targets of this poetic reaction. The "romantic" nature of this anti-Romantic group explains in part their affinity with Flaubert. They too extolled impassibility as a cardinal virtue in art. For the Parnassians, artistic perfection was to be sought in plastic effects. Hence the importance of the statuesque nude and the permanent search for a purity of sculptural lines. Théophile Gautier, for whom both Baudelaire and Flaubert felt much admiration, was from childhood on drawn to the plastic arts. Even when singing the beauty of the human hand, he felt compelled first to lend it the statuesque firmness of a sculptor's plaster cast. Firmness of line and of outline is indeed one of the characteristics of Parnassian poetry. The polished craft of the goldsmith, the glitter of jewels, the hard aristocratic surface of marble are recurrent images.

Sculpteur, cherche avec soin, en attendant l'extase,
Un marbre sans défaut pour en faire un beau vase

advises Banville.[18] And Gautier, whose poem "L'Art" is a true Parnassian credo, praises the beauty of Paros marble and calls for a poetic art whose sculpted and chiseled beauty can be achieved only through the artist's victorious struggle against a highly resistant material. The very titles of so many Parnassian works (*Emaux et camées, Les Stalactites, Améthystes*) betray this concern for a hard and almost icy perfection which the Symbolist poets were soon to condemn.

Victor Hugo's *Les Orientales* had done more than provide a pyrotechnical display of "visual" poetry. Its example, as well as its flashy preface, had encouraged poets to enter into competition with the visual arts and with music. Thus Gautier, in "Symphonie en Blanc Majeur," plays variations on a single color and indulges in true debauches of whiteness. The gratuity of art, its essential purity and nonutilitarian value, also was axiomatic with the Parnassian poets.

[18] Banville, *Les Stalactites*.

Art became an absolute, superior to the reality it described, superior even to Nature. "I prefer the painting to the object it represents," wrote Gautier in his preface to *Les Jeunes-France*. And with this preference for Art goes, of course, a preference for artifice, and ultimately a marked trend toward decadentism.

Strangely enough, however, despite its professed indifference to the issues of the day, Parnassian poetry is not isolated from the main philosophical and scientific currents. The influence of Auguste Comte and of his "positivism" can be detected in almost every work of these writers. A historical curiosity, concerned with pre-Christian religions and myths, and displaying a definite hostility to Christianity, can be felt. Not only has the historical curiosity been awakened (Leconte de Lisle, utilizing archeological data, is convinced that his poetic evocations have historical value), but philological and mythological research—for instance the revolutionary work of Creuzer—titillated the imaginations.[19]

The very choice of Carthage as a subject for a novel is symptomatic of this double Parnassian tendency: on the one hand, the desire to resuscitate a past through a combination of research and archeological intuition; and on the other, the focusing on a civilization so distinctly out of touch with the world of modern Europe as to ensure an almost hermetic purity. As for the other Parnassian traits, they are even more obvious. *Salammbô* seems conceived under the very sign of the "plastic" emotion. Flaubert's invocation at the end of his travel notes on Carthage ("A moi, puissance de l'émotion plastique! résurrection du passé, à moi, à moi!")[20] clearly indicates the spirit in which the novel was conceived. The sculptural and architectural metaphor almost becomes a mannerism in *Salammbô*. Hanno looks like an incompleted stone idol. The crucified

[19] For a concise discussion of this curious blending of science and art, see Pierre Martino's chapter "Positivisme et Poésie," in *Parnasse et Symbolisme*.
[20] Flaubert, *Notes de voyages*, II, 347.

Mercenaries look like "red statues." Salammbô, when her father promises her in marriage to Narr'Havas, stands "calm as a statue" (11). It would seem that during his "Oriental" trip, Flaubert was struck by the plastic nature of the very landscape. He found that the "form of the mountains" was as though "sculptured," that it offered more than in any other region "architectural lines."[21]

The architectural obsession is particularly striking. Numerous passages suggest a real choreography of geometric figures and patterns. The three levels of a tower are like three "monstrous cylinders." One of Hamilcar's apartments is built in the "form of a cone." At times the accumulation of geometric figures becomes truly oppressive. Early in chapter 4, Carthage is viewed as a vast amphitheater of "cubic" houses: it is a "mountain of blocks," with innumerable "intersecting" streets which "section" it vertically, and where emerge, here and there, enormous flat spaces of walls ("des pans énormes"). Viewed from the vast "quadrangular" court, the temple of Moloch is an "architectural mass" with eight uniform sides or sections, surmounted by cupolas and a rotunda, from which springs a "cone" with a "returning curve" terminated on the summit by a sphere. Not even Robbe-Grillet, with his compulsive taste for measurements and his predilection for lines and surfaces, has been more addicted to geometric images.

Even more ubiquitous are the images of precious gems, of sophisticated jewels—almost a museum display. ("I wallow in precious stones like a pig," Flaubert writes to his friend Jules Duplan.)[22] These images cluster around the key motifs of the novel, and chiefly stress the natural phenomena, among which the most important is of course the Moon. The shafts of its light bring out luminous glints, striking the gold necklace of some idol or the globes of glass glittering like enormous diamonds on the roofs of temples. The sea also, symbol of feminine caprice and fecundity, assumes a mineral quality: after the heat of the

[21] Flaubert, *Corresp.*, II, 296.   [22] Flaubert, *Corresp.*, IV, 226.

battle, it appears to Mâtho like a flat pavement of lapis lazuli (6). But even more characteristic is the association of precious stones and architectural effects. At the entrance of the temple of Tanit, a stone cone stands between a stela of gold and a stela of emerald. Inside, stone phalli appear. (Similarly, the pavilion of Khamon supports an ivory phallus bordered with a circle of gems.) And the coveted veil of the goddess, the sacred Zaïmph, close to a semispherical black stone and to an erected ebony cone, appears like a cloud of scintillating stars, "diaphanous" and "glittering." The temple of Moloch is also embossed with jewels in the best Parnassian manner. Chased flowers, chalices of diamonds, brazen horns, black mysterious stones, bronze standards, mother-of-pearl lozenges constellate this somber, awesome sanctuary. Even private locales are heavily ornamented. The family sepulcher in Hamilcar's house contains an almost surrealistic collection of gems—some of them (like the carbuncles formed by lynxes' urine) the products of an esoteric fantasy: stones fallen from the moon, *tyanos*, beryls, *sandastrum*, opals from Bactria, the twelve kinds of emerald—all of them flashing like splashes of milk, blue icicles or silver dust (7). Amethysts and topazes also adorn the ceilings of Salammbô's room. Even her snake's skin is "covered like the firmament with spots of gold . . ." (10). The described reality is here transmuted into a permanent metaphor.

This raises an esthetic problem. Does Flaubert's metaphoric style correspond to a metaphorical vision? This, in fact, as Harry Levin points out, is the very dilemma of Parnassian poetic practice: imagery seems deprived of "perspective" in a land where metaphors come true.[23] The emphasis on poetic jewelry work, this tourism through a kingdom of stone, have of course an immediate dramatic and thematic relevancy. But what ultimately matters is not the concrete application of this imagery (infinite resources for war, obsession with wealth, critique of a mer-

[23] Levin, *The Gates of Horn*, p. 277.

cantile society), nor even the peculiar eroticism dependent on the taste for the *clinquant* and which recalls Baudelaire's love of sonorous jewels, but the abstract, almost metaphysical potential of these images and rhythms. For the novelist's predilection for ternary rhythms, his massive and magnifying ends of chapters, as well as the use of ponderous adverbs frequently concluding a sentence—all bring about, no less than the lapidary imagery, a *fixation* of movement. An uncanny sense of immobility pervades the novel. Though the fortunes of war, the displacement of troops, the proliferation of battles suggest agitation, the overall impression is one of stasis and futility. The very fact that a dialogue between the culture of Carthage and our own is not possible, and that there exists, historically, a rupture of continuity, contributes to this sense of stasis and even of constriction. Perhaps it is one of the reasons why Flaubert was secretly drawn to a historical period which remains locked in itself. Certainly, the very structure and texture of *Salammbô* convey this combination of frenzy and immutability. No scene is more characteristic of the mood of the novel than the end of chapter 14 ("Le Défilé de la Hache") where the "bored" lions, who have fed on the corpses of the trapped army, lie satiated and "motionless as the mountains or as the dead." This combination of violence and of tedium represents a predominant feeling in *Salammbô*.

For the "bored" pose of the lions corresponds to an almost Baudelairean sense of ennui. Their yawns, which throughout the book accompany the cries of tortured men, are symptomatic—much like Baudelaire's "monstre délicat" —of an immobilization of life and of a chronic yearning for destruction. ("Ah, you understand what a horrible bore existence is!" Flaubert wrote to Baudelaire admiringly.)[24] Flaubert's own penchant, ever since his adolescence, led him to a poetry of ennui, combining dreams of infinity with a sense of despair. "I feel nothing but immense and

---

[24] Flaubert, *Corresp.*, IV, 205.

insatiable desires, an atrocious ennui and continuous yawns," he confides to his friend Ernest Chevalier.[25] Much of *bovarysme* seems to be implicit in this cry of frustration, in this diagnosis of his acedia. Moreover, the desire to create a poetry of ennui crystallizes, it would seem, around exotic images—images of the Egypt Flaubert discovered, or wanted to discover, during his long trip in 1850. "An immense ennui devours everything," he writes to Louise Colet. "When I will write Oriental poetry . . . that is what I will stress."[26]

Once again, the affinities with Théophile Gautier—even more so than with Baudelaire—are striking. The desert and the so-called "Orient" were favorite motifs of the poet. He too viewed Egypt, where the immutable sphinx yawned, as the ideal stage for *ennui*:

> Nul ennui ne t'est comparable,
> Spleen lumineux de l'Orient!

These lines from "Nostalgies d'Obélisques" sum up a certain Parnassian vision. Yet Flaubert's "oriental" poetry is not limited to the impassive yearning for a perennial stillness and mystery. The paradox of Flaubert's vision is that the very immobility seems to be in motion: monotonously, mercilessly rolling like the huge, clumsy tower construction, the outsized *helepolis* used during the siege of Carthage, which, on its iron-bound wheels, moves forward slowly toward the walls of the city like a mountain meeting another mountain. It is this sense of the hopeless continuity of eternal sameness—symbolized by the irresoluble tides of war and by the equally relentless struggle between Tanit and Moloch—which more than any other single factor endows the novel with a certain epic grandeur.

Contemporaries—provided they were well disposed—did indeed refer to the epic qualities of *Salammbô*. "Beaucoup trop de bric-à-brac mais beaucoup de grandeurs épiques

[25] Flaubert, *Corresp.*, I, 76.
[26] Flaubert, *Corresp.*, III, 136.

. . . ," Baudelaire wrote in a letter to Poulet-Malassis.[27] Théophile Gautier, in an article published in *Le Moniteur*, summed up his evaluation of the work: "It is not a book of history; it is not a novel. It is an epic poem!"[28] Similarly, Théodore de Banville praised the book as a "true epic narrative of modern times."[29] Flaubert himself, during the slow process of gestation and composition, repeatedly referred to *Salammbô* as an "epic" enterprise. "I have an epic itch" ("des prurits d'épopée")—is Flaubert's diagnosis of his condition after years of immersion in the petty, provincial world of *Madame Bovary*.[30] He now needs air and space: "grandes histoires" and "grandes gueulades." In one of the scenarios for the novel, he plans a "picturesque and epic enumeration" of all the African tribes; and in his correspondence, he evidences a certain uneasiness at the thought that his battles will be nothing but imitations of the "eternal epic battle" of Homer.[31] The epic, as a genre, had long fascinated him. To read the *Iliad* in the original was one of his dreams; for years he deluded himself into believing that he was almost ready to undertake this. As for the *Aeneid*, he was quite appropriately perusing it while working on his Carthaginian novel.

The predominance of military exploits, the massive displacement of troops, the lengthy sieges which allow for a theatrical display of both individual and group action— all this unfolding of seemingly inexhaustible resources in energy and men easily lends the novel an "epic" physiognomy. War transforms the trivial into the monumental, and extends finite action into time and space. Flaubert, always drawn to encyclopedic catalogues, indulges in endless *dénombrements*. With painstaking care, he describes in detail military equipment and military maneuvers. Complicated stratagems and ingenious devices give him particular delight. Both sides in this inexpiable war resort

[27] Baudelaire, *Correspondance générale*, IV, 129.
[28] Gautier, "Salammbô," in *L'Orient*, II, 322.
[29] Banville, *Critiques*, p. 159.
[30] Flaubert, *Corresp.*, III, 321.   [31] Flaubert, *Corresp.*, IV, 383.

to almost frantic expedients: the hair of female slaves is used for the war engines, the fat is taken from the dead to oil machines, fingernails and toenails of corpses are utilized to make breastplates, morsels of carrion are catapulted in what amounts to germ warfare.

But even more so than details of battle, conflicts of men and animals (the two, at times, are almost interchangeable) and the omnipresence of gods, idols and monstrous images, it is the very atmosphere of the book which inevitably conjures up epic reminiscences. Like its illustrious predecessors, *Salammbô* is a "Mediterranean" poem. When Flaubert, in one of his most spectacular light-and-landscape scenes, describes the dawn over Carthage ("Toward the east a luminous bar appeared . . ." 1), one recalls the Homeric "rosy-fingered dawn." A certain poetry of History emerges, which is based not so much on respect for sources as on a sense of the grandiose and the "collective." And the military action reveals not only the atrocious deed, but the exemplary and heroic one. The death of the last Mercenaries, their "invincible courage," their pathetic farewell to each other, their unswerving fidelity to their friendships, evoke the spirit of loyalty and sacrifice prevailing among the noblest battle companions in the epic tradition (14). As for the craft and cunning which traditionally temper and civilize the physical exploit, this element is here embodied by that decadent Ulysses, the former slave Spendius, who appropriately is also a Greek. In a context of total surrender to passion, whether that of love or of destruction, Spendius, plotter and agitator, represents the cunning mind.

Above all, however, it is the style, the very syntax of Flaubert, which brings about a characteristic wedding of Parnassian sensibility and epic massiveness. The paratactic use—and abuse—of conjunctions, the reliance on conjunctive locutions (*tandis que, pendant que*), have a cumulative and broadening effect. The action advances, and yet it seems part of the same immense, unchanging tableau. Adverbial articulations (*puis, alors*) introduce a certain "primitiveness" into the narration, create a link of necessity between contingent events, and provide a sense of the crescendo. The abundance of conjunctions is of course a chronic mania with Flaubert, one against which, on numerous occasions, he felt compelled to wage ruthless war; but it does serve here to create an epic rhythm. This tendency is further accentuated by strikingly characteristic epic similes which seem to derive straight from Homer or Virgil:

> Like a pruner cutting off willow branches, endeavoring to lop off as many as possible in order to gain more money, he advanced mowing down Carthaginians on all sides of him. (13)

> Swinging his heavy shoulders covered with furs, he reminded his companions of a bear leaving its cavern in the spring to see if the snow has melted. (14)

But the most significant epic "device" in *Salammbô* is Flaubert's own ability to fuse action and description, his skill at transmuting an action in progress into a seemingly arrested tableau. This mixture of movement and immobility is best illustrated by the altogether original use of the imperfect tense to describe a finite action:

> Hamilcar tira deux larges coutelas; et à demi courbé, le pied gauche en avant, les yeux flambants, les dents serrées, il les *défiait,* immobile sous le candélabre d'or. (7)

This gesture of defiance, which according to all the customs of French syntax would require a preterit, or *passé simple,* is here fixed, and so to speak liberated from contingency, by the *imparfait* of description. This grammatical transposition no longer shocks us: the Naturalist writers, in the wake of Flaubert, have often exploited it. Basically it is a painter's device, and corresponds historically to a period when literature often attempted to rival its sister art.[32] The immediate effect of this syntactical anomaly is to immobilize movement into a pose, and to provide a sense of statuesque grandeur. Suddenly, all human action seems to be amplified and projected against an immense, almost universal screen.

The basic "unit" of *Salammbô* is unquestionably the sexual image as crystallized around the divine couple Tanit and Baal, and as symbolized by the cosmic polarity of Moon and Sun. On the human level, Salammbô embodies the spirit of Moon-Tanit, while Mâtho incarnates the Sun-Baal. Tanit is the "humid" goddess, the goddess of fertility. She is "like an amorous woman who runs after a man in a field" (10). Baal, on the other hand, is the god' of terror, voracity and destruction. He "possesses" Carthage with a male's vindictiveness.

Such images and such concepts are, however, somewhat abstract. Flaubert very deliberately textures his novel with a profusion of sensuous images—all of which support the basic erotic motif. Odors (good and bad), scents, exhalations are evoked with particular frequency. Whether the emanations of sweaty crowds, or the mixed smells of perfumes, leather and spices, these stifling sensations all contribute to a latent lasciviousness. The association is often explicit. Thus Mâtho, about to ravish Salammbô, dilates his nostrils to breathe in more freely the perfume exhaled from her body. "It was a fresh undefinable emanation which nonetheless made him dizzy like the fumes from a censer. She smelled of honey, pepper, incense, roses, and yet another odor" (11). This evocation of an *odor di femmina* has upset many prudish readers.

More concrete, more physical still than these olfactory sensations are the many images of blood and violence, and in particular the recurring metaphor of the wound. Immediately upon falling in love, Mâtho is shot through the arm by the jealous Narr'Havas. His "gaping wound"

[32] See the suggestive comments on Alphonse Daudet's use of the imperfect in Ferdinand Brunetière, *Le Roman naturaliste*, pp. 81–110.

appears dramatically under a ray of moonlight (1). The siege of Carthage develops into a feverish blood-orgy with unmistakable sexual undertones. "The women, leaning over the battlements, shrieked. They were dragged forward by their veils, and the whiteness of their sides, suddenly uncovered, shone between the arms of the Negroes, as they plunged their daggers into them" (13). As for the public torture of Mâtho, at the end of the novel, it is a festival of cruel carnality.

Characteristically, Flaubert exploits images of warfare for what might be called sexual effects. The siege of a town and the possession of a woman are almost set up as explicit parallels. "He would never possess her; he could not even succeed in capturing a town" (6). Openings, breaches, battering rams are among the recurrent, almost obsessive images. The motif of *penetration* (into the temple of Tanit, into Salammbô's room, into the city· of Carthage) is particularly insistent. Mâtho and Spendius discover a "breach" in the city wall, they find a "slit" in the temple wall, they "penetrate" into a small round room, they discover a "narrow opening," they enter into a "narrow passage," they glimpse "small openings." The entire chapter describing the nocturnal penetration and profanation of the temple of Tanit is filled with similar suggestions (5). On occasion, as with the scene describing the mystic deflowering by the sacred serpent, the images are distinctly obscene (". . . its body, shiny and bright, gradually emerged like a blade half drawn from the scabbard" 10). This atmosphere of lubricity is further strengthened by the expressions "défit," "dénoua," "ses vêtements . . . tombaient," "il se leva tout droit," "dardaient," "se renversait," "haletait," "pliaient," "se sentait mourir." The erotic use of the snake-image again occurs in the tent scene, when the golden chainlet linking Salammbô's ankles snaps and the two ends fly apart, striking the tent "like two leaping vipers" (11). The image recalls the frantic undressing of Madame Bovary in the hotel room, when the thin corset-lace is made to hiss about her hips "like a gliding snake."

But the sexual imagery points to larger and more significant themes. Mâtho, literally bewitched, experiences love as an initiation to destruction and to death. He is oppressed by his own boundless desire, his very being seems to dissolve in an irresistible torpor, "like those who long ago have partaken of some potion of which they must die" (2). Love is here linked with the idea of a fateful inebriation. Above all, the love-motif corresponds to a spiritual malady recurrent in the works of Flaubert. The sexual quest thus becomes the physical expression of a self-destructive yearning for the unattainable absolute.

Repeatedly, sex and annihilation are linked in *Salammbô*. The martial context only stresses this association. But even the less military passages provide images of undoing. The scent of Salammbô is "more fragrant than wine and more terrible than death"—the language is almost Biblical. The fertility symbols in Tanit's temple, the perfumes and the exhalations "overcame" Mâtho. This sense of *accablement*, of succumbing to a weight, pervades the scene of the symbolic love-ritual with the serpent. "Salammbô panted under this great weight; her loins gave way, she felt that she was dying" (10). The sex and war imagery, already predominant in the opening chapter, provides the connective texture which from the "vertige de destruction" of the Mercenaries' feast leads to Moloch's "possession" of Carthage, and finally to the sadistic killing of Mâtho.

Death and destruction are thus the price for impossible dreams. For what really counts in *Salammbô*—as in most other works of Flaubert—is the drama of an impossible desire. This quest for the unattainable, this boundless appetite for that which can never be seized, and much less appropriated, is without a doubt the main tragic theme of the novel. The permanent presence of walls is a reminder not only of Salammbô's almost holy virginity, and of the distance which separates the Carthaginian patrician girl from the foreign plebeian, but of all sense of *distance* and indeed of the very notion of inaccessibility. And it is revealing that Flaubert had the high priest Schahabarim fall in love with Salammbô. A eunuch, he is condemned to consume himself in a hopeless and sterile desire.

The notion of sacrilege, so recurrent in *Salammbô*, acquires its full meaning in this context. For sacrilege—whether the soldiers' killing of the sacred fish or Mâtho's violation of the temple—ultimately proves to be a mad enterprise. A fundamental prohibition places the coveted object beyond reach. Mâtho knows it; during the entire expedition in search of the sacred veil, the very idea of sacrilege haunts him and terrifies him. It is as though the Flaubertian hero himself felt the instinctive need for barriers that would set a limit to his dangerous desires. His *libido sentiendi* as well as his *libido cognoscendi* condemn him to frustration and defeat. Schahabarim rebukes Salammbô, who is burning with a sinful "curiosity," and who wants to "see" the very form of Rabbetna: "Your desire is sacrilege. Be satisfied with the knowledge that you already possess" (3). The warning corresponds to a deeprooted Flaubertian wish—embodied by Madame Bovary, Saint Antoine, as well as Bouvard and Pécuchet—to transcend the limitations of one's own being.

We are coming close here to the very core of the Flaubertian sense of tragedy. For *bovarysme* is not merely—as Jules Gaultier put it—the wishing oneself other than what one is. It is an almost metaphysical eroticism: "desire" in its essential form. And it implies a condemnation to an unmedicable sadness—the kind of sadness which, on the most sordid level, Mâtho experiences when he attempts to satisfy or forget his desire with the handmaidens of Tanit (". . . he descended the hillside in sobs, like one returning from a funeral" 2). Prostitution with Flaubert is, as it were, the reverse of an ideal image. It is also the symbol of a reality which condemns life to betrayal and unfulfillment.

All the typical stages of *bovarysme* are reenacted in *Salammbô*. The first period of the disease is a state of vague exaltation, which combines sensuous and spiritual aspirations. In a revealing letter written to his friend Louis Bouilhet in 1850, Flaubert hesitates between three equally tempting subjects. The first is "a night of Don Juan." The second is the story of Anubis, the woman who wants to be loved by a god. The third is that of a mystic Flemish virgin who lives and dies in her provincial town. Quite clearly the last project is echoed in *Madame Bovary* and in *Un Coeur simple*, and the story of Anubis eventually became part of *Salammbô*. But what is more interesting than mere concern for origins is that the three projects, though superficially very dissimilar, bear a fundamental resemblance to one another. Flaubert himself was fully aware of it: "What worries me is the kinship between these three plans." All three stories, dealing with the double form of love (sensuous and spiritual), were to illustrate "l'amour inassouvissable"—insatiable love.[33]

Thus vague exaltation leads to an almost hysterical surrender to sensation, in quest of precisely that which refuses to be possessed. The second stage in this tragic disease is marked by an ungovernable tension, an almost demented convulsive distortion of the sensibility, resulting in paroxysms of possessiveness. The Barbarians, symbolizing Mâtho's delirium, "did not even know . . . what they wanted"—but they wanted with fury (12). Obstacles only exacerbate this ferocious desire. Mâtho begins to dream of "terrible and extravagant things," while Spendius frantically strives to invent "frightful engines of war such as had never been constructed before" (13). The Flaubertian protagonist, in this assault on the impossible, in this attempt to violate a secret, is doomed to will violence and his own destruction.

The madness of love—for love, with Flaubert, is a "mad-

[33] Flaubert, *Corresp.*, II, 253–254. In fact, as Thibaudet points out, Flaubert has repeatedly been drawn to studies of women tormented by the sensuous dream of the impossible (*Gustave Flaubert*, p. 128).

ness," a "curse," a "malady"[34]—is linked both to a dilection for the unbounded and to the fundamental impotence of all desire. The debauches of the imagination infallibly bring about a sense of sadness, tedium and even disgust. The mystic virgin who commits a sacred prostitution to recover the Zaïmph is also the woman who discovers the bitterness of dreams come true. "Elle restait mélancolique devant son rêve accompli" (11). This quasi-metaphysical sadness becomes most oppressive at the very moment the dream seems realized. Emma Bovary experiences the same mournful disenchantment. A sense of emptiness and despair invades the Flaubertian heroine as she measures the permanent distance that separates her chimera from reality. Paul Bourget diagnosed the disease of *bovarysme* most accurately when he saw it as a dramatization of the law which condemns satisfaction (*jouissance*, in the largest sense) to be forever out of harmony with desire.[35]

Bourget's diagnosis, developed in one of the best of his *Essais de psychologie contemporaine*, is relevant because it raises the entire question of desire and frustration to a philosophical plane. The disproportion and lack of harmony become symptomatic of an intellectual disease, indeed of the very *disease of intellect* by which modern civilization is being slowly eroded. Emma Bovary, Salammbô, Frédéric Moreau, Saint Antoine, Bouvard and Pécuchet—all of them are victims of their own nefarious imaginations, all of them have either read too many books or heard too many legends, all of them have "known the image of reality before reality."

Salammbô, like all of Flaubert's works, insists on the bewilderment and abdication of reason in the face of a devastating multiplicity of phenomena. The very first scene, with its unending variety of dishes and tribal habits, betrays an encyclopedic obsession. This mania for inventories appears throughout the novel. And Africa, the ex-

[34] See the letter to Sainte-Beuve (Flaubert, *Corresp.*, V, 59).
[35] Bourget, "Gustave Flaubert," in *Essais de psychologie contemporaine*, I, 127–196.

ceedingly fecund breeding ground of races and religions, was an appropriate symbolic setting for this obsession with polymorphism. The apocalyptic parade of gods, beliefs and heresies in *La Tentation de saint Antoine* also takes place on African soil. Flaubert obviously enjoys displaying his erudition or pseudo-erudition. He lists the camp customs of the various national groups among the Mercenaries, their clashing practices and cults, the cacophony of their idioms, the profusion and confusion of weapons and apparel, the medley of burial rituals. This array of colorful details is, however, not aimed merely at creating picturesque effects. The stage of this implacable war becomes a museum of artifacts, as well as a graveyard of civilizations. And knowledge itself—or the catalogue of knowledge—turns out to be no more than a symbol of sterility.

The figure of Schahabarim embodies this sterility. The eunuch-priest who betrays his goddess has been everywhere and learned everything. He has studied at Borsippa, near Babylon; he has visited Samothrace, Ephesus, Pessinus, Judea and the temples of the Nabathaeans; he has descended into the caverns of Proserpine and witnessed the five hundred columns of Lemnos revolve. His curiosity and knowledge extend to natural sciences as well as theologies. But the result of this intellectual tourism is idiosyncrasy and perverse indetermination. Intellectual aridity leads to all manner of heterodox aberrations. At the end of the novel, lonely and spiritually crippled, Schahabarim places himself entirely in the service of horror and extermination. Flaubert's taste for excess, his obsession with the proliferation of forms and concepts always points to a simultaneous love and terror of the monstrous. The temple of Tanit contains winged bulls, serpents with feet, flowers blossoming from crocodiles' jaws. Infinite shapes seem to undergo a perpetual nightmarish metamorphosis. "All the forms were found there!" (5). Flaubert observes in *Notes de voyages* (II, 356) that excess "is a proof of ideality." Above all, however, it is—in the Flaubertian context—a principle of annihilation, and as such one of the permanent tragic themes of his works. Polymorphism—perpetual change and modification—is bound up with its corollary: nothingness.

The attraction to nothingness is indeed the ultimate stage of the tragic sickness which erodes the spirit of all Flaubert's protagonists. *Salammbô* is not merely a book of death, but of annihilation. Sepulchral images and images of decomposition, profuse though they be, are probably less numerous than images of lassitude and dissolution. Death, to be sure, is omnipresent. In retrospect, all the characters—much like the survivors of the entrapped army —appear like "half-opened tombs, living sepulchres" (14). But the frenzy of destruction, the consuming desire to "anéantir," the "vertige" which makes the destroyer lose himself in that which he destroys, overshadow the simple reality of death. It is characteristic that the battle-orgy, when all the butchery is done and the soldiers are wearied from too much slaughter and screaming, ends in a collective desire for sleep. Many lie down next to lifeless bodies, "hoping never to awaken again" (12). Similarly, in the "Défilé de la Hache" chapter, the starving Mercenaries surrender to a "torpor" that benumbs them.

"Torpor" and "numbness" are indeed favorite expressions with Flaubert. They betray the lethal fatigue, the *tedium vitae*, which recurrently make him yearn for a total loss of consciousness and of self. Confiding his profound ennui, his total sense of discouragement to Edmond de Goncourt, he once spoke of his aspiration to be dead "without metempsychosis, without an afterlife, without resurrection, to be forever divested of his own self."[36] The closing line of *La Tentation de saint Antoine* should no doubt be read in the light of this confession. But *Salammbô* also communicates this longing for dissolution and nonexistence. Dreams of obliteration are suggested through images of "melting away" which convey unmistakable erotic undertones. The patrician virgin wants to "dissolve"

[36] Goncourt, *Journal*, X, 99.

herself in prayers "like a flower in wine"; she longs to "lose" herself in the night mist, in the water of the fountains, in the sap of the trees; she wishes to "leave" her body, become as immaterial as a breath of air (3). During the expedition through the aqueduct—a typical descent into the nether regions (the air is "heavier than that of a sepulchre")—Mâtho and Spendius experience a frightful fatigue, as though their limbs were about to "dissolve" in the water (4).

Such patterns of images correspond to a profound feeling of dejection, a heaviness of heart, an unredeemable discouragement. "The situation was unbearable, above all because of the idea that it would become worse" (9). Carthage's predicament aptly sums up the prevailing pessimism and gloom of Flaubert's total vision. Flaubert himself has alluded to the despondency which permeates the very conception of this novel. "Few people will guess how much sadness was necessary to undertake the resuscitation of Carthage!"[37] In fact, it is worse than mere "sadness": the emasculated priest of Tanit, having betrayed his cult, is left without a faith—a priest without God. Flaubert's own sense of anguish seems to parallel that of Schahabarim. His writings exhale a chronic blasphemy against the very principle of life. And like all true blasphemies, Flaubert's not only imply an apostasy (and the accompanying regret for the recused faith), but a deep and permanently frustrated taste for the absolute. Did not Flaubert call himself a mystic who was unable to believe anything?[38]

This perverse combination of mysticism and nihilism makes of much of Flaubert's work, and of Salammbô in particular, a forerunner of "decadent" art. Salammbô appears indeed as a direct precursor of some of the fin-de-siècle creations of Huysmans, Wilde, Mallarmé and Moreau. The characteristic obsession with sterility, the blending of eroticism and religiousness, the chaos of the setting and the taste for violence and putrefaction are all

[37] Flaubert, *Corresp.*, IV, 348.
[38] Flaubert, *Corresp.*, II, 412.

significant "decadent" traits. (The Marxist critic Georg Lukács goes so far as to consider Flaubert the "initiator of the inhuman" in modern literature.)[39] And it is revealing not only that Huysmans, in *A rebours*, has granted *Salammbô* a position of honor in the sophisticated library of Des Esseintes, but that Flaubert, at the very time he was composing the novel, was assiduously perusing Apuleius' *Golden Ass*.[40]

Flaubert's cult for the Rome of Nero, proclaimed so often ever since his adolescence, found its oblique way into his literary creation. His *retorica neroniana*—as Luigi Foscolo Benedetto calls it—is precisely what lends *Salammbô* its garish colors. "In my novel on Carthage, I wanted to do something purple," he once explained.[41] The North African settings, the "orientalism," only serve to stress the typically decadent combination of refinement and cruelty. It has often been said that Flaubert's imagination has been fired by Victor Hugo's *Les Orientales*, which he read as a young boy. But although his admiration for Hugo the poet remained almost boundless, Flaubert's "Orient" is far removed in tone and spirit from that of Hugo. It is in part related to a cult of experience and to dreams of a former life ("I have been a boatman on the Nile . . ."[42]); but, mostly, it reveals an almost desperate escapism through images of alienation and violence. "I carry in me the melancholy of the Barbaric races, with their migratory instincts and their innate weariness of life which made them leave their countries as though to be freed from themselves."[43]

The glorification of the Barbarians, which in *Salammbô* appears most clearly in the scenes of their epic courage in death, is of course one of the most recurring "decadent" motifs. Tired races, like the spiritually exhausted senators

---

[39] Lukács, *The Historical Novel*, p. 194.
[40] See Luigi Foscolo Benedetto, *Le Origini di "Salammbô*," pp. 116ff.
[41] Goncourt, *Journal*, IV, 166–167.
[42] Flaubert, *Corresp.*, V, 240.
[43] Flaubert, *Corresp.*, I, 217–218.

and consuls in Cavafy's "Waiting for the Barbarians," have a secret hope that the Barbarians will soon arrive. The entire nineteenth century, especially after the first wave of Romantic poets, liked to think of itself as a somewhat bloodless, overcivilized civilization that had reached its period of decline. The Latin decadence was a frequent subject of meditation, and poets considered Paris the capital of a new *Bas-Empire*. As early as 1836, Alfred de Vigny described the Parisian spirit as a "démon du Bas-Empire." Baudelaire's vision of the modern capital constantly conjures up decadent images. As for Flaubert, he quite clearly expressed this secret affinity with this *Bas-Empire* atmosphere in a letter to his friend Turgenev: "I feel the sadness of the Roman patricians of the IVth century."[44] As usual, Flaubert's feelings were ambiguous: on the one hand, he pretended to be deeply affected by disintegration and devaluation (blaming the mythical "Bourgeoisie" for its lack of backbone), yet he also relished witnessing what he considered the death-agony of the modern world.

Salammbô is thus representative of a moral and intellectual climate. But it is also very much a *roman personnel*, a novel expressing some of the most intimate attitudes and yearnings of Flaubert. Far from being the marginal work, the eccentric aberration that some readers saw in it, the novel about the greatness and horror of Carthage is indeed central to an understanding of some of the most permanent obsessions of Flaubert. Were the thought not so heretical, one might even venture to say that in many ways *Salammbô* is more truly representative of the patterns of Flaubert's imagination than *Madame Bovary*. And not merely because it is filled with personal reminiscences of the crucial journey to North Africa and the Near East in 1850, nor because it reflects Flaubert's lifelong taste for history and erudition (the original idea of the novel was probably inspired by a text of Michelet), but because

[44] Flaubert, *Lettres inédites à Tourgueneff*, p. 45.

the novel reënacts a personal drama—the drama of a man haunted by a desire for the absolute, and capable only of finding the human substitutes of destruction and death. Sartre is probably right: Flaubert lived out fully and without issue the conflict between the synthetic myth of religion (in which he wanted to, but could not, believe) and the materialistic "bourgeois" spirit of analysis.[45] Sartre, in typical fashion, probably attributes too great an influence to Flaubert's father, the Voltairean physician, in crushing the innate temperamental idealism of his son. But unquestionably, a work such as *Salammbô* reveals an explosive mixture of a godless religion and a naïve *scientisme* which makes of Flaubert himself a kind of "priest" in search of a cult. His solitude, his lugubrious pessimism, coupled with his dreams of perfection go a long way toward explaining his faith in the redeeming virtues of Art. "Art is the search for the useless," Flaubert jotted down at the time he undertook his documentary voyage to the site of Carthage. "It is in the field of speculation what heroism is in ethics."[46] It is characteristic that the notion of Art should be so intimately bound up, in Flaubert's mind, with the idea of a glorious and tragic futility.

[45] Sartre, *Critique de la raison dialectique*, p. 92.
[46] Flaubert, *Notes de voyages*, II, 358.

L'Éducation sentimentale:

PROFANATION AND

THE PERMANENCE OF DREAMS

The Bordello:
In the End Is the Beginning

Ten years after the publication of *L'Éducation senti-mentale*, Flaubert was still pained by the critics' hostile reaction. To his friend Turgenev, he wrote in 1879: "Without being a monster of pride, I consider that this book has been unfairly judged, especially the end. On this score I feel bitter toward the public."[1] Few endings of novels have indeed baffled, even outraged more readers. The hero's flat assertion that an adolescent excursion to a brothel has been the most precious experience of a lifetime confirmed suspicions that Flaubert was an incurable cynic. It was bad enough that the "hero," Frédéric Moreau, after a life distinguished by failure, returns to the somnolence of a provincial existence, a death-in-life which corresponds to a total abdication and to a permanent vocation for nothing. But did the author have to bring Frédéric and Deslauriers together in this scene, pointing up the weakness and bad faith inherent in their reconciliation? Did he have to indulge in an inventory of decay? And does the exalted expedition to the provincial bawdyhouse not cheapen whatever might have been salvaged (the very memory of Mme Arnoux!) by stressing venal love and by

[1] Flaubert, *Lettres inédites à Tourgueneff*, p. 206. Complete citations for all notes may be found in the Bibliography.

[125]

linking almost perversely the prurient excitement of early adolescence with the impotence of precocious senility?

Yet Flaubert felt surer of the validity of this scene than of almost any other scene in the novel. Endings were for him a matter of utmost concern even when, as in *Madame Bovary* or *L'Éducation sentimentale*, they may at first appear like an unfunctional appendix. But the anticlimactic last three chapters in *Madame Bovary* are far from gratuitous. In *L'Éducation sentimentale*, the ending is even more intimately bound up with the very structure and meaning of the book. Paradoxically, it almost engenders the very beginning. It is an epilogue, no doubt: but this epilogue echoes and parallels one of the earliest passages in the book. I refer to the second chapter, which is partly a flashback to Frédéric's and Deslauriers' childhood, and partly an early conversation between the two friends as they look forward to the future, but already have a past to talk about. Thus the book can be said to begin and to close with a conversation between Frédéric and Deslauriers in which projects or reminiscences take priority over action. The immediate effect of this extension in time (the prologue carries us back to 1833, the epilogue forward to the winter of 1868) is a feeling of temporal circularity and erosion. All the dreams have come to nought. And already during the first conversation, the light the two friends can see shining from the small window of the *maison basse*, the house of ill repute, seems like a shimmering symbol of unattainable desire. "I am of the race of the disinherited," says Frédéric, convinced before the event that no worthwhile woman will ever love him. In the meantime, they do not have enough money to respond to the blinking light. But they do remember a common adventure of some years back, the same adventure that, twenty-seven years later, they will tell each other, agreeing that it had been the best moment of their lives. "C'est là ce que nous avons eu de meilleur."

If, however, we look at this last scene more closely, we

must notice that the bordello motif is not exploited for its sheer anecdotal value, nor even primarily to allow for the devastating final comment. The episode, as remembered by the two friends—though it occurred some time before the events of the novel itself—does in fact sum up, in miniature fashion, a whole pattern of events and meanings. What happened is banal enough: on a late Sunday afternoon, the two boys plucked some flowers, gathered them into bouquets and proceeded furtively to the house of "La Turque."

> Frédéric presented his bouquet, like a boyfriend to his fiancée. But the heat of the day, the fear of the unknown, a kind of remorse, and even the excitement of seeing at a glance so many women at his disposal, affected him so much that he grew very pale and could neither move nor speak. They all laughed, amused at his embarrassment. Thinking that he was being made fun of, he ran away; and since he had the money, Deslauriers was forced to follow him. (III.7)

Several aspects of this passage deserve analysis. To begin with, the author provides here a subtly nuanced sketch of Frédéric's character. The naïve gesture of appearing with flowers at a brothel points up a latent and ineffectual idealism. The comparison with the boyfriend and his fiancée is touching enough, but suggests a tendency to see reality through a deforming imagination. The heat which paralyzes him reminds us of many other states of dreamy indolence in Frédéric's life. The vague sense of guilt, which, one must assume, is here related to a mother-image, is elsewhere associated with the pure and "maternal" image of Marie Arnoux. The multiplicity of women making the choice impossible corresponds not only to the constant and inconclusive wavering, within the novel, from one woman to another, but to Frédéric's basic inability to focus on anything and impose a single direction on his life. The immobility, the speechlessness and the ultimate flight underline a chronic timidity, the fear of judgment and humiliation. Thus he also tears up his first letter to Mme Arnoux: ". . . he did nothing, attempted nothing—paralyzed by the fear of failure" (I.3). And the flight itself corresponds, of course, to a flight from the realities of the capital and a return to the sheltered life of the province.

But there is more to this passage. The naïve arrival in the whorehouse, the flustered departure, the very *fiasco* of the expedition symbolize the poetic illusion that clings tenaciously to unfulfilled love. It symbolizes the orgyless orgy, the love-dream remaining pure because it was unrealized. After all, Frédéric leaves "La Turque" chaste! The debauches have been of the imagination: mere velleities. So that the final comment ("C'est là ce que nous avons eu de meilleur"), far from being exclusively a cynical remark, or a symptom of arrested development, must also be interpreted as a lasting nostalgia for innocence.[2] This preference for the past conceals another form of idealism. Memory illumines. And although both friends seem to have lost everything, this final dialogue between the man who sought Love and the man who sought Power reveals that it is the search for Love (no matter how clumsy and frustrating) which retrospectively bestows the only meaning. The episode thus combines, in the most ambiguous manner, touching illusion and adult disillusionment, flights of fancy and retreat into the self, attraction to the multiform manifestations of life and paralysis caused by the very proliferation of forms and possibilities, eternally youthful memories and the pathos of aging. In other words, it is a retrospective prolepsis of the very essence of the novel. Even the relationship of Frédéric and his friend is prefigured in the terse remark that since the one had the money, the other was obliged to follow him!

The bordello motif, or in a more general sense the image of the Prostitute and the theme of Prostitution, is at the core of *L'Éducation sentimentale*. Frédéric's erotic

[2] A nostalgia for innocence which, as Harry Levin suggests, goes hand in hand with the need to be "sheltered from the contingencies of adult existence" (*The Gates of Horn,* p. 229).

sensibility and erotic dreams as a boy crystallize around visions of satin-covered boudoirs where he and his friend will experience "fulgurant orgies with illustrious courtesans" (I.2). Such exotic passions are inevitably linked to dreams of success. He and Deslauriers spend so many hours constructing and peopling their harems that they are as exhausted as though they had indulged in real debauches. Later, when Frédéric actually penetrates into the world of Parisian women, he is almost overcome by the luxurious *odor di femmina*. There is, to be sure, a certain literary tradition behind this particular mystique of the senses. Romanticism had cast the eternal hetaera, whether simple *fille de joie* or high-class courtesan, in the role of initiator into the deep mysteries of life. Even social, artistic and political success—in nineteenth-century literature—is often related to one form or another of prostitution. Such literary expressions no doubt correspond to certain social and psychological patterns: the bourgeois adolescent looked at the prostitute with mixed feelings of admiration, contempt, desire to redeem and even a yearning for profanation. There is for instance a curious letter from Alfred Le Poittevin to Flaubert which tells of the young man's desire to desecrate in the company of a whore places where he has been "young and credulous."[3] As for Flaubert himself, it is clear that he is haunted by the image of the prostitute, whom he associates, in an almost Baudelairean manner, with equally complex monastic and ascetic urges.

In the novel, the bordello motif and the theme of prostitution assume in part a satiric function. The world of the *lorettes* into which Frédéric is ironically introduced by Mme Arnoux's husband, appears to him at first in the guise of a masked ball, where the most tempting display of flesh, costumes and poses inevitably brings to mind the variegated offerings of an elegant house of prostitution providing "specialties" for every whim. Frédéric is so dazzled that, during the first moments, he can distinguish

[3] Le Poittevin, *Une Promenade de Bélial et oeuvres inédites,* pp. 194–195.

only silk, velvet and naked shoulders. Then, gradually, he takes stock of the contents of this Parisian seraglio: the languorous Polish beauty, the placid and falsely modest Swiss siren, the provocative Fishwife, the Primitive with peacock feathers, the avid Bacchante, the carnival Workwoman—all the "refinements of modern love" dance before him, and the beads of perspiration on their foreheads further suggest a hothouse atmosphere (II.1). This scene, ending in a collective hangover the following morning, recalls the famous Taillefer orgy in Balzac's *La Peau de chagrin*: the same display of available carnality, the same specter of disease and death, the same garish coupling of the lascivious and the macabre. Only Flaubert is not concerned with sheer pyrotechnics. He is not out to rival Petronius' description of decadence in the *Satyricon*. His aim is neither sensational nor allegorical. He works and weaves his images patiently and deliberately into the general pattern of the novel. But there are some immediate effects, and the most noteworthy is a vertiginous proliferation of forms and gestures which ultimately transforms human beings into mechanized objects. In her drunken stupor, one of the women imitates "the oscillation of a launch."

The easy-virtued world of Rosanette is not the only one to be described in terms of lupanar images. Frédéric's suggestive vision imposes these very same images onto the assembly of elegant feminine guests in the salon of Mme Dambreuse (II.2). The upper-class ladies all sit in a row, "offering" their bosoms to the eye; the rustling of their gowns suggests that dresses are about to slip down. The lack of expression on their faces is in perverse contrast to their "provocative garments." The animal-like placidity of these ladies in décolleté evokes the "interior of a harem." Flaubert's intention becomes quite explicit, for he adds: "A more vulgar comparison came to the young man's mind." Here too, the salon provides a sampling of physical and regional types to satisfy every possible taste: English beauties with keepsake profiles, Italians with ardent eyes, three Norman sisters "fresh as apple trees in April"—an alluring and appetizing display of sophisticated impudicity. The total effect is once again dehumanization: the crescendo of feminine chatter sounds like the cackle of birds.

Even public locales (cafés, restaurants, *bals publics*) are seen as places of prostitution, for instance the Alhambra, where, according to Deslauriers, one can easily get to know "women." The exotic name corresponds to fake exotic architecture, or rather to jarring elements of architecture: Moorish galleries, the restaurant side in the form of a Gothic cloister, Venetian lanterns, a Chinese roofing over the orchestra, neoclassical painted cupids (I.5). This shocking combination is not merely a sign of vulgarity. It represents the particular attempt at facile poetry, or rather at facile estrangement, which is the special function of all purveyors of bought pleasures. In this light, the bordello becomes the convenient metaphor for any catering to the thirst for illusion. The Alhambra provides sensual pleasures for the public. The reader witnesses a collective debauchery: the last firecracker of the evening provokes an orgastic sigh. But in reality, nothing really happens. The policemen who wake up Frédéric on the boulevard bench where he has fallen asleep, and who are convinced that he has "fait la noce," are as wrong as his own mother concerning his visit to "La Turque." For Frédéric, it has been an innocent orgy, combining in characteristic fashion exposure to depravity with an exacerbated yearning for ideal love. Frédéric's only activity right after the Alhambra is to stare at Mme Arnoux's window.

This aspect of the metaphorical unity of *L'Éducation sentimentale* is further strengthened by the presence of key characters who, in one form or another, are for sale. The most important of these is Rosanette Bron, "La Maréchale." That Rosanette is a kept woman, and most often kept by several men at the same time, is of course no secret. Her true calling is perhaps never more graphically suggested than by her portrait, commissioned by

M. Arnoux, eventually purchased by Frédéric, but which in the meantime stands exposed in the window of a gallery with the following words written in black letters underneath: "Mme Rose-Annette Bron, appartenant à M. Frédéric Moreau, de Nogent" (II.4). True to her vocation, she specializes, one might say, in sexual provocation. Innumerable passages in the novel stress this talent. Her laughter has a whiplike effect on Frédéric's nerves. At times, she assumes the poses of a "provocative slave." Most often, her sex appeal is less indolent: her way of pulling up her stockings, her movements, her very chignon are "like a challenge" (II.2). When she eats, and the redness of the fruit mixes with the purple of her lips, the insolence of her look fills Frédéric with mad desires. As for her innumerable caprices, her disconnected cravings, they correspond to the usual versatility associated with the prostitution metaphor; only here the multiplicity of forms and possibilities is internalized. The capricious, unpredictable nature of Rosanette also corresponds to her treachery—and in a broader sense, to the theme of treason so important in this novel. Hers is partially an irresponsible type of cruelty best exemplified by her coldly abandoning Frédéric at the Café Anglais after accepting from de Cisy a bracelet with three opals.

A far more cold-blooded selfishness is the main feature of the "grande dame," the regal prostitute Mme Dambreuse. Frédéric finds that she has something "languorous" and "dry" (II.4). Her sterile cupidity appears in full light when, after the death of her husband, and in the presence of her lover, she stares, disconsolate, into the empty strong box! As for the perfidious Vatnaz, the eternal procuress, she provokes only disgust. The mere touch of her "thin, soft hand" sends shivers down Frédéric's spine. The world of Paris thus insistently proposes to Frédéric images of prostitution: *lorettes* at the hippodrome; streetwalkers under the gaslight; scenes of slave markets with lewd sultans and cheap puns in boulevard plays. At the horse races, he glimpses an obscenely made-up queen of the burlesque theater known as the "Louis XI of prostitution." Everywhere he turns, it would seem that, as in Baudelaire's *Tableaux parisiens*, "La Prostitution s'allume dans les rues."

But actual prostitution is of course not the only form of prostitution. There are less literal manifestations, all pointing to some manner of depravity. For the bordello motif is closely bound up with Frédéric's apprenticeship of life. His "education" in Paris—the subject as well as the title of the novel place it squarely in the tradition of the *Bildungsroman*—is to begin with the discovery of one type or another of pandering, cheapening or desecration. One could almost take one by one every character and every activity. The very name of Arnoux's hybrid establishment, *L'Art industriel*, is like a profanation of art. And his career sadly illustrates this profanation: an amateur painter, he is in turn director of an art magazine, an art dealer, the owner of a pottery factory manufacturing "artistic" soup plates and mythological decorations for bathrooms. With every chapter he takes a step down. After designing letters for signboards and wine labels, and going bankrupt through shady deals, he has the idea of a *café chantant* and of a military hat-making business, and he finally winds up dealing in beads and cheap "religious art." The very word "décadence" (III.4) aptly sums up his career. There is the same brutal deflation in the life of Pellerin, the painter who wanted to rival Veronese, then places his art in the service of politics, and ends up being a professional photographer. The actor Delmar, a coarse histrion, similarly illustrates the prostitution of art: he sells out his vulgar talent to political parties, and gives public recitals of humanitarian poetry on . . . prostitution (III.3). This propensity for selling out is most strikingly symbolized by the epitaph-like résumé of the life of the financier Dambreuse, who "had acclaimed Napoleon, the Cossacks, Louis XVIII, 1830, the working-man, every régime, adoring Power with such intensity that he would have paid in order to have the opportunity of selling himself" (III.4).

As for Frédéric himself, much could be said. In a letter to Amélie Bosquet, written some ten years before the publication of *L'Éducation sentimentale*, Flaubert makes this revealing confession: "One has spoken endlessly about the prostitution of women, but not a word has been said about that of men. I have known the tortures of prostitutes, and any man who has loved for a long time and who desired no longer to love has experienced them."[4] Unquestionably Frédéric's ambiguous situation vis-à-vis the Arnoux household, combining the duplicity of an adulterer, the frustrations of an unsuccessful suitor and the embarrassment of being Arnoux's rival not only with his wife, but with his mistress, exposes him to complex compromises and turpitudes. His dilettantish vacillations and reliance on others are almost those of a "kept" person. Frédéric is not only weak (Flaubert often depicts strong women and weak, virginal men), but passive and "feminine." He holds, for his friend Deslauriers, "un charme presque féminin" (II.5). The projected marriage to Mme Dambreuse, for money and social prestige, shows us Frédéric morally at his most depraved.

Finally, the prostitution motif provides a link between individual and collective attitudes. Society itself, as represented by various groups, corporations or institutions, is the great whore who always embraces the winner. Like Rosanette, who after despising the revolutionaries now declares herself in favor of the Republic, so do all the representative authorities—"as his lordship the Archbishop had already done, and as the magistracy, the Conseil d'Etat, the Institut, the marshals of France, Changarnier, M. de Falloux, all the Bonapartists, all the Legitimists, and a considerable number of Orleanists were about to do with a swiftness displaying marvelous zeal" (III.1). Politics in

<hr>

4 Flaubert, *Corresp.*, IV, 352.

particular, which held a somewhat perverse fascination for the apolitical Flaubert, is viewed as a slattern. During the obscenely violent and profanatory sack of the Tuileries palace, a slut is seen, on a heap of garments, assuming the motionless, allegorical pose of the Statue of Liberty.

The bitterness of an image such as this stresses the coarseness and the fickleness of political allegiances. But it is part of a more general theme of betrayed ideals. *L'Éducation sentimentale* is a novel of bankruptcy and of pathological erosion. Certain chapters accumulate one form of betrayal on top of another, until the feeling is that of an immense desertion. Friendship, ambition, politics, love—nothing seems immune from this chronic deterioration and devaluation.[5] The most brutal manifestation of this aspect of the novel is the double betrayal of the political turncoat Sénécal, the former Socialist now turned police agent, who during the coup d'état of 1851 coldbloodedly kills the sentimental revolutionary Dussardier. This stunning act, which leaves Frédéric agape, is like an allegory of treason destroying idealism.

And it is no gratuitous coincidence that makes Frédéric the witness to this despicable deed. The images of prostitution and degradation exist primarily in relation to Frédéric's personal vision, to his longings, his sadness, his disappointments and his defeats. The bordello motif may permeate the novel as a whole and may have a universal significance within its context. It represents ersatz on all levels, transmuting almost every gesture into parody: the duel with de Cisy is no real duel; the props Pellerin uses for his "Venetian" portrait are fake props; all creative efforts are derivative. But it is in relation to Frédéric's "sentimental education" that all this counterfeit acquires dramatic meaning. No matter how obviously depraved the objective world may be, it is his sentimental life which, subjectively, is most affected by the principle of degrading

[5] For instance, in chapter 2, Part II, Rosanette betrays both Arnoux and Frédéric, Arnoux betrays his wife, and Frédéric betrays the confidence of Arnoux.

vicariousness. Thus Frédéric bounces from one woman to another, permanently oscillating between contradictory desires and contradictory experiences, always driven to seek a poor substitute for the *authentic* experience he dreams of, and which, in the process, he steadily defiles. One desire awakens a contradictory desire, suggesting a repetitive discontinuity. "The frequentation of the two women provided, as it were, two strains of music in his life, the one playful, passionate, amusing; and the other almost religious . . ." (II.2). And there are not two women in his life, but four—if one includes the young girl, Louise Roque. This oscillation at times obliges Flaubert to resort to devices which appear extraneous: chance encounters, unexpected letters, coincidences which further underline the passivity of the hero and his easy surrender to the easiest path. Almost symbolically, at one point, the "strumpet" Rosanette (Flaubert actually uses the word "catin") interrupts a love scene in progress, thus making the ideal "irrevocably impossible" (III.3).

What is worse, Frédéric *uses* the image of one woman in his relationship with another. It is bad enough that he has learned to make one sentiment serve multiple purposes: in his courtship of Mme Dambreuse, he "makes use of his old passion" for Mme Arnoux (III.3); he repeats to Mme Dambreuse the very oath he just uttered to Rosanette, sends them both identical bouquets and writes them love letters simultaneously (III.4). Even more sadly, he has to rely on substitute images to stimulate himself sexually. "He found it necessary to evoke the image of Rosanette or of Mme Arnoux." (Thus Flaubert himself once told the Goncourts that "all the women he ever possessed were no more than the mattress for another woman he dreamed of.")[6] In the novel, this sexual substitution takes place quite literally when Frédéric, desperate because Mme Arnoux failed to show up at their rendezvous, makes

6 Goncourt, *Journal*, VI, 172.

love to Rosanette on the very bed he had so devoutly prepared for Mme Arnoux.

Such a pattern of substitution and profanation—under-
lined by the permanent prostitution motif—leads to contradictory results. On the one hand, we witness a strange
paralysis, reminiscent of the scene in the brothel when
Frédéric could not make his "choice." Life is a planned
orgy which never quite amounts to one. As boys, Frédéric
and Deslauriers had such extravagant dreams that they
were "sad as after a great debauch" (I.2). Frédéric feels
destined to accept defeat before even attempting a victory. He has a keen sense of loss before even having possessed. His imagination builds and furnishes Moorish
palaces (always the exotic yearning!); he sees himself
lounging on cashmere divans listening to the murmur of
fountains—and these sensuous dreams become so precise
"that they saddened him as though he had lost them"
(I.5). Make-belief and mental aphrodisiacs turn out to be
manifestations of impotence.

The other result appears as a complete contrast to this
atony: a vertiginous proliferation. But this proliferation,
much like the dizzying display of women at "La Turque,"
only leads to another form of futility. Innumerable examples in *L'Éducation sentimentale* illustrate this coupling
of diversity with sterility: the different esthetic "theories,"
the contradictory literary projects, the cacophony of political ideas, the jarring clash of opinions and inept clichés.
Polymorphism, in the Flaubertian context, is nearly always
a sure sign of an almost hypnotic attraction to nothingness, a suicidal yearning for annihilation. "Exhausted,
filled with contradictory desires, no longer even conscious
of what he wanted, he felt an extraordinary sadness, the
desire to die" (II.4).

It is significant that this allurement to nothingness, so
explicitly stated, should be experienced by Frédéric while
in the company of a high-class prostitute. For somehow,
in Flaubert's own imagination, prostitution and an almost

ascetic staring into the emptiness of existence are closely related. To Louise Colet he writes that the sight of street-walkers and of monks "tickles" his soul in its deepest recesses, that prostitution evokes simultaneously "lewdness, bitterness, the nothingness of human relations. . . ."[7] The theme of sterility and even abortion in *L'Éducation sentimentale* is illumined by a comment such as this. Flaubert's admiration for the marquis de Sade, which he shares with Baudelaire, makes him suspect Nature and explains in part why he views the Prostitute both as an antiphysis and the very incarnation of sterility. With bitter irony, Flaubert describes the "maison de santé et d'accouchement" where Rosanette gives birth to a sickly offspring in terms that are most equivocal: the chambermaid looks like a "soubrette," the director of the establishment is called "Madame," the establishment itself (with its closed shutters and continuous sounds of piano playing) is called a "maison discrète" (III.4)—leaving little doubt as to the analogy the author had in mind. Originally, Flaubert had even planned to have the "Madame" explain to Frédéric how to dispose of the newborn baby! And when the sickly child soon after dies, Rosanette's grief coincides with the grief of Mme Dambreuse as she realizes that her husband has left all his wealth to someone else. "A mother grieving beside an empty cradle was not more pitiful than Mme Dambreuse at the sight of the open strong-boxes" (III.4). The theme of sterility could not possibly be pushed much further.

Profanation, betrayal, sterility . . . and yet. And yet the reader is never permitted to forget the ideally pure figure of Mme Arnoux. Frédéric may use other women, and forget himself with them; they are nothing but substitutes for an ideal. One might even say, paradoxically, that profanation is here in the service of purity. Ever since *Mémoires d'un fou*, written at the age of seventeen, Flau-

[7] Flaubert, *Corresp.*, III, 216.

bert was haunted by the contrasts between idealized woman (*le ciel*) and cheap love (*la boue*). The narrator of *Mémoires d'un fou*, still writing under the recent impact of his meeting with Mme Schlésinger, the model for Mme Arnoux, feels guilt and shame because he has lost his virginity with a promiscuous creature, "as though my love for Maria were a religion that I had profaned" (16). In *Novembre*, written at the age of twenty, he attempted to synthesize in one figure the dual visage of woman. *L'Éducation sentimentale* again insists on a polarity. It is clear that the very concept of immaculate beauty required, in Flaubert's imagination, the drama of inaccessibility, as well as the antithesis of corruption.[8]

This persistent idealism, strengthened by profanation as though made holier by it, is implicit in the bordello exploit, the subject of the last scene of the book. Just as the narrator of *Mémoires d'un fou* was haunted by the loss of virginity, so here Frédéric is filled with nostalgia for a lost innocence. For the memory is altogether a chaste one, and even on the level of sheer venery, the incident is marked by a sort of poetry of unrealized love. The memory, however, coming as it does at the end of the book (and especially after the ultimate, deeply moving encounter with Mme Arnoux), acquires an additional aura. And it is significant that Frédéric says not a word of this unforgettable last meeting to Deslauriers. For this is a private realm, a regal chamber open to no one. All throughout the novel it is Mme Arnoux's image that shines forth from behind the Parisian fog, keeping alive an "invincible hope." The very name Marie (the same name as in *Mémoires d'un*

---

[8] From the notebooks published by Marie-Jeanne Durry, it is obvious that these two elements are associated in the earliest stages of the novel's genesis. Frédéric is attracted simultaneously to "Prostitution" and to "ideal exaltation." Flaubert explains to himself that "cynicism hides timidity." As for Mme Arnoux, the notebooks reveal a compelling need to *purify* her. In some of the earliest scenarios she actually does show up at the rendezvous. The author's yearning for purity, visible in the very act of creation, is at the heart of the novel (*Flaubert et ses projets inédits*, pp. 137–138, 150, 163). On the profanatory urge, see Philip Spencer, *Flaubert*, in particular pp. 39, 51 and 79.

fou and in *Novembre*) suggests purity. And in the service of this "image," despite all his weaknesses and abdications, Frédéric acquires nobility. For the sake of this "image," he has in the long run given up everything.

In fact, Marie Arnoux is more than an image, she is a *vision*. But this carries us from the last scene back to the very first scene of the novel.

The River and the Boat:
In the Beginning Is the End

On September 15, 1840, Frédéric—a young man about to begin the study of law—is traveling on a riverboat. *L'Éducation sentimentale* begins among the whirlwinds of smoke, on a vessel which is about to steam away. The destination is Nogent, where Frédéric is to remain with his mother until the fall term begins.

Flaubert was obviously in no way compelled to begin his novel with a river journey. Yet the earliest, very sketchy outline of the novel—not even twenty lines in length—already envisions this as a key scene: "—traversée sur le bateau de Montereau un collégien."[9] The special care with which the scene was eventually written is revealed by the number of drafts—at least seven, it would seem. But such statistics are hardly needed to communicate the importance and suggestive power of these opening pages. Not only does the river journey establish the geographic poles of the novel (the capital and the provincial home), but it provides an ideal setting for the fleeting encounter with Mme Arnoux. Flaubert knew only too well the hopeless dreams that can crystallize around a figure met under ephemeral circumstances: his first meeting with Elisa Schlésinger took place on the beach in Trouville. The boat provided an even more dramatic setting.[10]

The symbolic potential of the scene is more significant

9 Durry, *Flaubert et ses projets inédits*, p. 137.
10 Elsewhere in the novel Flaubert himself associates travel, especially ship travel, with the "amertume des sympathies interrompues" (III.6).

still. For this is not an exotic sea voyage, with the excitement of hoped-for discoveries and possible adventures. Although there is the hustle and bustle of a real departure, nothing could be more prosaic, more commonplace, than the itinerary of the *Ville de Montereau* and the bourgeois vulgarity of its human cargo. It is a departure which fails to bring about an authentic voyage. So too, the movement of the boat is only another form of immobility. A passenger is not an active agent. But here the passivity is double: the boat itself merely follows the inevitable course of the river. Submissiveness to an ineluctable flow, the monotony of the landscape as it slowly glides by, the ability to see its details and yet the inability to hold on to impressions as they merge and fade away—these characteristics of the river navigation are exploited here as an almost prophetic symbol of Destiny and Time, and anticipate the drifting, languid and perpetually dreamy quality of Frédéric's life.[11]

For passiveness and the propensity to dream are closely bound up. The vibrations of the ship are conducive to drowsy well-being. The two banks "unroll" like "two large ribbons": the image almost suggests a film in slow motion. And there is a curious harmony between the outer landscape, slowly gliding by, and the inner landscape with its permanent mutations. To these evanescent forms the mind of Frédéric easily surrenders. Motion, real or imagined, will in fact always be for him an invitation to dream, a liberation from reality. Gaston Bachelard's observations about the excitement of railway travel could easily apply to Frédéric's experience on the boat: "The trip unfolds a film of dream houses . . . with the salutary prohibition of ever *verifying*."[12] As the ship passes by a hill, a vineyard, a windmill—Frédéric's imagination sketches out entire novels of his many unlived lives. His mind is filled with *projects*. And this tendency, which the distance be-

[11] Albert Thibaudet, who rightly insists on the water imagery of this beginning, speaks of the "images flottantes de la vie qui se décompose" (*Gustave Flaubert*, p. 143).
[12] Bachelard, *La Poétique de l'espace*, p. 69.

[141]

tween the boat and the land brings out literally and symbolically, will remain a constant trait of his character. Frédéric "dreams his life" (as opposed to Emma Bovary, who dreams about life), explains Albert Thibaudet.[13] But at the origin of this trancelike state there is the habit of projecting himself into time and space: "he saw Mme Arnoux, ruined, crying, selling all her furniture" (II.2); he "glimpsed, as though in a flash, an immense fortune . . ." (II.2); "Already he saw himself in a waistcoat with lapels and a tricolored sash" (III.1). Often the very "projection" is closely bound up with an image of motion or travel (thus dreams engender dreams): "They would travel, they would go to Italy, to the East!" "He saw her standing on a little hill, gazing at a landscape" (II.6); "He saw himself with Her at night in a post-chaise; then on a river's bank on a summer evening" (III.1). The result is an almost self-hypnotizing, almost hallucinated state. The word "hallucination" actually occurs on several occasions. ("His daydream became so intense that he had a kind of hallucination.")[14] The riverboat, in the first scene of the book, provides an initial setting in which the capacity to dream is closely linked with the attraction to the impossible: movement and distance are inseparable.

But there is also irony in the fact that dreams take shape in the midst of the floating mediocrity of public transportation. The passengers are not exactly models of refinement. Except for a few "bourgeois" in first class, they are representative of humanity at its shabbiest. Flaubert goes to great length in describing a repulsive assembly: sordid clothes, worn-out hats, dirty shirts, torn ties.

[13] Thibaudet, *Gustave Flaubert*, p. 145.
[14] D. L. Demorest, with the support of striking quotations, has shown that the tendency to exaltation at times leads to states akin to "somnambulism" (*L'Expression figurée et symbolique dans l'oeuvre de Gustave Flaubert*, pp. 531–532). Flaubert himself seems to associate such states with movement. See the comparison, in *L'Éducation sentimentale* (II.1): "He felt somewhat stunned, like a man who gets off a ship." For a most interesting discussion of Flaubert's "hallucinatory" style, see John C. Lapp, "Art and Hallucination in Flaubert," *French Studies*, October 1956, pp. 322–334.

People eat and sleep pell-mell. The deck is soiled with nut-shells, cigar butts and garbage. A sordid "reality" thus seems to engender the very dream-world. But does the presence of this "reality" not also soil the dream? Or does it heighten its beauty?

The fact is that Flaubert very deliberately placed this scene of grotesque filth and crudeness immediately before the dazzling first encounter with Mme Arnoux. "Ce fut comme une apparition." The word *apparition* must be taken here in its strongest sense: the earthly manifesta-tion of an unworldly being. Mme Arnoux is like a vision—a vision made concrete, and yet so splendent that it im-mediately obliterates all that which surrounds it. She sits alone, or so it seems, for Frédéric suffers from a momen-tary blindness ("éblouissement") caused by too great a splendor. Everything in this passage suggests the vision of an angelic creature. The rays which emanate from her eyes, the spiritualized oval contours of the face, the fea-tures that stand out against a blue sky which here is like a background in a Fra Angelico painting, the "splendeur" of her brown skin, her delicate, almost immaterial hands through which light flows—all this, as seen through Fréd-éric's eyes, and Flaubert's art, transmutes a woman into an apparition, and makes of her, in the midst of a nine-teenth-century scene of everyday life, a sister to Beatrice.

> e par che sia una cosa venuta
> da cielo in terra a miracol mostrare.

Frédéric might have recited to himself these lines from Dante's *Vita Nuova*. He, too, feels a "deeper yearning," a curiosity that knows no limits. The mystical overtones of these pages are further stressed by Frédéric's giving "alms" to the harpist, a gesture which vaguely corresponds, in his own mind, to an idea of blessing and to an almost religious impulse.

These images of spirituality are of the utmost thematic importance. One of the earliest sketches indeed sums up this initial meeting with the single word: *éblouissement* (dazzlement).[15] Throughout the novel, Mme Arnoux repeatedly "appears" as a vision (". . . Madame Arnoux parut" I.4). Her role as Madonna is brought out by a number of scenes in which she is shown together with her children in the "tranquil majesty" of a maternal pose.[16] Her hands seem forever ready to spread alms and wipe away tears. Frédéric frequently sits and merely "contemplates" her (I.5). Most often, however, her figure is associated with a particular quality of light. "Madame Arnoux was sitting on a big rock with this incandescent light at her back"—the image here is one of a halo. Her glances penetrate his soul "like those great rays of sunlight which descend to the bottom of the water" (I.5). When Frédéric meets her in the street, "the sunlight surrounded her" and her entire person seems invested with an "extraordinary splendor": an "infinite suavity" emanates from her eyes (II.6). At times Frédéric uses nothing but the capitalized personal pronoun *Elle* when he thinks of her. Her entire person is not only extraordinarily radiant (light pours from her as from a glory), but even the tiniest part of her body is infinitely precious. "Each of her fingers was for him more than a thing, almost a person."[17] In short, Frédéric places her "outside the human condition" (II.3). She fills him alternately with religious awe and with an "undefinable beatitude" (II.6). Nothing better illustrates Flaubert's skill at objectively presenting a subjectivity—and of simultaneously stressing the drama of this subjectivity—than the manner in which he idealizes Mme Arnoux through the eyes of Frédéric. One wonders how Henry James could have reproached Flaubert for what is precisely one of the main achievements of this novel: the fact that Mme Arnoux is offered us preponderantly

[15] Durry, *Flaubert et ses projets inédits*, p. 163.
[16] One of Flaubert's most striking early impressions of Elisa Schlésinger was the sight of her nursing her baby.
[17] II.6. Is it not likely that this remark concerning Madame Arnoux's fingers corresponds to the curious notation in Flaubert's notebooks which baffled Marie-Jeanne Durry: "toutes les dents sont des personnes" (*Flaubert et ses projets inédits*, pp. 192–193)?

through Frédéric's vision. Henry James obviously missed the point.[18] What matters is not whether Frédéric is a worthy medium through which to view so noble a soul, nor even whether the lady really is so sublime a creature (a futile question!)—but the tragic urge to create such a figure, to believe in her, and to cling stubbornly to the beauty of a vision engendered, as it were, by the very banality of existence.

The thematic importance of the first scene is further brought out by the fact that the image of Mme Arnoux is very frequently associated with the idea of travel. In part this corresponds to a characteristic Flaubertian yearning for the exotic. Thus already in the first scene, on the boat, exotic elements are introduced and amplified by the hero's imagination. He attributes Mme Arnoux's complexion to an Andalusian origin; when he sees her Negro servant, he imagines that she has brought her from the West Indies, and that she herself is a Creole. The harpist on the boat plays an "Oriental ballad" all about daggers, flowers and stars. And later in the novel when Frédéric dreams of Mme Arnoux, he sees himself traveling with her to distant lands, on dromedaries, elephants or elegant yachts. Such images are to some extent ironic, but not altogether. They also represent a genuine lyricism.[19] For Frédéric, just as for Flaubert, the ideas of love and passion are commonly associated with ideas of motion and travel to distant lands. Frédéric frequently fancies himself *in movement* with "Her." (It is in a carriage that he almost dares touch her hand!) But movement can also mean separation; travel can mean remoteness, estrangement, inaccessibility. It can mean that the loved one is elsewhere. Thus, already on the boat, Frédéric's destination and Mme Arnoux's destination are not the same: he will get off in Nogent, while she will proceed with her husband

[18] James, *Notes on Novelists*, p. 86. On James' curious antagonism to Flaubert, see Edmund Wilson, "The Ambiguity of Henry James," in *The Triple Thinkers*, pp. 141–142.
[19] On the non-ironic qualities of exoticism in *L'Éducation sentimentale*, see Raymond Giraud's *The Unheroic Hero*, pp. 159–160.

to Montereau, and from there to Switzerland. When his mother later talks to him, his mind tries to follow the image of Mme Arnoux: he pictures her sitting in a diligence, wrapped up in her shawl, her head leaning against the cloth of the coupé. There is a similar image of departure and separation almost at the end of the book: he conjures up a vision of her, sitting in a railway carriage or on the deck of a steamship "like the first time he met her" (III.5). The very reference to the first scene of the novel testifies to the permanence of the dual themes of encounter and separation. The very symbol of an exalted meeting thus tragically turns out to be a symbol of an irretrievable loss.

The travel motif is thus broadly speaking charged with a sense of poetic bitterness. Frédéric perpetually dreams of "distant countries and long voyages"—yet the only long voyage takes place during the hiatus which precedes the epilogue. He travels to forget, and appropriately the trip itself is barely mentioned: it is forgotten, swallowed by Time and meaninglessness. It is a void, a vacancy—almost an initiation to death.[20] As for his other trips, they are all derisory. His second arrival in Paris, at the beginning of Part II, is by coach. The trip begins in exhilaration, but as the heavy carriage, slowed down by rain, moves through the outskirts of the capital, the prevailing mood becomes one of ugliness and sterility, as Frédéric glimpses empty lots, branchless trees, chemical works, puddles of dirty water, sordid courtyards littered with refuse, midwives' signboards. Similar effects of disenchantment are achieved through other scenes of locomotion. The excursion to Creil to see Mme Arnoux in her husband's factory ends in discomfiture. The hedonistic journey to Fontainebleau with Rosanette (the lovers are constantly on the move) is made trivial by Rosanette's inept comments during the

---

[20] It is significant that Marcel Proust should have prized above all in L'Éducation sentimentale this "blank" which communicates, by means of a stupendous "change of gears," the poetical qualities in the rhythmical fluctuations of time (Chroniques, p. 205).

visit to the château. The impetuous trip to Nogent after the double rupture with Rosanette and Mme Dambreuse only leads to another "defeat": Frédéric arrives just in time to witness the marriage of Louise Roque to Deslauriers. And even in town, vehicles and motion most often communicate a feeling of interrupted flow, for instance during the traffic jam after the races. The entire book seems to be conceived under the ambiguous sign of continual motion and stasis, which correspond to Frédéric's contradictory need to escape outside his solipsistic self and yet to seek refuge, to *dissolve* within it.

Images of dissolution, of liquefaction, are indeed extremely important in the metaphorical texture of the novel. *L'Éducation sentimentale* begins with a scene of travel, but it is travel by water. The Seine is where the destinies of Mme Arnoux and Frédéric meet, and it is also where, in the very first pages, they prophetically separate. The Seine is part of the Parisian landscape—and it occupied an even greater portion of the landscape Flaubert himself had constantly before his eyes from his room in Croisset. But although Flaubert was far from insensitive to its beauty, it is, in *L'Éducation sentimentale*, a river of sadness and of cruel indifference. Frédéric, in his despondent moments, watches the river flow between the somber quays blackened by the seams of the sewers. (How different from the graceful, carefree Seine of Hugo, the melodramatic Seine of Balzac, the picturesque Seine of Zola!) Flaubert's Seine has no definite color (it is "jaunâtre"—vaguely yellow). It is a river associated with loss and tragic unconcern. An old man cries; his son was probably killed during the uprising: "The Seine flowed calmly" (III.1). Tears and dirty water—they are part of the same scenery.

Albert Thibaudet has admirably shown the omnipresence of the river image in Flaubert's description of Parisian traffic and in the "liquid continuity" of the imperfect tense.[21] In fact, at one point the Champs Élysées are quite

[21] Thibaudet, *Gustave Flaubert*, p. 144.

explicitly likened to a river. But the Parisian crowds also—whether peaceful strollers on the boulevard or riotous mobs—are compared to liquid masses in motion. What Frédéric surveys near the Madeleine is an "immense flot ondulant" (I.5). The revolutionary mobs, later in the novel, are seen as "flots vertigineux" (III.1): images which appropriately suggest ineluctable forces, as well as an energy that eventually flows away or evaporates.

For images of liquid in *L'Éducation sentimentale* are intimately related to images of vapor. At the beginning of the novel, a wandering haze covers the surface of the water. As the novel progresses, the poetic mist (still associated with hope in the scene where Deslauriers and Frédéric contemplate the delicate haziness in the direction of the river) becomes a tenacious fog. The characteristic weather in Flaubert's Paris is a steady drizzle and a depressing fog. At times rain becomes torrential: streets are transformed into waterways. But most often an almost anesthetizing fog seems to settle. Frédéric feels himself surrounded by "damp air" (I.4); a "humid gloom" (I.3) descends into the depths of his heart. But it is also a strangely luminous fog: from behind it shines the invisible, but effulgent figure of Mme Arnoux. This opaque luminosity is one of Flaubert's most notable achievements in *L'Éducation sentimentale*. It makes of him not only one of the outstanding poets of Paris, together with Hugo and Baudelaire, but also a brother to the Impressionist painters.[22]

This vaporous liquefaction admirably conveys states of passiveness and expectancy, and a strange mixture of stubborn hope and inherent defeatism. Thus while waiting interminably in a café, Frédéric (though not in the least bit thirsty) absorbs one "liquid" after another: a glass of rum, then a glass of kirsch, followed by a glass of curaçao, then various hot and cold grogs (II.1). Variety once more

[22] Harry Levin, in a perceptive discussion of this city-poetry, links Flaubert's art with that of Monet, Degas, Renoir and Pissaro (*The Gates of Horn*, pp. 230–231).

betrays futility. Drinking becomes almost literally a manner of "killing time." And repeatedly liquids and liquefaction evoke the erosive quality of Time, as well as a sense of dissolution and loss. Sitting near the river with Louise Roque, Frédéric plays with sand, letting it slip through his fingers, while close by the sound of a cascade and the bubbling whirlpools can be heard (II.5). The sand, trickling through fingers as though liquefied, no doubt signifies Time slipping away. And this dissolving quality of Time, so central to the meaning of *L'Éducation sentimentale*, is almost redundantly imparted by means of "liquid" associations. Thus while the rain pours outside, Frédéric, sitting in the café and still waiting, looks at the clock in such a manner that, if objects could be worn out by looking at them, "Frédéric would have dissolved the clock" (II.1). The same image of dissolution recurs as Frédéric waits for Mme Arnoux, who does not show up at their rendezvous: "He felt himself dissolve from utter dejection." Even the political disintegration of Louis-Philippe's regime is expressed in terms of a liquefaction (which is of course also a liquidation): "the Monarchy was melting away in rapid dissolution" (III.1).

L'Éducation sentimentale, viewed in this light, appears as a novel of steady flow and indefinite expectation. No final catastrophe ever interrupts the fluidity of existence. Tragedy here stems not from the brutal interruption of life, but from its hopeless and self-destructive continuity. The gradual bankruptcy of an entire generation is experienced, often circuitously, through the consciousness of an individual who himself is the victim of slow disintegration. The auction sale of Mme Arnoux's private belongings, toward the end of the novel, admirably symbolizes this impression of a whole life being liquidated. As Frédéric witnesses the profanation of her most intimate objects— her hats, her shoes, her lingerie—he experiences a sense of "dissolution," a mournful torpor akin to spiritual death (III.5). This feeling of slow disintegration, this wearing down by life itself, is perhaps one of the reasons why young readers are so often impatient with this book. But the theme of progressive deterioration is only one of the strands in *L'Éducation sentimentale*. The poetic power of the novel is largely to be attributed to its inner contradictions reflected in the enigmatic double ending of the epilogue, which juxtaposes a scene of transcending love and one which almost smugly surveys a life of defeats. And there is a double irony here. For just as the dreams associated with lovely images of travel and water are doomed to a fiasco, so the apparently cynical memories of the brothel in the final scene mask a never defeated and never satisfied craving for innocence and beauty.

The Ambiguities of Love

In his discussion of *Madame Bovary*, Percy Lubbock declares that there is not the least shade of ambiguity in this novel. Flaubert's art, according to Lubbock, is so much in control of his subject that there is no way of mistaking or misreading it. "Flaubert has only one word to say, and it is impossible to find more than a single meaning in it."[23] This more than questionable assertion fits Flaubert's craft and vision in *L'Éducation sentimentale* even less. Few novels in French literature are indeed more ambiguous—though the uniform surface may suggest impassive control. Nothing in fact could be further removed from the truth than this image of an author who tolerates no enigma. Even the final scene with Mme Arnoux, to which I have referred as a scene of transcending love, is very far from unambiguous.

It is a deeply touching scene. Many years have elapsed since the two saw each other last. There once had been a period of intimacy which almost led to adultery, but events, and above all their own characters, made such a liaison irrevocably impossible. Now, sixteen years later (he is over forty, she well over fifty), Mme Arnoux unexpectedly

23 Lubbock, *The Craft of Fiction*, p. 60.

comes to visit him. The ostensible reason is to return some borrowed money. At first, there is the silence of deep emotions. Then they talk. She tells him of her present life in a remote part of Brittany, of the bench facing the sea on which she likes to sit and dream, and which she has named *le banc Frédéric*. Upon her request, they go out for a short walk, and this walk among the early evening lights and shadows of Parisian streets recalls another walk, many years earlier, on a cold, foggy winter afternoon. They walk as on dead leaves, singing out their duet of memories, like an already transposed, purified and serene song of passion. It is the meeting of two phantoms. Their gestures suggest a certain timelessness and also a curious sense of poetic finality.

Yet there is something about this scene that can disturb the reader. The very style of the conversation constantly borders on the cliché. It is filled with sentimental phraseology drawn from Romantic books. When Frédéric refers to the "music" of her voice, when Mme Arnoux mentions the "distant echo" of his words which come to her "like the sound of a bell carried by the wind," the reader remembers the many occasions on which, in *Madame Bovary* as well as in *L'Éducation sentimentale*, Flaubert had satirized precisely this kind of language. This impression seems to be confirmed by Mme Arnoux's explicit reference to "love passages in books" and by Frédéric's curious (to say the least!) remark that he now understands Werther, who is not appalled by "the twaddle of Charlotte." How is one to account for this? One could of course invoke an artistic flaw. Thus John Middleton Murry believes that Flaubert is here carried away by his inveterate need to parody second-rate Romanticism. "For the sake of a worn-out metaphor, Flaubert was willing to make his heroine speak out of character."[24] The other explanation would be to interpret the scene as a conscious and cruelly ironic subversion of whatever idealism was latent in their

[24] Murry, *Countries of the Mind*, pp. 159–160.

relationship. The main characters would thus be shown, up to the very end, as pathetic victims of their illusions.

The idea of a final unveiling and mocking of all illusions would seem to be supported by another disturbing element. When Mme Arnoux takes off her hat, and Frédéric can see her white hair and the ravages of time, he is utterly shaken. But he flings himself on the floor, at her feet, and makes to her the most ardent love declaration of his life. This he does to conceal from her (and from himself) his sense of disillusionment. The scene could thus easily be interpreted as one of insincerity. Frédéric succeeds in half convincing himself. But is not that also an ironic twist which sums up Frédéric's propensity to get drunk on his own words? And does it not also stress the literary, highly subjective quality of his love for Mme Arnoux? According to one critic, Flaubert here somewhat cruelly suggests that Frédéric perhaps never really loved her.[25]

But there is worse. At one point, Frédéric has the suspicion that the aging Mme Arnoux has come to "offer herself" to him! Already once, much earlier, he suspected her of being the accomplice of her husband in having him intervene in their interest with the banker Dambreuse. But the suspicion in the final scene is of course far more serious. And if it casts a somewhat equivocal light on Mme Arnoux, it casts an even worse light on Frédéric himself. For he not only feels a sudden desire to possess her which is fiercer than ever, but at the very same time he is held back as though by a fear of incest (for Mme Arnoux is the mother-image), as well as by the more pedestrian fear of involvement and complications. The final touch of irony is provided by Mme Arnoux, who interprets Frédéric's equivocal passivity, when he turns his back to her and calmly rolls a cigarette, as a sign of supreme delicacy: "Comme vous êtes délicat. Il n'y a que vous."

The scene is, however, very far from a final debunking

25 D. L. Demorest. *L'Expression figurée et symbolique dans l'oeuvre de Gustave Flaubert*, p. 530.

of every ideal. Quite the opposite. It is probably one of the most beautiful love scenes in all of literature. And the use of clichés is not the least of its deeply touching aspects. It is not the first time that Flaubert places the banal in the service of intense emotion. When, after a long separation, Frédéric meets Mme Arnoux by chance in the street, their conversation is of the utmost triteness: questions about her children, a few words about the weather—and yet this encounter is for Frédéric more exciting than "the most beautiful of adventures." In the last scene, the effect is even more powerful. The use of literary clichés suggests not that life imitates art, but that it has caught up with art, that it has become art.[26] Or rather, it is as though the two characters were now dictating to each other the very terms of their own romance.

Time seems to replace narration. The use of the *futur antérieur* ("... Nous nous serons bien aimés—We shall have loved each other truly") indicates not merely anticipated retrospection, but the kind of retrospection from a final and almost hypothetically aloof vantage point capable of bestowing upon the past the beauty that belongs exclusively to supreme destinies. To such beauty, achieved through the alchemy of loss and memory, Flaubert was sensitive ever since his adolescence. "Memory is a beautiful thing, it is almost a desire one mourns," he writes to his friend Ernest Chevalier in 1842.[27] And many years later, in a letter to Mme Roger des Genettes, memory endows the past with an almost spiritual glow: "... the days of yesteryear begin to sway softly in a luminous mist."[28] This sentence could have come straight out of *L'Éducation sentimentale*. Frédéric and Mme Arnoux, during their final encounter, become poets of the past. They speak about their common memories as one speaks of a dear departed one. Theirs is a lyric funeral oration of their own love.

[26] D. L. Demorest is right: for Mme Arnoux memory has become "presqu'un roman"—almost a novel (*L'Expression figurée et symbolique dans l'oeuvre de Gustave Flaubert*, p. 534).

[27] Flaubert, *Corresp.*, I, 102.

[28] Flaubert, *Corresp.*, VI, 426.

This lyricism and the sense of a rich past carry them both out of time. But there is also a new sense of freedom in this ecstasy. No longer the possible victims of passion, they now dominate their love, much as the artist, when his life's turmoil has been transmuted into art, dominates his work and himself through it.[29] As for the willful blindness of Frédéric, who chooses not to look at Mme Arnoux's gray hair and pays the most ardent tributes to the woman she has ceased being, far from casting doubt on Frédéric's sincerity, this gesture only stresses his perennial need to love. What more striking illustration could Flaubert provide of the desire to be taken in by the beauty of one's dreams? The negation of reality is here not an elusion, but a stubborn affirmation.

L'Éducation sentimentale thus sings the poetry of the unattained. Although nothing seems to protect Flaubert's protagonists from the snares of time and disillusionment, although life itself seems to defeat them, the novel ultimately metamorphoses this defeat into a victory. Is it because for the author it represents a work of compensation ("Il ne regretta rien.—He regretted nothing. He felt compensated for all he had suffered in the past.")? Whatever the echoes of his personal life—it would seem that Mme Schlésinger did come to pay him a similar visit in Croisset —the novel marks a victory for the *vieux troubadour*. The theme of adultery, which haunted Flaubert ever since his earliest writings, has here been exorcised. By transforming Marie Arnoux into an explicit mother-image ("l'effroi d'un inceste"), Frédéric not only "frees" himself from one of his most persistent obsessions, but he poetically justifies the involuted pleasure he took in being denied. Where he dreamed of possessing an older, married woman, he learns the beauty of renunciation and of dreams that survive as dreams. The final scene with Mme Arnoux is a masterpiece of nuances, nostalgia, echoes and veiled luminosity.

[29] Albert Thibaudet puts it excellently when he says that Mme Arnoux can now "possess" her dream, instead of being "possessed by it" (*Gustave Flaubert*, p. 150).

Even its ironies give support to the music of this scene. For Frédéric's reticence, his so-called "prudence," his fear of getting involved, are but the flattest ways (and why should Frédéric be able to interpret this complex fear?) of suggesting that this fear of reality, this fear of possession are in fact manifestations of a basic defense against disillusionment, of a quest for purity which ultimately leads to a monastic withdrawal.

Yet ironies and ambiguities there are, and it seems difficult to agree with Martin Turnell that in *L'Éducation sentimentale* Flaubert takes romantic love so seriously that "there is no trace of irony in his treatment of it."[30] This is scarcely the case. The apparent inconsistencies can in part be attributed to the very genesis of the novel, to the survival of certain elements in the original plans which Flaubert modified in the process of elaborating the plot. In one of the earliest scenarios, Frédéric was to "possess" the married woman. But Flaubert then crossed this out, and added the alternative "elle s'offre." The expression "elle s'offre" appears again in another sketch, followed by the comment that she no longer interests Frédéric.[31] Of these original ideas, only Frédéric's "suspicion" that she came to offer herself to him has survived. Quite clearly, in the process of gestation, the figure of Mme Arnoux underwent serious changes, and in particular a gradual idealization.[32] But more important still than these changes in intention, and also more elusive, are the author's reactions to his writing at the very moment of composition. The very process of writing involves a drama beyond the action and suffering of the protagonists. Words evoke and provoke. The writer becomes his own reader, as he battles with his memories and his desires. His book does not remain an

[30] Turnell, *The Novel in France*, p. 281.
[31] Durry, *Flaubert et ses projets inédits*, pp. 138, 174.
[32] Jean Bruneau argues very convincingly that a similar process of idealization of Mme Schlésinger takes place in Flaubert's mind at the time he writes *L'Éducation sentimentale*. Writing about his old flame rekindled it. (*Les Débuts littéraires de Gustave Flaubert, 1831–1845*, pp. 373–374).

inert and obedient mass; his mind refuses to be in a state of quiescence. This other drama—the spontaneous reactions to the very process of creation—places the author in a state of tension vis-à-vis his own work, and makes of him (far more than in a strictly autobiographical sense) the hero of his own poem.

The Ambiguities of Politics

Even the supposedly objective account of historical events is fraught with personal tensions. Although Flaubert indulged in orgies of documentation concerning the events of 1848 (political pamphlets, history books, eye-witness accounts, his own and his friends' memories),[33] his description of the 1848 revolution and of the events that led up to it hardly reflects a dispassionate attitude. Here, too, the intentions of the author were ambiguous. This novel, which many readers now interpret as a pungent social and political satire, and into which some go so far as to read the death sentence of bourgeois society, was originally not at all focused on political or social issues. The first sketches are centered exclusively on the trio: wife, husband, lover. Only later—progressively and dimly—does Flaubert begin to show interest in the social and historical background, as he establishes, in his mind, a parallel between the "sentimental" fiasco of the protagonists and the political fiasco after 1830.

Gradually the subject became fascinating in itself. "I want to write the moral history of the men of my generation . . . ," he confides to Mlle Leroyer de Chantepie in 1864.[34] The very difficulties of maintaining a balance between the historical drama and the drama of individual destinies was a challenge to Flaubert, who loved difficulties for their own sake. The artistic "problem" for a while seemed to take priority over the social issues. The primary

---

[33] For a discussion of this documentation, see Alexis François, "Flaubert, Maxime Du Camp et la Révolution de 1848," *Revue d'Histoire Littéraire de la France*, 1938, pp. 183–204.
[34] Flaubert, *Corresp.*, V, 158.

problem was how to prevent his characters from being swallowed up by the huge setting and the turmoil of events. Hence Flaubert was almost compelled to attribute to his main characters a solid dose of selfish indifference in order to prevent History from becoming all-absorbing. ("I am afraid the background might devour the foreground.")[35] But of course there is irony and bitterness as well behind their indifference. Flaubert was evidently satisfied neither with providing a background that would broaden the horizon, nor with the stimulus of a difficult artistic problem, nor with coolly diagnosing France's ills by means of a "historical novel" written at such short range that the consequences could still be felt. Ultimately, he could not resist the temptation to let his accumulated bile overflow in what amounts to an almost militant debunking of all the nonsense and turpitude he associated with politics.

Flaubert's bias, or ill will, is evidenced by the many parallels he establishes between individual and collective treasons. The very structure of the novel clearly divulges his ironic view of the events of 1848. The revolution breaks out at the point at which Rosanette becomes Frédéric's mistress in the apartment prepared to receive Mme Arnoux, and consequently begins under the double sign of indifference and defeat. And the revolutionary aspirations die out in utter apathy in early December 1851, at the very point at which Frédéric's love life ends almost simultaneously in a triple fiasco. Thus also, by a kind of malevolent logic, Sénécal's betrayal of the revolution takes the concrete form of his betrayal of friendship, as he kills the idealistic Dussardier.

Flaubert the *bourgeoisophobus* (so he once signed a letter) is filled with rancor against his own social class, much as he tried to make of "bourgeois" a moral rather than a social category. André Gide once called *L'Éducation sentimentale* an "epic of disgust."[36] And indeed disgust there is. The smugness of the *époque pantouflarde*, the boorish

35 Flaubert, *Corresp.*, V, 363.
36 Gide, *Journal* (1889–1939), p. 805.

reign of *muflisme*, the belief in investment (the famous *trois pour cent*) and in the army as an instrument to repress popular uprisings, all these were for Flaubert objects of indignation as well as uncomfortable reminders of his own traits or social allegiances, a fact which only further exacerbated Flaubert's disgust and his hatred of his favorite bugbear, the philistine bourgeois.

Characteristically, however, his satirical wrath in *L'Éducation sentimentale* seems directed primarily against the popular uprisings and its parasitical fellow travelers. The revolution is certainly not presented in a glorious light. The description of the mob's invasion of the Tuileries (III.1) is a crescendo of violence and obscenity in four movements. Frédéric and Hussonnet first see the onrushing crowd, and hear a huge *mugissement* (roar) and *piétinement* (tramping) suggesting a herdlike stampede. "Heroes don't smell good," tersely comments Hussonnet. Then, after the throne is occupied by a brutish representative of the proletariat, joy becomes frantic. The "canaille," the vile rabble, begins to tear, break, defile. Finally, a lecherous curiosity propels them to the queen's chamber, and delinquent types wallow in the beds of the princesses, possessed by a bestial desire to commit vicarious rape.

Elsewhere, Flaubert insists on the epidemic of stupidity which spreads in the wake of the uprisings, and which is epitomized by the Club de l'Intelligence (III.1). In one of the most acrid scenes of the novel, Flaubert accumulates the targets of his ire: conformistic imitations of historic "models" such as Marat or Danton, vulgarity (the poem glorifying the workman's cap), foolish projects (for a universal language, for a decree against misery), orgies of abolitions, foggy notions about the apostolic mission of the proletariat, aimless chatter and obnubilating clichés. The incomprehensible speech in Spanish by the "patriot" from Barcelona aptly sums up this pandemonium of absurd and contradictory claims. And behind the stupidity, Flaubert points to the futility of it all. The mob storms a prison in order to liberate fifty prisoners who are not even there! Incompetence and betrayal are the distinguishing features of a revolution doomed to miscarry. Inadequate leadership, tiresome debates, the selfishness of various guilds, the lip service of late-joiners and of the established institutions, even fear and cowardice, all condemn it to flounder and collapse under its own ineptness.

There is unquestionably some historical truth to this appraisal. But it is very limited and one-sided. Louis Berniawski, in the Conard edition of the novel (pp. 630–631), has pointed out the many gaps in the social, political and intellectual tableau presented by Flaubert. Nothing is said, for instance, about the dynamic and liberal neo-Catholic movement, almost nothing about the great variety of socialist schools and doctrines, nothing about *napoléonisme*; and the description of the public press leaves very much to be desired. There is little doubt that these are willful gaps, for Flaubert had documented himself, and was certainly quite capable of further documentation. The omissions are conscious, just as the perspective remains slanted. Only—what complicates matters—the slant is not always the same.

Sartre, who never forgave him his silence at the time of the reprisals following the Commune, points out that Flaubert hated the worker ("il mange de l'ouvrier") even more than he despised the bourgeois.[37] Certainly Flaubert felt suspicion and distaste for all socialist theories; he accused socialist thinkers of being doctrinaires and potential despots. His correspondence is studded with biting, and at times scatological remarks about the myth of the "people." The People is for him the imbecile rabble, and Socialists are, he feels, imbued with a fanatical hatred of freedom.[38] Sénécal is obviously meant as a caricature of

[37] Sartre, *Critique de la raison dialectique*, pp. 703–704. Sartre has recently insisted again on Flaubert's bad faith ("La Conscience de classe chez Flaubert," *Les Temps Modernes*, May, June 1966, pp. 1,921–1,951; 2,113–2,153). See also "Flaubert: du poète à l'artiste," *ibid.*, August 1966, pp. 197–253.
[38] Flaubert, *Corresp.*, III, 349–350; V, 148–149. Despite his immense admiration for Victor Hugo, Flaubert was appalled by Hugo's utopian faith in the People.

this type. Yet matters are not quite so simple, and Sartre's reproaches are not altogether fair. For if there is the sinister figure of Sénécal, there is also the generous and lovable figure of Dussardier. A close look at Frédéric's own hesitations and oscillations during the revolutionary events proves to be most instructive. At first he is a passive spectator, then he is stirred by the public enthusiasm, finally he feels ashamed of his neutrality and reproaches himself for not being in the midst of the fight "with the others" (III.1).

Certainly Flaubert was not insensitive to a certain epic grandeur of revolutionary events. Granted that this kind of sensibility is above all of a plastic nature, it nevertheless produced some moving and even grandiose scenes, filled with tragic resonances. The passage describing Frédéric's nocturnal arrest (the fleeting shadows behind the blazing windows of the Pitié hospital, the Guard's exclamation cast in the midst of silence, the stamp of heavy footsteps, the confused masses melting into the darkness, the statuesque dragoon on his motionless horse, the heavy rolling sounds that seem to intensify the black silence in which ghostlike figures appear and disappear) could come straight out of one of the apocalyptic novels of André Malraux (III.1).

Nor do the socialist doctrines and popular uprisings have a monopoly on unintelligence. When it comes to diagnosing imbecility, Flaubert is of the most devastating impartiality. "How fed up I am with the filthy worker, the inept bourgeois, the stupid peasant and the odious clergyman," he was to write to George Sand in a typical moment of global exasperation.[39] And in a letter to Turgenev, he refers to the conservative forces as the "infâme parti de l'ordre."[40] Yet this very talent for exasperation indicates not indifference, but a deep-seated propensity to moral indignation. Raymond Giraud's surprising, but astute, statement that Flaubert was by temperament a "preaching

[39] Flaubert, *Corresp.*, VI, 276.
[40] Flaubert, *Lettres inédites à Tourgueneff*, p. 154.

moralist" is certainly confirmed by *L'Éducation senti-mentale*.[41]

It would be most revealing to undertake a systematic study of Flaubert's *moral* reactions in the novel. But no-where, I believe, is his sense of indignation and of pity more vehement than in the somber passage describing the atrocious treatment inflicted on the political prisoners gathered under the terrace of the Orangerie, exposed to hunger and unspeakable brutality, and agonizing in their own excrements among the decomposing bodies of their dead comrades (III.1). The scene prefigures in sordid and dramatic power the most ferocious descriptions inspired by our own fanatical and genocidal period. The mere fact that Flaubert chose to describe in detail this infamous episode is a clear indication that his attitude is far from impassive.

The Author's "Presence"

Such ambiguities in handling the themes of politics and love, as well as clear undertones of moral commitment, raise once again the problem of Flaubert's so-called "ob-jectivity." True enough, Flaubert himself has proclaimed objectivity, or "impassibility," as a fundamental dogma of his art. His letters to Louise Colet in particular (maybe he felt that "La Muse" badly needed the advice?) repeat tirelessly that the great writer ought to seek a "super-human impersonality," that he should avoid "singing about himself," that he must be a hidden god, that the imper-sonality of the artist is his true sign of strength, that his work must be "serene" and "enigmatic" ("incompréhensi-ble"), that he should strive to create the illusion that he him-self never really existed.[42] These precepts Flaubert unques-tionably attempted to follow; they were of immense help to him in overcoming his early tendency to uncontrolled lyrical and autobiographical outbursts. But can one agree

[41] Giraud, *The Unheroic Hero*, p. 146.
[42] Flaubert, *Corresp.*, II, 380; III, 61–62, 321–322. See my dis-cussion of the *Correspondance* in chapter 1.

with those readers who view his novels as a systematic application of these principles, or who maintain, like Erich Auerbach, that Flaubert's opinion of his protagonists and events "remains unspoken"?[43] In fact, Flaubert "intervenes" far more often than would appear at first. A detailed, nuanced study of these interventions would unquestionably yield some illuminating results. For this is not only a matter of technique (although the technical problem is in itself interesting enough), but a problem which involves the complex relationship between a writer and his creation. When, for instance, does the author intervene? Is there a pattern to his commentary? What are the methods of intervention? And are these intrusions conscious—or are they the spontaneous reactions of a sensibility fighting its private battles? These questions are all related to the novelist's themes and vision.

L'Éducation sentimentale provides a surprising variety of author's intrusions. The most flagrant, of course, are those —quite numerous—where Flaubert supplies an explicit appraisal of his characters. Arnoux's "roguish tricks" come very close to "turpitude" (II.2); the banker Dambreuse is "as subtle as a Greek and as laborious as a native from Auvergne" (I.3); the actor Delmar has a "vulgar face, made like a stage set to be viewed from a distance" (II.1); the young snob de Cisy keeps "spouting forth nonsense" (II.4); Deslaurier's manner of speaking and thinking betrays "the man of mean extraction" (II.1). It is Frédéric, however, who is most often exposed to the author's disparagement and sneers. He himself suffers from his own "prodigious cowardice" at the beginning of his relationship with Rosanette (II.2); later his pride and manhood founder in a "bottomless cowardice" ("une lâcheté sans fond" II.4); his spineless character makes him the victim of a "lâcheté immense" (II.6). This is the very kind of surrender which, at the time of his vague political ambitions, compels Flaubert to denounce his protagonist as an "homme de toutes les faiblesses"—a man prone to every

[43] Auerbach, *Mimesis*, p. 429.

manner of weakness (III.1). Groups also come under direct attack as they mix with legitimate grievances "the most inept complaints" (II.6) or display their incompetence and baseness among "clouds of idiocies" (III.1). Flaubert's appraisals are, however, not uniformly disparaging. In referring to Dussardier's generosity, he makes this statement, which is strictly an author's judgment: "He was one of those persons who throw themselves under vehicles to bring aid to the horses which have fallen" (II.2).

Brief appraisals of the characters' motivation and of their psychological reactions are another form of intervention. Here again, Flaubert is not at all reticent. Mme Dambreuse, sitting on a small sofa, keeps brushing off the red flock from a Japanese screen "no doubt in order to show off her hands" (II.2). At the auction sale she casts insolent looks at Rosanette, "perhaps envying the latter's youth" (III.5). The attenuating "no doubt" and "perhaps" seem to be introduced here as though to suggest the author's lack of solidarity with his own comments. A similar impulse or device can be noted in various evaluations of Frédéric's behavior. He forces himself to despise Delmar "in order to banish, *perhaps*, the kind of envy he felt" (II.1). If he feels attracted to the art dealer Arnoux, "this was, *no doubt*, due to some deep-rooted affinities" (II.3). In the tête-à-tête with Mme Dambreuse, the conversation languishes: they talk very little, "distrusting themselves, *no doubt*" (III.3). These repeated *sans doute* and *peut-être* do more than disengage the intervening author; they almost suggest that the interpretation might be vaguely formulated by the characters themselves.

Sometimes, indeed, it is difficult to ascertain whether it is the characters' or the author's point of view that is being communicated. A certain telescoping occurs. When Frédéric remains in the café "without knowing why—out of weakness, stupidity, vague hope" (I.5), is it the author alone who judges him? Similarly, when Flaubert writes that his hero has "learned from his visits to the Dambreuses" (III.3), it is not altogether sure that this opinion is not also vaguely shared by Frédéric himself. Flaubert's comments are of course often far less equivocal. On the subject of Deslauriers, for instance (perhaps because he was venting his resentment against his former friend Maxime Du Camp whom he here uses as a model), Flaubert can be more brutal in his assessments and disparagements. Generally speaking, however, direct judgments about characters are more frequent than interpretations of motives or speculations about the psychology of action. This would be in keeping with the author's de-emphasis of plot causality and with his characteristic tendency, in *L'Éducation sentimentale*, to establish a cleavage between motivation and action.[44]

The conventional and clumsy narrator's devices (omniscient explanations, summings-up of past or collateral action, digressions on personal opinions and documentation, sudden and unjustified shifts of point of view) Flaubert is careful to avoid. But there are slips. Occasionally the author confirms a fact; but very seldom does he project his narration outside the strict chronology, and even more rarely does he indulge in the conditional sentences by means of which Stendhal, for instance, so often toys with hypothetical situations to bring out ironically the charming innocence of his heroes. But when it comes to the structure of his novel, Flaubert unquestionably loads the dice. There his presence is felt as a permanent form of intervention, often ironic, at times deliberately cruel. Thus the entire visit to Creil is planned as a series of mortifications (clumsy love declarations covered by the noise of machinery, constant interferences with Frédéric's attempt to establish contact) leading up to the final vexation as the author has his character take the wrong road upon his return! Such "arranged" situations are typical of Flaubert. He likes, in particular, to play variations on the subject of cruel coincidences and chance meetings. Frédéric en-

---

[44] For a very perceptive discussion of this absence of causality ("unkausale Situationsabfolge"), see Hugo Friedrich's excellent chapter on Flaubert in *Die Klassiker des französischen Romans*, and in particular, pp. 136–142.

counters Mme Arnoux at the races while in the company of Rosanette; the man his carriage besplatters with mud is none other than Deslauriers; the presiding chairman at the Club de l'Intelligence happens to be the vindictive Sénécal; the shabby-looking individual he meets after seducing Mme Dambreuse is once again Deslauriers. And what could be more savagely ironical than to have Dussardier shed bitter tears of compassion over the fate of the very man who will coldbloodedly murder him? Flaubert takes a far from "impassive" delight in planning such dissonances.

Often the intrusions are of a strictly stylistic nature. It is not uncommon that in an otherwise "objective" sentence a single term betrays the author's judgment. When Flaubert calls the insurrectionist crowd a "populace," when he refers to their drinking as a "godaille" (III.1)—this is not impartial reportage. A study of Flaubert's adverbs and adjectives would likewise bring out his affective presence throughout. "Everybody *nevertheless* formulated an irrevocable judgment . . ." (III.2); "Frédéric, seized with an *inexplicable* self-confidence . . ." (II.2); "Then, with his *usual* levity . . ." (II.4). At times the single epithet reaches out as though to define an essence.

Proust felt that there was hardly a single beautiful metaphor in all of Flaubert. The fact is that even during the composition of *Madame Bovary*, Flaubert was struggling hard to repress his metaphorical verve ("I am devoured by comparisons as by lice"),[45] partly because he did not want to indulge in purple prose, partly also because he knew there was nothing more personal, in a literary sense, than a comparison. The simile is an expression as well as an imposition of the author's vision. The metaphor-hunt was, however, not as thorough as Flaubert might have wished. And some of the comparisons ("France, being without a master, began to shriek with terror, like a blind man without his stick or an infant who has lost his nurse"

---

[45] Flaubert, *Corresp.*, III, 79.

III.1; "Rosanette, before going to bed, always exhibited a little melancholy, just as there are cypresses at the door of a tavern" III.4) are decidedly heavy-handed and not in the best of taste!

Finally Flaubert's voice clearly emerges through generalizations, aphorisms in the style of La Bruyère (whom Flaubert greatly admired) and in sentences which have the ring of incisive historiography. Some of Flaubert's phrases display the lapidary quality one associates with a Voltaire or a Montesquieu:

> En effet, avoir combattu l'émeute, c'était avoir défendu la République. Le résultat, bien que favorable, la consolidait; et, maintenant qu'on était débarrassé des vaincus, on souhaitait l'être des vainqueurs. (III.2)

The biting elegance and concision are like a personal seal of the author. So too are the somewhat more conventional maxims and generalizations often suggesting a so-called "experience of life"; these constitute a traditional ingredient of many French novels ever since *La Princesse de Clèves*. When Flaubert writes

> There is nothing so humiliating as to see fools succeed where we have failed. (I.5)

> there always remain in our conscience some of those sophistries which we pour into it. (II.3)

> in the midst of the most intimate confidences, there will always be found restrictions, false shame, delicacy and pity. (III.1)

one perceives the voice of the *moraliste*.

If, however, one compares the intrusions of Flaubert—even the conventional ones—with those of the other major novelists of the nineteenth century, Flaubert's uniqueness comes into clear focus. Balzac attributed the sociological and historical importance of his own novels in large part to his lengthy digressions. ("The digressions were so to speak the main subject of the author," he explains in a concluding note to the first episode of *L'Histoire des Treize*.)[46] Flaubert would never agree that a fictional text should become a pretext. As for Stendhal's peculiar irony—both lyrical and self-protective—it was alien and incomprehensible to Flaubert. Stendhal's paternal scoldings of his characters, his sarcasms and pretended surprises, paradoxically grant his protagonists the existential freedom to discover themselves in the very act of living. His ironic staccato lyricism through which he avenges himself of his own heart's bondage (while rejoicing in it) also provides a vicarious compensation for his own defeats. These tensions between the author and his creation are the very measure of Stendhal's affective involvement. Flaubert's intrusions are of a totally different cast. Far from entering into conflict with his characters (or pretending, as Gide does so self-consciously, that they escape his control), Flaubert, even when his personal voice can be heard, tends to *merge* with his characters to the point of undifferentiation. This double perspective, which tends however to overlap and melt into a single vision, is one of the distinguishing features of Flaubert's so-called objectivity. It thrusts the reader both inside and outside the character, while reducing the distance between subject and object. We always know a little more about the characters than they themselves know, but what we know is not in conflict with what they know, as is the case in Stendhal's novels, where the blindness of the protagonists ensures their naïveté.

Symptomatically, the very intrusions of Flaubert are of an ambiguous nature. Many statements which appear like an author's intervention could also be attributed to the protagonists. Or rather, they fall somewhere in between the author and the character, and curiously belong to both. The famous "Ce fut comme une apparition" of the first chapter, though presented as an objective fact, corresponds to Frédéric's "vision." But the same is true of what may

[46] Balzac, "Notes de la première édition de *Ferragus, Chef des Dévorants,*" Première partie de *l'Histoire des Treize, Oeuvres complètes*, XXII, 393.

at first seem to be personal judgments of the author. When Frédéric, in a heated conversation at the Dambreuses, "uttered one silly thing after another" (II.4), it is quite clear that he himself is aware of his foolish behavior, and that the expression is one of indirect self-blame. When the author writes that the guests of the Dambreuses "would have sold France or mankind in order to protect their fortune," it is equally clear that this precisely is Frédéric's appraisal of these men (II.4). When Mme Arnoux replies to Frédéric's compliments on her children "without any exaggeration of maternal silliness," it is again not so much the author who emits an opinion, as Frédéric who admires (II.2). This skillful fusion of points of view, which allows for no distance while creating the illusion of distance, is perhaps nowhere more apparent than in the pseudo-objective imperfects which lie halfway between description and indirect "represented" speech. "It was impossible to know her" (II.2) is really less the author's opinion than Frédéric's assessment of Rosanette. As for the great compensation of the last encounter with Mme Arnoux ("Il ne regretta rien. Ses souffrances d'autrefois étaient payées"), it may strike the reader as an objective appraisal, but it is primarily the equivalent of an interior monologue.

Objectivity is in fact, with Flaubert, a permanent state of *immersion*. The elements of autobiography, which always tempt critics, are here so broad and all-pervasive as to become irrelevant. One could point of course to this or that detail which has been transposed from Flaubert's life experience. One could even show how a chronic "mood" has been translated into fictional terms. Flaubert's correspondence is filled with expressions which cast light on the moral atmosphere of the novel. "I am made to live to an old age, and to see all about me and in me perish," he wrote to Louise Colet soon after he became her lover. And many years later, to George Sand: "How many corpses in our hearts! Each one of us carries within him a necropolis."[47] But such parallels become pointless in studying

[47] Flaubert, *Corresp.*, I, 235; V, 247.

works from which the author never truly absents himself, in which neither he nor his fictional characters lead an independent life. It is surprising that so much emphasis has been placed on Flaubert's proclaimed impersonality, and so little on what, in his own mind, this impersonality implied—namely, a thorough and pervasive presence. "The author in his work must be like God in the universe, *present everywhere* and visible nowhere."[48] Poetry, Flaubert knew—even when controlled—had to remain subjective: hence his insistence that in art there are no beautiful subjects per se.[49] The practice of a fictional art in which object and subject tend to merge explains, better perhaps than any other single factor, why *L'Éducation sentimentale* is at the same time such an original achievement, and yet, for many readers, such a frustrating experience. Flaubert himself, puzzled by the novel's lack of success, provided a revealing diagnosis: "It is too true, and—esthetically speaking—it lacks the distortion of perspective" ("la fausseté de la perspective").[50]

This combination of an objective precision and a "closeness" which tends to blend and blur is one of the characteristic traits of Flaubert's art. The vision of both the author and his characters is at times distinctly myopic. When Emma Bovary notices Léon's fingernails or the texture of his skin just above his collar; when Frédéric distinguishes the beads of perspiration on the dancers' foreheads or when he admires the glistening sclerotics of Mme Arnoux's eyes—one rightly suspects that the author has internalized within his protagonists a vision which he alone, as all-seeing narrator, is privileged to have.

The one device which more than any other corresponds to this ambiguous perspective, and suggests a curious telescoping of points of view, is the *style indirect libre*. In her study of this "free" indirect discourse, Maguerite Lips claims that it is the ideal stylistic expression of imper-

[48] Flaubert, *Corresp.*, III, 61–62. Italics mine.
[49] Flaubert, *Corresp.*, III, 249.
[50] Flaubert, *Corresp.*, VIII, 309.

sonality.[51] This is, however, only partially the case, and a simplification. For if it is true that the *style indirect libre,* by juggling away all pronominal antecedents, allows the author to "disappear" as narrator, it is equally true that this disappearance is due to a camouflage *inside* the characters, a camouflage which—to put it paradoxically—could be described as intrusive self-effacement. What happens in fact is that the author himself replaces the pronominal antecedent. Hugo Friedrich, in his excellent chapter on Flaubert, alludes to this "flipping into" the characters, to this impersonation by which the author "acts out" his own fictional creatures.[52] It is a subtle and elusive form of intervention, one which the German expression *verschleierte Rede* (veiled discourse) very aptly describes. "Hussonnet was pensive: the eccentricities of the Revolution exceeded his own" (III.1). Is it Flaubert or Hussonnet who judges the eccentricities? Or is it both? The veiled presence lends itself to a particular form of Flaubertian bitterness: "Since they were the victors, they must needs amuse themselves" ("Puisqu'on était victorieux, ne fallait-il pas s'amuser?" III.1).

Any discussion of Flaubert's art must take into account the subtle uses to which the *style indirect libre* is put. It is Flaubert's favorite method for presenting flashes of interior monologue—often mere exclamations. "Did she have a lover? What lover? Was it the diplomat or another? Martinon, maybe? Impossible!" (II.4). Almost always the thought is only half formulated by the character; it is the author who, in a typical act of "collaboration," provides the verbal articulation. The most important function of this grammatical device is, however, as a stylization of direct discourse, and consequently as a substitute for dialogue. Flaubert considered the abuse of dialogue a serious

[51] Lips, *Le Style indirect libre,* p. 195. See also Stephen Ullmann, "Reported Speech and Internal Monologue in Flaubert," in *Style in the French Novel.* Ullmann has excellent remarks on the mimetic value of this device.

[52] "Er wird zum Schauspieler seiner Gestalten" (Friedrich, *Die Klassiker des französischen Romans,* p. 124).

flaw; he set out deliberately to create a series of gradations which would allow him to play with dialogues, either by condensing them and pushing them into the background, or by translating them into a stylized rhetoric. The *style indirect libre* allows for precisely the kinds of shortcut and ellipsis Flaubert desired. But it does more. Its very indirectness and artificiality help bring out triteness on all levels: the gossip and the *idées reçues* of the unintelligent; the pretentious formulas of the pseudo-elegant; the comedy of social ritual, with its formalities, amenities, insincere protestations and diplomatic prudence. The language of the Dambreuses, self-conscious and insidious, lends itself particularly well to such stylization. The device is moreover an excellent mode for communicating shades of insincerity, perfidy and hypocrisy. It admirably evokes the very essence of ingratiating discourse. Turpitude is thus ironically stressed by the very technique which, on the surface, seemed to do away with the author's commentary.

In fact, the *style indirect libre* is an extremely sharp instrument of intervention. The elimination of standard dialogue imprisons the characters at a distance from each other. Without having to comment openly, the author thus brings out the pathos of incommunicability. Frequently, the device is used as an oblique instrument of critique (inept thoughts, silly projects, ineffectual dreams, the eternal clichés of political discussions) which only technically maintains the author offstage, but which turns out to be more damning than Balzac's diatribes or Stendhal's most impertinent intrusions.

The artistic skill of Flaubert is evidenced not only in the uses to which he puts this "free" indirect discourse, but in the manner in which he weaves it into other rhetorical modes. The mixture—and clash—of direct speech and *style indirect libre* (for instance in the scene where Frédéric attempts to justify her husband's lies to Mme Arnoux, II.2) represents, on the stylistic level, the impossible dialogue between the young man who talks in a tentative, conventional and half-felt manner and the woman who, wounded

[171]

in her affection and her pride, reacts altogether spontaneously. At times, Flaubert plays with the *style indirect libre* in an even more complex fashion, creating contrapuntal effects between the private thoughts of different characters, and setting those off in turn against regular dialogues and the voice of the narrator.

The very "presence" of the author is thus an integral part of the fictional construction. The telescoping of the author's point of view with that of the characters provides a sense of unity. But this unified and controlled multiple perspective also makes for a certain elusiveness: the author plays at being absent. In reality his very impassibility is loaded with passion—often the passion of hatred or contempt. Technically, Flaubert's achievement is his ability to be simultaneously inside and outside a given consciousness. The described subjectivity imposes itself with such concreteness and immediacy that it becomes a reality felt from within and formulated from without. Flaubert's fiction could be called a phenomenology of the subjective.

Though largely opaque as an object, the consciousness of Frédéric is transparent to the extent that it is a medium "through" which we can see. In this respect the reader is plunged into the protagonist's awareness. But as Erich Auerbach very rightly suggests, language in Flaubert's work "interprets itself."[53] It is an instrument not only of representation, but of criticism. And one should add, an instrument of self-criticism and even of self-punishment. Through language (and the *style indirect libre* is only one of its aspects), the power of Flaubert's presence is so all-pervasive that he can "hide" inside his work and abolish all distance. With Flaubert, the artist becomes truly the center of his creation. No writer has been more concerned with the integrity of point of view.[54] (Stendhal's achievement was in this respect brilliantly amateurish.) But the

[53] "In the Hotel de la Mole" in Auerbach, *Mimesis*, p. 429.
[54] See Jean Rousset's brilliant essay, "*Madame Bovary* ou 'le livre sur rien' " in *Forme et signification*, pp. 109–133.

[172]

very respect for this integrity—even when the point of view of a character was that of a temperament alien to the author—implies the strong hand of the author. Control may not be the greatest virtue in a writer. But if one were to judge by this criterion alone, then certainly no novelist has ever held his fiction more firmly in hand.

Assessments

The smugness of culture-custodians under the Second Empire explains in part why the reaction to *L'Éducation sentimentale* was almost unanimously unsympathetic. The book was, to begin with, denigrated on "moral" grounds. The critic of the *Journal des Débats* accused Flaubert of having degraded all that which soars, of having soiled everything noble: science, patriotism, "well-acquired wealth" (the juxtaposition is revealing!) and social amenities.[55] Another reviewer, Saint-René Taillandier, complaining of the author's destructive misanthropy, and shocked by the brutal irony and "scandalous" conclusion of the novel, denounced Flaubert for having written a contemptful and insulting book.[56] Such views were echoed by later critics. Henry James' less myopic assessment is still tainted with priggishness. Viewing Frédéric as an abject human specimen, James complains of the emptiness of this "ill-starred novel."[57]

An artistically more damning criticism leveled at Flaubert was that the novel amounted only to a series of documents, social and personal, and not to an authentic work of the creative imagination. Maxime Du Camp, the perfidious friend of Flaubert, did much to spread the notion that *L'Éducation sentimentale* was entirely autobiographical. Flaubert's evidently painstaking historical documentation misled others into reading the novel as a subspecies of history rather than as a work of literature. Edmond

[55] Cuvillier-Fleury, "La Satire dans le roman," *Journal des Débats*, December 14, 1869.
[56] Taillandier, *Revue des Deux Mondes*, December 15, 1869.
[57] James, "Gustave Flaubert," in *Notes on Novelists*, p. 85.

Schérer, in a review for *Le Temps* dated December 7, 1869, complained that this was not a novel but a series of memoirs. A more recent, if not more charitable critic, John Middleton Murry, diagnosed Flaubert's passion for documentation as a "morbid condition," and concluded that *L'Éducation sentimentale* (according to him, even less significant in scope than *Madame Bovary*) was "a work of history rather than literature."[58] Even admirers of Flaubert have contributed to these distorting perspectives.[59]

The most surprising complaint, however, centered on the so-called "poor composition" of the novel. With the unanimity of a well-rehearsed chorus, critics deplored its "fragmentation." According to Cuvillier-Fleury, it was studded with disjointed episodes. He called it a "pot-pourri" and, with academic solemnity, denounced Flaubert for having mixed several *genres*.[60] His colleague of the *Revue des Deux Mondes* was equally severe: "What kind of art is it, the result of which is to suppress composition, to make unity impossible and to replace a tableau by a series of sketches?"[61] Even Émile Faguet and Jules Lemaître, several decades later, though less intolerant, thought that the total effect of *L'Éducation sentimentale* was disconnected, that the novel was lacking in organic unity.[62]

Two types of readers tend to belittle *L'Éducation sentimentale*: the unsophisticated who usually finds the "plot" boring and unedifying, and—at the other extreme—the literary snob who smiles at the author's stubborn quest for

[58] Murry, *Countries of the Mind*, pp. 161–167.

[59] Gilbert Guisan, discussing Flaubert's documentation of the revolution of 1848, begins with the assumption that "the element of invention in the narrative was quite limited" ("Flaubert et la Révolution de 1848," *Revue d'Histoire Littéraire de la France*, 1958, pp. 183–204). As for the fervent Flaubertiste Gérard-Gailly, he is so fascinated by his own biographical detective work that he succeeds in convincing himself that the novel "is a confession and not a fiction" (*Flaubert et les "Fantômes de Trouville*," p. 175).

[60] Cuvillier-Fleury, *Journal des Débats*, December 14, 1869.

[61] Saint-René Taillandier, *Revue des Deux Mondes*, December 15, 1869.

[62] Émile Faguet, *Flaubert*, pp. 108–124; and Jules Lemaître, "Gustave Flaubert," in *Les Contemporains*, p. 86.

perfection. A Stendhal or a Gide does more to flatter this type of reader: he makes of him almost an accomplice. Such a complicity hardly exists in the work of Flaubert: the author does all the work himself. Some do resent this all-controlling hand. A public whose taste often goes to the revealing sketch rather than the completed canvas finds Flaubert's art weighted down and condemned to immobility. Such objections are not altogether unjustified. The novel is at times contrived. It is slow-moving. A certain tedium accompanies the unheroic existence of the protagonists. Flaubert himself was the first to express misgivings. He knew what problems he faced, having willfully chosen them. The most difficult was no doubt how to fuse individual destinies into the current of History without either submerging his characters or losing the sense of historical momentum. "I have much trouble fitting my characters into the political events of 1848," he confided to his friend Jules Duplan. He was aware also of the "artifice of the composition" and of the lack of climax: "the *facts* are lacking. I can see no key scene, there is no pyramid."[63] Worst of all, Flaubert knew that "inactive heroes" were not likely to fascinate.

But the qualities of this book are to be found precisely in its apparent defects. Flaubert's love for precision and perfection are those of a poet. No poem is in fact more "constructed" than *L'Éducation sentimentale*. This composition is, however, not to be sought in the concatenation of events, in the conventional plot causality, but in the more subtle, and also more intricate metaphoric structure and texture of the book. It is a structure which dramatizes stasis and erosion. Firmly incased between an epilogue which points to the beginning (the theme of the bordello) and a prologue which points to the end (the themes of water, travel and unattainable love), the substance of *L'Éducation sentimentale* appears confined, locked within itself. The novel begins with a departure and ends with a

[63] Flaubert, *Corresp.*, V, 363; *Supplément*, I, 323; II, 208.

return. The appearance and disappearance of the various women who play a role in Frédéric's life leave him, at the end, as he was at the beginning, lonely and with his dreams unfulfilled. The structure, circular and repetitive, betrays in fact a psychological state. Frédéric's withdrawal to the province, his almost instinctive retreat into a solipsistic shell, correspond to a fatigue of living and to an almost incestuous yearning for the maternal womb. Toward the end of the novel, Frédéric dreams of curling up. Through a deathlike somnolence he apparently seeks the innocence of his prenatal life. This image of the return, this concept of circularity also correspond to the theme of failure. In his ultimate conversation with Deslauriers, Frédéric in fact suggests a diagnosis for their common unsuccess: "C'est peut-être le défaut de ligne droite" ("Perhaps it was the absence of a straight line").

A similar care in sustaining images can be noted in Flaubert's use of recurring objects. The chandelier first seen at *L'Art industriel* and later glimpsed, in a totally different environment, in Rosanette's apartment, serves as a symbol of profanation. Mme Arnoux's little silver box becomes an accompaniment and almost a commentary of an entire life. Flaubert is moreover a master at the art of preparations. This is particularly evident in the handling of the political scenes. Quite early in the novel, and repeatedly—whether by means of discussions or allusions in the conversations—Flaubert succeeds in introducing the pertinent political facts (which announce and prepare the events of 1848) and in establishing the sense of a historical "time" which punctuates the dramatic episodes of the novel. Thus even the political structure of *L'Éducation sentimentale* suggests a mournful circularity. The early chapters (particularly chapter 4 of Part I, centered on the events of 1841–1842) are studded with proleptic political intrusions. Part III is largely taken up by the explosive and derisory events of the 1848 revolution: mob actions and social turmoil occupy the center of a much enlarged stage. Finally, toward the end of the book, the

political intrusions are mostly in the nature of post-mor-
tems, sadly pointing to the total fiasco of revolutionary
ideals and to the general apathy which characterizes the
events of 1851. A narrowing of the perspective takes place,
as the individual, with his frustrations and sense of futility, takes ironic precedence over the collective tragedy.

The underlying structural unity of the book, the functional value of all the episodes—even those which at first
may appear digressive or gratuitous—are perhaps nowhere
more evident than in the pages describing Frédéric's and
Rosanette's excursion to Fontainebleau (III.1). Over sev-
enty pages of rough drafts testify to the care with which
Flaubert composed this admirable passage. For the expedition to Fontainebleau represents not merely a selfish
escape from the battle-torn capital, a respite for intimacy
and an occasion for pointing up Rosanette's ineptness.
Frédéric indeed feels guilty for his lack of solidarity with
those who are exposing their lives: "he reproached himself for not being there with the others." The entire episode is an exercise in irony which never loses sight of the
Parisian tragedy. But it also replaces this tragedy in the
larger context of a metaphysical meditation. Fontainebleau forces upon Frédéric a double sense of History:
human history in the château (kings and their mistresses
who fill him with "retrospective lust") and natural history (the trees and rocks of the forest, whose patriarchal
majesty and cataclysmic chaos fill him with awe). Quite
clearly, the details of the episode are dramatically and
thematically relevant. There is irony in those trees which,
on the one hand, join each other high up in the air like
immense triumphal arches, and on the other seem to be
"falling columns." The Parisian revolution is never forgotten, and the apparent digression is really a circuitous
commentary, mournful and almost desperate. The political revolution is measured against the geological "revo-
lutions." The "immobilized Titans" remind us, in their
angry pose, of the revolutionary furor. But they also point
up the insignificance of all human endeavor in the face

of eternal change and death. The Fontainebleau landscape assumes an apocalyptic grandeur which further underlines the futility of "human" events. It is an almost religious awe which the "gravity" of the forest ("le sérieux de la forêt") inspires.

Ironies and antitheses such as these carry us to the heart of the Flaubertian sensibility. The poetry of immobility and universal silence which emanates from these pages, the pantheistic exultation in front of eternal Nature, the infinite depth of the sky, induce a dizziness and ultimately a yearning for dissolution and nothingness. The very proliferation of phenomena and their immutable profusion cause a feeling of numbness and torpor which corresponds to the despondency of the typical Flaubertian hero (whether Madame Bovary, Saint Antoine or Bouvard and Pécuchet) as he takes stock of the "eternal wretchedness of all things." The exhalation of the centuries is like the "perfume of a mummy." Death and the death-wish preside over these pages. The inhuman rocks seem to multiply in surrealistic fashion, and end up by filling the entire landscape like the "unrecognizable and monstrous ruins" of some vanished city. Almost terrified, but irresistibly drawn to this dismaying spectacle, Frédéric and Rosanette surrender to their dizziness, and lose themselves in a trancelike contemplation of universal nothingness.

L'Éducation sentimentale is ultimately a tragedy-in-Time. Its most authentic achievement rests in the author's "temporal" awareness of permanence and death. The appreciation of Proust is significant: he recognized in his predecessor, although he was basically not drawn to him, a master-poet of "Time."[64] It is certain that, ever since his early adolescence, Flaubert has been haunted by Time, Change, and Death. They were for him more than oppressive metaphysical categories: almost physical realities. To his mistress Louise Colet he confided that the sight of a child always made him think of old age: the cradle re-

[64] Proust, "A propos du 'style' de Flaubert," in *Chroniques*, p. 205.

minded him of the tomb. He was convinced—and it turned
out to be the case—that he was destined to see everything
around him perish. "I have already attended a thousand
inner funerals," he wrote at the age of twenty-four.[65] These
are to some extent Romantic poses. But the obsession is
also quite real in Flaubert's case; it explains, in part, his
lasting fascination with History. Flaubert is probably the
first major novelist to understand that the novel is essentially an experience *in time*, and who proceeded to exploit
this tragic potential. Thus the Flaubertian novel focuses
not so much on the event, as on the gap between events.
It deals not with what occurs during a crisis, but with
what takes place between crises. Or rather, its subject is
what happens *instead of* the crisis.

The technical virtuosity of Flaubert in handling time
has no doubt its origin in the author's own "temporal"
anxiety. The frequent projections into a hypothetical future, the even more frequent mental returns to a past
that weighs on the present, are not surface features in
L'Éducation sentimentale. They correspond to a typical
Flaubertian rumination. Thus during his Nile voyage,
Flaubert sits in his boat, watching the water "flow by,"
reminiscing with "profound intensity." Forgotten things
come back, like old nursery songs. And characteristically,
he asks himself: "Is this the beginning of a new period?
Or of total decadence?"[66] As novelist, Flaubert discovers
qualitative time. The subtle interplay of the preterit and
imperfect tenses underlines the periodic awakening from
an almost hypnotic routine, and clearly suggests the unresolved conflict between dreams and the deceptions of
reality. Thus, also, the narration oscillates between extreme precision of dates ("On the 15th of September,
1840"; "at ten minutes after seven"; "three days later") and
a trancelike vagueness ("one day"; "often"; "toward the
beginning of that winter"). These constant changes of
speed, this elasticity of time plunge the reader into the

[65] Flaubert, *Corresp.*, I, 221, 235.
[66] Flaubert, *Corresp.*, II, 201.

nonchronological, psychological time of the protagonist. Flaubert thus succeeds in incorporating memory and illusions within a perpetual *present* that is indifferent to them.[67] But his greatest achievement as virtuoso of Time lies in the slow movements—in what Jean Rousset so aptly calls the "adagios" of the novel, where time seems redundant and emptied of its own substance.[68] Unquestionably, the very subjectivity of the point of view (all being more or less consistently experienced through Frédéric's consciousness) slows down the rhythm of the novel. Time and subjectivity are intimately related.

The technical prowess in the manipulation of time is thus entirely in the service of tragic themes. On the most obvious level, *L'Éducation sentimentale* is a novel about "aging"—a pathetic, pointless growing old, which transforms Frédéric at best into an overripe adolescent. The novel appropriately ends with a catalogue of metamorphoses: Rosanette, for instance, has now become enormously fat. "Quelle décadence," comments Deslauriers. To this transforming and destructive force of time, Flaubert opposes, in contrapuntal fashion, the poetry of the timeless. The Fontainebleau episode stresses the two poles of the Romantic imagination: the awareness of the futility of all human endeavor, and the almost mystic awe in the face of eternal Nature. This poetry of the timeless has its psychological counterpart in the unrealized love of Frédéric and Mme Arnoux. They both know it is because their love has not been consummated that it has remained pure. But this freedom from the contingencies of time, this preserved purity in an "arrested" survival, is a privileged and rare condition in the world of Flaubert. And it can exist only where there is a denial of life. *Lived* life is either filled with the ironies of imperfect synchronization where, as in Proust, desire and fulfillment never coincide;

---

[67] For some very keen observations on Flaubert's ability to "dilate reality with imagination," see Margaret Mein, "Flaubert, a Precursor of Proust," *French Studies*, July 1963, pp. 218–237.

[68] Rousset, "*Madame Bovary* ou le 'livre sur rien,'" in *Forme et signification*, pp. 109–133.

or it is steadily dissolved by the erosive nibbling of time. The interval between desire and possession is repeatedly illustrated in *L'Éducation sentimentale*. When Frédéric, after exasperating difficulties in locating the Arnoux, finally manages to present himself at their new address, he is surprised to experience no "spasms of joy." ("The calmness of his own heart astonished him" II.1—the observation might come straight from *A la Recherche du temps perdu*.) Such gaps—or *décalages*—were an important feature in the original synopsis of the novel: "But the hour of agreement is past."—"She loves him when he no longer loves her."[69] The more fundamental tragic experience is here related to the steady wearing down of life by life itself. Time, in Flaubert's work, is the very underlying principle of a pathological process.

Once more, we are driven back to Flaubert's central obsession: disease and death. His tragic imagination focuses without respite on the *chronic* aspects of life, on those aspects which either signify irremediable loss or induce men to take consenting steps toward annihilation. Consenting—for Flaubert's originality as tragic novelist rests in part on the characters' urge, deeply felt by the author himself, to accelerate the movement carrying them toward ruin, as though under a hypnotic spell. This attraction to nothingness is symbolized by the desire to return to the "funereal peacefulness" of provincial life: the province, like the maternal womb, invites to cozy drowsiness and oblivion. Here again the words *torpeur* and *assoupissement* are among the favorite terms of the author, and they usually point to a process of disintegration. Toward the end of *L'Éducation sentimentale*, Frédéric feels altogether "shattered, crushed, annihilated, no longer conscious of anything except a sensation of extreme fatigue" (III.5). *Anéantir* is another key word of Flaubert, corresponding to a permanent yearning for nothingness. Sooner or later, all the characters of Flaubert share Saint Antoine's desire

[69] Durry, *Flaubert et ses projets inédits*, p. 138.

to dissolve into *la matière*. After the Alhambra ball, Frédéric, walking through the dark streets of Paris, meditates on the "nothingness of all things" (I.5). But this nothingness is not merely something external: the protagonist carries within himself the disease of undoing, and—as it were—a calling for nonbeing. His answer to his mother's question is ironically revealing. He tells her of his determination to live in Paris. "And what do you plan to do there?"—"Nothing" (I.6).

The suicidal tendencies are obviously related to the theme of failure. The poetry of *unrealization* no doubt protects the purity of sentimental ideals. But ultimately, though he sings of unrealized pure love, Flaubert is the poet of ruin. Dussardier, contemplating with "ineffable sadness" the broken bits—the "ruines"—of his beloved pipe, experiences a foretaste of the steady deterioration which is the pathology of the entire human condition. Images of death seem to intrude throughout the novel. Frédéric's departure for Paris coincides with the death of Louise's mother ("The idea of this corpse so near them threw a funereal gloom over their parting" I.6.) His Parisian life begins, as it were, under the sign of death. His search for Mme Arnoux is likewise darkened by funereal images. One day, in the street, he believes that at last he has found her; but a hearse and a procession of mourning coaches prevent him from crossing over. When the procession has passed, the "vision" has disappeared also. As for the auction sale of Mme Arnoux's private belongings—almost an autopsy of an entire life—it is an episode heavily loaded with images and symbols of death: her handkerchiefs, her hats, her shoes are "relics." And as her private belongings are profaned by greedy hands, it seems to Frédéric that he is watching "ravens tearing away at a corpse." In the airless room his own being seems to dissolve in a "torpeur funèbre" (III.5).

Yet the true achievement of the novel—at least for our own epoch—goes beyond the tragic handling of the themes of Time and Death. Far more so than *Madame Bovary*, whose Romantic anti-Romanticism does recall the "subversive" qualities of *Don Quixote, L'Éducation sentimentale* appears as the ancestor of our present-day anti-novel. It is in relation to this book that Rémy de Gourmont stated peremptorily: "The subject, in art, is of interest only to children and illiterate people."[70] What indeed is the "subject" of *L'Éducation sentimentale*? This precisely—despite impressive elements of social and psychological realism—is what irritates many readers. Henry James, hardly "illiterate," simply could not understand what interest there could be in writing hundreds of pages about so "inferior" a person as Frédéric. "Why, why him?"[71] But such an unconventional approach to subject matter was one of the chief self-imposed challenges of the artist.

Modern French writers and critics are likely to honor *Bouvard et Pécuchet*—partly because of its incompleteness, partly because it refuses throughout to play the fictional "game"—as an archetype of the *roman nouveau*. There is, however, a great deal of misunderstanding and even of mystification in this attribution of paternity. Certainly *L'Éducation sentimentale*, which strains conventional forms and techniques in a far more original way (the originality of *Bouvard et Pécuchet* is of a different nature) provides a better parallel with the experiments of recent years. And some critics, without necessarily sympathizing, have been aware of the phenomenological elements in the novel. Martin Turnell complains of Flaubert's obsession "with bricks and mortar, with distance, size and shape" which tends to dwarf his fictional creatures and dehumanize his work. And Sartre, despite unadmitted affinities with Flaubert's sensibility (the same sense of the viscousness of existence and of the proliferation of matter), blames him for having "petrified" reality.[72]

Dehumanization—to the extent that the world of phe-

---

[70] Gourmont, *Le Problème du style*, p. 25.
[71] James, *Notes on Novelists*, pp. 82–83.
[72] Turnell, *The Novel in France*, p. 290; Sartre, *Situations*, II, 172.

nomena acquires priority over the world of meaning—is indeed one of the characteristics of the most recent French experiments in fiction. Writers such as Alain Robbe-Grillet, Nathalie Sarraute, Claude Simon and Michel Butor refuse the moral and intellectual comfort provided by an essentialist and anthropocentric view of the world. A real antipsychological trend has set in: the writers of our generation refuse to believe in an "ultimate deep." The very word "psychology" now almost sounds insulting in literary criticism. As for the literature of "character" or "types"— it appears totally discredited. Contemporary French writers and critics simply could not care less about the wart on the tip of a character's nose! This antipsychological mania has led to the excesses of a nonfigurative literature which has plunged the reader into an undefinable verbal space. As the distance between the writer and reality vanishes, the traditional polarity of subject and object also disappears. A systematic devalorization, symptom of a deep malaise, has set in. But this subversion of the traditional subject-object relationship also carries a tragic potential: it underlines the discordant, gratuitous nature of life.

The insistence on contingency, on the *thusness* of experience becomes a significant, though unsystematic feature in the work of Flaubert. Time and experience are here no longer abstracted, disengaged realities to be analyzed and categorized; they impose themselves with an immediacy which, most often, destroys all sense of distance and cozy perspective. Together with the protagonists, we are thrust into what seems like a perpetual, and slightly opaque present. No secret signs or omens endow the present with *a priori* dramatic significance: the protagonists appear caught in a permanent indetermination. Flaubert exposes them to the banal, haphazard, fragmented and essentially undramatic experience of unfiltered, uninterpreted reality. Despite the sense of flow symbolically suggested by the river-image, much of *L'Éducation sentimentale* is an exercise in discontinuity. Even the conventional link between motivation and action is here frequently absent.[73] Jules Lemaître, with his usual irony, sensed this disjointed quality (which he, however, attributed in part to poor composition) and pointed to the "anti"-novelistic tendency of the novel: "You believe that something will happen? Come on! Does anything happen most of the time? Is life a play? And do you mistake *L'Éducation sentimentale* for a novel, for one of those invented stories where each action of the hero precipitates a dramatic event, where each of his steps starts off some fireworks?"[74] This separation between the experience of art and the experience of "existence"—as well as the attempt to find a stylistic equivalent for the latter—will be at the very heart of Sartre's *La Nausée*.

And this almost subversive exploration of the frontiers of fiction, ushering in the experiments of later novelists, is directly related to Flaubert's tragic imagination, which—beyond the tragedy of time and of erosion, beyond the ironies of unfulfillment—obsessively concentrates on a desolation which has no precise cause.

[73] On this rupture of causality between motivation and action, see Hugo Friedrich, *Die Klassiker des französischen Romans*, pp. 137ff.

[74] Lemaître, *Les Contemporains*, p. 87. For a claim that Flaubert is an ancestor of the "new novel," see Nathalie Sarraute, "Flaubert le précurseur," *Preuves*, February 1965, pp. 3–11.

La Tentation
de saint Antoine:

THE DEBAUCHERIES OF THE MIND

J'ai pris en dégoût la forme . . .
The Gymnosophist

The "Chambre Secrète"

This pandemonic prose poem is, according to Baudelaire, the secret chamber of Flaubert's mind. Baudelaire knew only those fragments which Flaubert had published during the winter of 1856 in *L'Artiste*, but he felt immediately drawn to this dazzling and disquieting text. In this compendium of Romantic motifs, he no doubt recognized his own literary heredity. For Baudelaire believed that Romanticism had been for the writers of his generation a celestial (or infernal) grace to which they all owed eternal stigmata.[1] More specifically, he could appreciate the peculiar blend of lyricism and irony in the *Tentation*—an irony in the Baudelairean sense: a self-destructive lucidity and tedium which accompany the gloomy tête-à-tête with one's self. The solipsistic anguish of Saint Antoine evoked self-tortures in which Baudelaire himself was of course a refined specialist.

To speak of a secret chamber is quite appropriate. The first version of the book was begun in 1848, the last version was published in 1874: over twenty-five years were

---

[1] Baudelaire, "Madame Bovary," *Oeuvres complètes*, p. 657; *Salon de 1859, Oeuvres complètes*, p. 1,062. Complete citations for all notes may be found in the Bibliography.

devoted to the elaboration of the work—indeed a whole lifetime, if one also takes into account some juvenilia such as *La Danse des morts* (1838) and *Smarh* (1839), where appetite for knowledge is already bound up with a historical imagination, and the exhilaration and terror of a cosmic flight also lead to a yearning for nothingness. Scholars have examined the three different versions (1849, 1856, 1874) in great detail, and were able to demonstrate Flaubert's painstaking artistic self-consciousness as revealed through the changes the work underwent.[2] In fact, however, despite much condensation (the 1849 version which Maxime Du Camp and Louis Bouilhet condemned was intolerably verbose), despite considerable reshuffling and much new strategy, there is little true evolution. The basic vision remains the same, obsessively so. Flaubert's tenacity is remarkable. More than any other writer, he clings to his most cherished nightmares.

La Tentation de saint Antoine is a summa of attitudes and beliefs. It echoes the conflicting philosophies of an entire period, reaching to the heart of what is most significant in Romanticism, summing up its tragic and poetic tensions, rehearsing its unalterable dilemmas. On the surface, it may appear like a repertoire of Romantic clichés: the taste for sensationalism and violence, eroticism of an adolescent nature, permanent cravings for the impossible. The monstrous snake in the first version calls itself the "universal devourer" and complains of a never-ending thirst. These hackneyed motifs point to a metaphysical uneasiness. The saint experiences a tedium which is very much akin to the Baudelairean *ennui*. For Saint Antoine's spiritual depression cannot be accounted for alone by the sense of futility which accompanies the eternal sameness of life ("Manger, c'est toujours la même chose" p. 350*) or the

---

2 See in particular Jacques Madeleine, "Les Différents 'Etats' de 'La Tentation de Saint Antoine,'" *Revue d'Histoire Littéraire de la France*, 1908, pp. 620–641; and Henri Mazel, "Les Trois Tentations de Saint Antoine," *Mercure de France*, December 15, 1921, pp. 626–643.

* All page references are to the Conard edition, which very con-

eternal recurrence and multiplication of phenomena. It has its roots in a persistent acedia, such as Baudelaire has evoked in some of his most oppressive and airless poems. The saint complains that he will never be able to cure himself of this "colossal ennui" which crushes him. Corroded by his disease, he no longer even has the will to want to will (pp. 426–427). Baudelaire's disease of ennui—also satanic in nature, for it leads him "loin du regard de Dieu"— presents a similar syndrome: sense of weight, desolation, sterility, paralysis of the will and desperate imprisonment in the self.

Escapism in the *Tentation* parallels the efforts toward liberation from solipsism in *Les Fleurs du Mal*. Saint Antoine, at the beginning of the book, watches with envy the movement of birds and of departing ships. Spatial and temporal exoticism are strong allurements for the unhappy hermit. Apollonius, in a rhythmical and evocative passage, conjures up images of voluptuous southern regions where time and space are immeasurably expanded ("ton esprit s'élargira . . ." p. 112). Flaubert's long-standing yearning for multiple incarnations finds a natural outlet in a work which surveys and amalgamates conflicting cultures and beliefs. He dreams in turn of being a soldier, a publican, an adviser to the emperor, a martyr. This desire for "many lives" is one of the most potent stimulants for his creative imagination. It operates in two temporal directions: as a projection into the future, as an exploitation and self-indulging multiplication of the self (thus Emma Bovary *sees herself* leading other existences, and the narrator of *Novembre* experiences a narcissistic wish to become a woman so as to be able to "admire himself"); but also as a hypothetical and nostalgic search into the past in quest of former selves. Flaubert not only enjoys visiting the "catacombs" of his own past, even as a young man, but likes to think that his being contains the débris of a thousand former lives. This Romantic dissatisfaction

veniently includes in one single volume the three versions of *La Tentation de saint Antoine*.

with reality, which propels the Flaubertian hero to wish to be anything but himself, leads eventually to dreams of dissolution, and ultimately—as in the *Tentation*—to pantheistic reveries. Baudelaire, whose modes of escape are in a different poetic register, likewise speaks of a *moi* which is insatiable for the *non-moi*.[3]

The very form of *La Tentation de saint Antoine*, blending dramatic, epic and lyric tones, is a clear example of the Romantic breakdown of genres and of a tendency toward "total" literary expression. Its most characteristic mode is a rhythmic, sonorous and poetic prose—or, to be more accurate, a prose-poetry which places it in a direct line running from Chateaubriand and Quinet to Rimbaud and other more recent practitioners. No technical feature is at the same time more symptomatic and richer in consequences than this new concept of the capabilities and function of prose. The very first sentence of the saint introduces the reader to rhythmic patterns which reach a level of high craft in passages such as the speech of the queen of Sheba ("Ah! bel ermite! bel ermite! mon coeur défaille! . . ." p. 30). As for the texture of the language, and the structural patterns they evoke, one is again reminded of the lapidary and plastic qualities of Parnassian poetry. Virtuoso displays of color, jewelry and geometric designs (Alexandria appears as a mass of curves, cones and angles) show affinities—which are not only external—with Flaubert's other African poem, *Salammbô*. Africa is once again the symbolic setting for the birth and death of cultures and religions, and for the apocalyptic clash of elemental forces. Although Flaubert achieves highly sensitive effects, especially in his poetry of time and of silence, the predominant mood is one of violence. His orgiastic rhetoric corresponds to the very theme of orgy, so dear to the Romantic writers. Like Balzac, he is fascinated by the *priapées antiques*, and like him he associates images of orgy with visions of death and decomposition.

[3] Baudelaire, *Le Peintre de la vie moderne, Oeuvres complètes*, p. 1161.

The larger issue is decadence, which literally haunts the entire nineteenth century. The exciting and distressing notion that civilizations grow and perish is a direct consequence of the historical relativism developed during the Age of Enlightenment. The metaphysical repercussions during the Romantic period are far-reaching. Thus *La Tentation de saint Antoine* cannot be reduced to the story of a saint tempted in the Thebaid by a cortège of sensuous allurements and of heterodox beliefs. Flaubert's ambition was in part to write a philosophic and theogonic poem. In this he follows the taste of his period for *grandes machines*, for large-scale, almost cosmic accounts. To the obvious influence of Goethe's *Faust* has to be added the example of allegorical and didactic works which is clearly felt as early as in *La Danse des morts* and in *Smarh*. Flaubert's bent of mind and acute historical imagination, moreover, predispose him to account for religious and metaphysical constructions from the viewpoint of historicism. According to Jean Seznec, Flaubert's *Tentation* anticipated Renan's *Origines du Christianisme*.[4] Indeed, Flaubert's fascination for change and transformation appears already in his juvenilia. In one of the colorful pages of the first *Éducation sentimentale*, Jules surveys the evolution of "love" from Genesis to the Directoire, only to experience a sense of lassitude and oppression.

For the historical imagination points not only to cycles and metamorphoses, but to decay and death. Flaubert thus conjures up images of disintegration. The 1849 version, in its insistence on the undoing of gods, is a true Götterdämmerung. Juno is heard lamenting:

> What! no more noise! I come, I go, I run all over Olympus. All are asleep, or gone. I call; Echo itself seems dead! (p. 461)

In documenting himself for the book, Flaubert consulted with special interest legends of an eschatological nature—

[4] Seznec, *Nouvelles Études sur la Tentation de Saint Antoine*, p. 38.

those which announced the twilight of the gods and a final apocalypse.[5] In fact, the death of the gods is not only a Romantic obsession ("Plus d'autels; ô passé! splendeurs évanouies!" writes the otherwise optimistic Victor Hugo), but is at the very heart of *La Tentation de saint Antoine.* Hercules has lost his vigor, and Neptune, whose trident no longer arouses tempests, complains that "all is dead." But it is not merely the death of the pagan world that is bewailed. When Buddha explains that his role has come to an end, that "the great period is fulfilled," that all must now die (p. 127), he refers to the larger principle of the eventual demythification of any given religion. It is the eternally recurrent obliteration of all things which is involved in this theological evolutionism.

Flaubert quite consciously exploits some of the parallels of comparative religion. Buddha's birth and exploits are brought into juxtaposition with those of Christ. Strange resemblances are suggested by Hilarion. Similarly, the high priest of Cybele alludes to the blood which will redeem all sins, and the mourning figure of the woman bent over the corpse of Atys reminds Saint Antoine of the mother of Jesus. It is dramatically logical that it is Hilarion who points up the resemblances of the "false" gods with the true one: Saint Antoine understands that it is a ruse of the Devil. But the parallelisms are subversive in a larger sense also. For syncretism is not only a challenge to any orthodoxy; the effort at reconciliation or coalescence of different beliefs symbolizes the tendencies and dangers of modern culture. After such knowledge, what forgiveness? The very age of all-embracing science is also the age of greatest doubt and greatest despair.

"Science recognizes no monsters . . ." discovers Jules in the 1845 version of *L'Éducation sentimentale.*[6] The nineteenth century's ambivalent attitudes toward science are paralleled by equally ambiguous attitudes toward the con-

[5] See Jean Seznec, *Les Sources de l'Épisode des Dieux dans la Tentation de Saint Antoine,* p. 25.
[6] Flaubert, *Oeuvres de jeunesse inédites,* III, 260.

cept of the "monstrous." Much remains to be said about
the prevailing fascination with monsters and monstrosities
as manifestations of the exceptional, violations of a law
and aberrant revelations of a deeper truth. There is hardly
a writer of the first and second Romantic generations who
was not captivated by the misshapen and the repellent.
Freaks and hideous forms entranced the young Flaubert
long before he saw the Breughel in the Palazzo Baldi in
Genoa. The delight at seeing this painting was really but a
shock of recognition. Ever since his childhood, he was
partial to the *grotesque triste*, just as Baudelaire found an
echo to his own sensibility in the hallucinations, the
witch's sabbath and the *comique fantastique* of a Goya. To
be sure, Flaubert exploits the satiric potential of distortion.
But deformity raised more significant problems. Ugliness
became part of an esthetic system. " 'T is the tempestuous
loveliness of terror," writes Shelley in the wake of the
marquis de Sade, who openly proclaimed the superiority
of hideousness. Such attitudes reveal the notion of art as
a form of protest. The artist, faced with chaos, has to impose his own order. Ultimately the taste for chaos and
horror betrays a desire to transcend the human. Flaubert
is convinced that the craving for weird forms is really
the craving for the infinite—a "convoitise de l'infini."[7]

Flaubert's dilection for monstrous forms must thus not
be attributed to facile sensationalism. It is in fact the key
to a dialectical tension between nihilistic impulses and in-
tuitions of the absurd on the one hand, and on the other a
compelling expectation that behind these forms lies hidden
a metaphysical secret. Each period tends to define its own
humanity against its notions of the nonhuman. Monsters
are masks through which man can read into his own face.
What distinguishes the Romantic period is that its monsters stress simultaneously the breakdown of values and
the profound need for an underlying but invisible unity.
The most horrendous shapes sired by the imagination be-

[7] Flaubert, *Oeuvres de jeunesse inédites*, III, 264.

come assurances of a mysterious link in Nature. Saint Antoine assumes that the supernatural shapes of ithyphallic deities, or of human figures with the head of a cow or a snake, carry him to "other worlds" and initiate him to a fundamental mystery. Implicit is a basic philosophical tension of Romanticism. Heteroclite phenomena bring despair and mystic impulses into permanent clash.

Dilemmas of Romanticism

Flaubert's *Tentation* illustrates the pivotal dialectic conflicts of Romanticism. These dramatic and largely unresolved tensions are related to four major themes: Solitude as suffering or joyful redemption; Knowledge as Promethean hope or self-inflicted curse; Time as dynamic force or as principle of disintegration; Nature experienced in hostility or in mystic communion.

Antoine's very temptation is evidently conceived in a climate of desperate solitude. So is, explicitly or implicitly, the fate of every Romantic hero, caught between the realization that he is alone in a desert (that desert may be "un désert d'hommes") and the proud joy he takes in his aloneness. Nothing is more characteristic than this dual view of claustration as a feared reality and as a happy state. The whole complex of prison imagery, in which the nineteenth century indulges repeatedly, is suffused with this fundamentally ambivalent attitude. The prison cell resembles the monastic cell.

Flaubert unquestionably conceived of solitude as a baneful condition. His adolescent work *Novembre*, though studded with literary clichés, is also a self-revealing document. Man, he feels, is condemned to emotional and spiritual isolation: "le coeur de l'homme n'est-il pas une énorme solitude où nul ne pénètre?" But instead of seeking communication, the narrator further wraps himself up in himself: "je me renfermai et me roulai sur moi-même." The moral climate is one of sterility. In the *Tentation*, the Gymnosophist, disgusted with the world, lives "enfoncé dans la solitude" (p. 85). The monotonous wail heard from the

Alexandria *ergastulum* echoes the voices of the chained slaves in the *ergastulum* at the beginning of *Salammbô*. At the very outset, Antoine complains: "Quelle solitude!" His eremetism is oppressive not only because of the self-imposed reclusion, but because of a permanent condemnation to immurement in the self. He feels incarcerated in his own mind. "My thought struggles to escape from its prison" (p. 49).

But it is precisely here that the saint and Flaubert are both guilty of a fecund duplicity. For Antoine luxuriates in those very pleasures of the mind which only solitude can grant. He indulges in that form of isolation and inactivity which permits reflection and voluptuous reveries. Hilarion, with the Devil's logic and lucidity, accuses him of self-deceptively transforming his penitence into exquisite pleasure. "You hypocrite, who wallow in your solitude the better to surrender to the debauchery of your desires!" (p. 42) The narrator in *Novembre* also experiences the "voluptés de la pensée," and himself analyzes the coupling of a chaste existence with the most ferociously voluptuous daydreams. "I lived solitarily in my desires," he observes. The observation goes to the heart of Antoine's (and Flaubert's) temptations. Both seek the ecstasies of dreams. A hermit's cabin, as Gaston Bachelard suggests in his poetic essay on space, is the very symbol of a "meditating universe."[8] For Antoine it becomes indeed the symbolic locus where dream and reality interpenetrate ("Quelle est la limite du rêve et de la réalité?" p. 393) and expose the consciousness to the most inordinate desires.

It is a Faustian craving for knowledge, far more so than an appetite of the senses, which most persistently exalts and tortures the saint. The temptation of the spirit is stronger than the temptation of the flesh. This *libido sciendi* is fully exploited by the satanic Hilarion, who grows in size, together with the hermit's appetite, until he assumes the shape of a luminous archangel. The pleasures

---

[8] Bachelard, *La Poétique de l'espace*, p. 46.

of knowledge are repeatedly suggested in erotic terms. Pride, in the 1849 version, describes its caresses and its "spasmes fous." The urge to embrace all phenomena, to penetrate into their secret (". . . je veux entrer jusqu'au noyau du globe . . ." p. 350), to stretch one's capabilities to the point of coping with the supernatural are related to a potency complex. The temptation of power is closely bound up with the temptation of knowledge. In his opening monologue, Antoine longs for the science of magic (another echo of *Faust*) by means of which he could manipulate the forces of nature. Hilarion, who represents both Science and the Devil, explains that his kingdom extends to the entire universe. Boundless desire and desire for the boundless are here synonymous. It is revealing that in his dreams he becomes Nabuchodonosor, whose expressed ambition it is to rebuild the tower of Babel and dethrone God. The invitation to rival God is later repeated by the Old Woman.

Images of verticality, flight and elevation correspond to this desire for power. The cosmic flight in Part VI (Part III in the first version and the space navigation in *Smarh* are earlier treatments) marks not only an exhilarating escape from the laws of gravity, but a latent dream of expansion and *envol*. Volitation is in fact one of the most recurrent motifs in Romantic literature. Whether these poetical aeronautics suggest the psychological need for rebellion or domination, the moral quest for progress or the metaphysical longing for redemption (a poet such as Hugo combines all three),[9] the flight of Icarus haunts the Romantic imagination.

These spatial images do, however, also involve a sense of terror. The flight which began in joy may well end with a tragic fall. Here again Flaubert's work reënacts one of the dialectical tensions of Romanticism. The sublime ascent is frequently paid for by an unredeemable tumble. Thus Antoine describes how his thought struggles in vain to

[9] See my article on Hugo's spatial obsessions, "Victor Hugo, la prison et l'espace," *Revue des Sciences Humaines*, January-March 1965, pp. 59-79.

escape from its "prison": ". . . during a split second, I feel as though suspended; than I fall again ("puis je retombe" p. 49)!" This terror of the fall is very clear in *Smarh,* where it is conveyed in a semicomical mode. After the experience of exaltation and dilatation comes fatigue in the face of immensity. Smarh begs for a safe landing. This terror corresponds to the inconsolable sadness which the Flaubertian protagonist always feels as he begins the inventory of phenomena. A strange dizziness accompanies desire, and habitually leads to a wish for total abdication (*anéantissement*). Knowledge turns out to be a suicidal allurement.

Flaubert's thought merges here, at least partially, with a persistent antirationalistic current. Not only Rousseau and his immediate disciples, but also Balzac, whose work Flaubert read with care, proclaimed the disease of thinking. Balzac's essay "Des Artistes" stresses the belief that intellectual effort "goes so to speak against Nature," that all creative efforts of the mind constitute a pathological abuse. The noxious and at the same time powerfully seductive attributes of knowledge assume in this context a metaphysical reality. Very appropriately, Antoine, in the 1849 version, throwing a stone at Logic, cries out: "No! away with reasoning, away with thought! You are damnation" (p. 486). And it is profoundly significant that both in the first and in the last version it is the Devil who gives Antoine his lesson in Spinozist philosophy—the very same Devil who, in *Smarh,* explained that all knowledge and metaphysics can be summed up by the words "doubt," "lies," and "nothingness." The Spinozist lesson leads indeed to a fit of depression. (The Pig, in the early version, wants to be reduced to ham.) Antoine, whose consciousness is stretched to a bursting point "in this dilatation of Nothingness," experiences a feverish dizziness.

Yet it is one of the most characteristic features of the Romantic sensibility to yearn precisely for this experience of vertigo in the face of the infinite. This dizzying dilatation, this *aspiration vers l'infini*, is for Baudelaire the indispensable condition of Romantic art.[10] Flaubert's hermit is assailed not only by the desire for immensity, but by a peculiar form of temptation which, for want of a better expression, must be called the voluptuousness of the infinite. The notion of *volupté* is indeed repeatedly linked with spirituality and unlimited space, to the point where any abuse of the senses seems to guarantee access to infinity. "Au delà des voluptés gît la Volupté," says the goddess of "obscene caprices" in the first version (p. 374). The allegorical figure of Lust, who wants to explore "bottomless" sensuality, is even more explicit. Through the madness of the senses, she claims to glimpse, as through the cracks in a door, unending perspectives. Is it a descent into Hell or an elevation into the sublime regions of dream? The meaning of the Flaubertian debauches of the imagination cannot be resolved in simple moralistic terms. The syndrome of *bovarysme* corresponds to this curious blending of frenetic sensuality with spiritual aspirations. This frenzy may destroy the body; but the weakness of the flesh, according to Hilarion, proclaims the vastness of the impossible.

Once again, the parallel with Baudelaire is unavoidable. Baudelaire's most erotic poems are also most heavily weighted with spiritual longing. The Sapphic partners in "Femmes damnées" are "chercheuses d'infini" in a landscape of temptations specifically associated with Saint Antoine. Elsewhere, the two lesbian addicts Delphine and Hippolyte carry "infinity" in their own hearts. In *Le Poème du Haschisch,* Baudelaire explains that man's vices are the very proof of his "taste for the infinite." Ultimately, in the Baudelairean context, the curiosity of the senses leads to the exoticism of death.

La Débauche et la Mort sont deux aimables filles . . .

The final meaning of the poem "Le Voyage" is a search

[10] See in particular "Qu'est-ce que le Romantisme?" in the *Salon de 1846*, Baudelaire, *Oeuvres complètes*, p. 879.

for new experiences in the as yet uncharted region of Death:

Plonger au fond du gouffre, Enfer ou Ciel, qu'importe?
Au fond de l'Inconnu pour trouver du *nouveau*!

These lines, probably written in 1859, bear an uncanny resemblance to the invitation extended by Death in the 1849 version of *La Tentation*:

Si tu veux le néant, viens! Si tu veux la béatitude, viens!
Ténèbres ou lumières, annihilation ou extase, inconnu
quel qu'il soit . . . Allons, partons . . .

This Romantic escapism is clearly not a naïve search for sensations through tourism to far-off regions. The notions of time and space become tragically interdependent. Spatial claustration and spatial escapism are closely related to temporal anxiety.[11] Apollonius' lyric outbursts on the theme of departure ("Nous allons au Sud . . ." p. 112) combine the reveries of space (the island of Junonia, distant cascades, even more distant stars) with the reveries of time (the lizard that wakes up every hundred years). Time for Flaubert signifies the death of each instant (in *Novembre*: "Each minute of my life was suddenly separated from the others by an abyss"), as well as the mummification of larger historical periods: the Egyptian gods, according to Isis, are now immobile statues whose shoulders are bleached by the droppings of birds. The Romantic imagination, aware of this endless dying, undertakes a struggle against Time. The attempt to bring eternity into time is in fact, according to Georges Poulet, one of the characteristic traits of the Romantic writers, obsessed as they were by the desire to be utterly absorbed by a reassuring present.[12] With Flaubert, however, temporal pessimism remains almost complete. Just as on the human level time means

[11] About this interrelation, see Gaston Bachelard's comments in *La Poétique de l'espace* (p. 28).
[12] Poulet, "Timelessness and Romanticism," *Journal of the History of Ideas*, 1954, pp. 3–22.

decay and death, so on the religious level time means at best a pathetic theological evolutionism. The dynamic movement of ideas, the eternal striving of the mind, are offset and rendered futile, it would seem, by a progressive exhaustion. "Mais la vie s'épuise, les formes s'usent," explains Hilarion (p. 122). No writer of his time seems to have so completely experienced the abstract notion of decadence. It is not surprising that Des Esseintes was to be an admirer of *La Tentation de saint Antoine.*

It is, however, on the complex subject of "Nature"—a subject closely related to the problems raised by decadentism—that Flaubert participates most obviously in the Romantic ambiguities. For Nature is the all-loving, all-consoling and all-absorbing mother; but it is also the cruel or indifferent spectator of man's tragic fate—or worse still: his most persistent foe. "Embrace Nature by every desire of your being, and wallow amorously on her vast bosom," advises Lust. But the spirit of Death, pointing to the callousness of Nature, immediately proposes the antithetical image: "No! No! Life is bad, the world is ugly. Don't you feel abandoned in the midst of this creation?" (pp. 433–434). The double lesson rehearses the dialectical tension embodied by the two exemplary figures of Rousseau and Sade. No Romantic writer could afford to ignore the dilemma altogether. For some, it remained a permanent tragic principle. Thus Baudelaire, while proclaiming the fundamental harmony of sensations and of spiritual experience, remained convinced that man's moral and esthetic values could only be achieved *against* Nature.

It is in this light that the Spinozist passages in the various versions of *La Tentation* must be assessed. Pantheistic reveries can be found in Flaubert's earliest writings. He himself has alluded to his "faculté panthéistique." Henri Grappin, in a remarkable though now forgotten essay, points up the expression, as well as a significantly pantheistic passage in *Par les Champs et par les grèves* where Flaubert and his companion Du Camp experience an extraordinary joy in *becoming* nature.[13] Repeatedly, Flaubert expressed his attraction to altitude, his combined love and terror of space and expansion, the "malaise voluptueux" associated with the desire to fly and to "be scattered" in the air.[14] The narrator in *Novembre* climbs on high towers to enjoy dizziness and the urge to "fly in the air and be dissipated with the wind."

Flaubert's mystical and monistic urges were no doubt stimulated by early readings in Spinoza, to whom he was initiated by his childhood friend, Alfred Le Poittevin. Significantly, it is to Le Poittevin that the final version of *La Tentation* is dedicated. All three versions contain indeed "lessons" in Spinozist philosophy, characteristically developed in cosmic flight. All three proclaim the unity and eternity of Substance. In the text of 1849, Antoine is told by the Devil (for it is he who philosophizes) that there exists a hidden breath in the heart of things, that God cannot be separated into parts, that matter and spirit are indivisible, that there can be no more than one infinity, and that the divine principle cannot be abstracted from the world. The lesson in the 1874 version (still given by the Devil) focuses more specifically on the attributes of divine essence: God cannot have existed before the "beginning"; he cannot have willed a multiplicity of causes; his will is not separable from his essence; he is not separable from matter; he cannot be engaged in dialogue. This philosophy of immanence, this panpsychism stressing the all-inclusiveness of reality and the continuity of experience, clearly echoes Part I of Spinoza's *Ethics*, and in particular Propositions V, VIII, XIII, XIV, XVIII and XX.

The monistic vision of Antoine, as he flies through outer space, abolishes the gap between the subject and the object. All interval disappears. The telescoping of dreams and reality, so characteristic of *bovarysme*, assumes here

[13] Grappin, "Le Mysticisme poétique et l'imagination de Gustave Flaubert," *La Revue de Paris*, December 1 and 15, 1912, pp. 609–629, 849–870.

[14] See in particular Flaubert, *Par les Champs et par les grèves*, p. 212.

a metaphysical significance. According to René Wellek, such an identification of object and subject, together with the deification of a dynamic, organic Nature, represents one of the essential tendencies of the Romantic imagination. The objection to a mechanistic universe as conceived by the eighteenth century (Goethe, for instance, was an enemy of Newtonian cosmology) went hand in hand with a neo-Platonism that tended to identify soul and body, God and world, and ultimately led to what Wellek calls the "at-homeness in the universe" of the great Romantic poets.[15] There is no question that Antoine's fervent pantheistic wish at the end of *La Tentation* ("être la matière!") beautifully fits this scheme.

At least at first glance. For Antoine's joyful wish to have wings, to divide himself, to be water, perfume or sound—in short, to *become* matter himself—is also somewhat of an anguished cry and a desire for self-annihilation. In reality, the concluding passage of the 1874 version (in the earliest version it appeared in the middle of the text, preceding the lesson in Spinozism), is one of the most difficult passages in all of Flaubert. And on it, because of its strategic placement in the final version, hinges the entire meaning of the book. For on the one hand, it is a clearly mystic drive which urges Antoine on, even to the point of wishing to annihilate himself in the divine creation: he wishes to become *God's thing*. Yet how is one to reconcile this interpretation with Flaubert's statement to Edmond de Goncourt that the "final defeat" of the saint is due to the scientific cell?[16] This assertion about "defeat" (despite the mystic élan and the prayers at the end) seems confirmed by Antoine's observing, just prior to the ultimate outburst, the vibrations of microscopic masses of protoplasm. Finally, there must be a meaning to the fact that in all three versions the Spinozist lesson is taught by the Devil. What further corroborates the subversive nature of

15 Wellek, "The Concept of Romanticism in Literary History," in *Concepts of Criticism*, pp. 162, 165, 182, 188.
16 Goncourt, *Journal*, X, p. 36 (October 18, 1871).

his teachings (not to speak of their clearly anti-Christian character) is that the first pantheistic longing to "penetrate matter" is expressed, in the version of 1849, by the laughable figure of Science as she whispers into the ear of Pride (p. 349).

Flaubert's Spinozism is thus paradoxically in the service of his pessimism. The negation of epigenesis seems to imply an oppressive materialism. According to the Devil there can be no dialogue with a God as boundless as matter. What is worse, according to strict Devil's logic, this infinite and indivisible God, just as he cannot be contained in any shape, cannot possibly stoop down to a given sentiment. God is indifferent to suffering ("Sans doute le mal est indifférent à Dieu . . ." p. 175). Pantheistic reveries thus seem to lead Flaubert to an ethical nihilism. "There is no aim!" explains the Devil (p. 171). As for God, who did not act before the beginning, he now appears "useless." Finally, as part of the Spinozist lesson, the Devil affirms the utter futility of prayers ("Et tu prétends le fléchir!" p. 174), thus casting an ironic light on the last words of La Tentation: "Antoine crosses himself and continues his prayers." This ambiguous return to a mechanical gesture is indeed the conclusion in all three versions.

Flaubert's ambiguities are, however, not unique. It would seem that the schemes concerning the fusion of object and subject, and man's spiritual reconciliation with Nature—profoundly meaningful though they may be as a Romantic ideal—need to be qualified to account for the full range of Romantic tragic tensions. Instead of the wished-for unity and harmony, there is often a sense of outer rift and of inner dédoublement. Spiritual cacophony is the subject of Baudelaire's poem "L'Héautontimorouménos," where he evokes the self-tortures of a mind facing its own "sinister mirror" and voracious irony. The lucid and gloomy dialogue with his own incompatible self is the subject of "L'Irrémédiable." One would be almost tempted to say that the reconciliation of Nature and Art, of reality and language, is the Romantic ambition to the precise extent that such reconciliation remains unattainable. Certainly that strain which runs from Sade to Vigny, and then to Baudelaire and Flaubert (and who could call them less significantly Romantic than Lamartine or Musset?) displays much less "at-homeness in the universe" than metaphysical rebellion, much less a deification of Nature than a defiance: Art itself becomes a form of protest.

"Nature seemed beautiful to me like a complete harmony," writes the narrator of *Novembre*. The aspiration toward universal joy and the wish for a loving Nature ("Nature aimante") are indeed permanent with Flaubert. Jules, in the first *Éducation sentimentale*, tries to develop an "intelligence aimante" for Nature; he sets out to enjoy the entire world "like a complete harmony."[17] But even more persistent is the anguished awareness of the formidable indifference of Nature. As Antoine watches the infinite varieties of animals, all he sees are digestive and reproductive activities: "il y en a qui accouchent, d'autres copulent, ou d'une seule bouchée s'entre-dévorent" (p. 408). Birth, and copulation, and death. . . . Like T. S. Eliot's Sweeney, Antoine might conclude: "That's all, that's all, that's all, that's all. . . ." His is no doubt a quest for harmony and meaning. As Jean Seznec very convincingly has shown, he anxiously searches for the principle of the continuity of creation.[18] But do the uninterrupted cycles (negating creative Providence) and the exhilarating diversity of forms really cure what Jean-Pierre Richard calls the "maladie de l'intervalle"?[19] One has the uncomfortable feeling that despite the apparent answer provided by the episode of the monsters, who seem to supply the secret of the great link, despite the intense wish to believe in a fundamental unity of life, Antoine is left profoundly dis-

[17] Flaubert, *Oeuvres de jeunesse inédites*, III, 164.
[18] Seznec, *Nouvelles Études sur La Tentation de Saint Antoine*, p. 79.
[19] Richard, "La Création de la forme chez Flaubert," in *Littérature et sensation*, p. 159.

tressed by what remains an unanswered question: "pour-
quoi les Formes sont-elles variées?" (p. 187)

The Essential Contingency

A writer haunted by images of death and decay may
well seek comfort in those very cycles of Nature which
imply decomposition. The poet tries to espouse the world
by proxy. To create artistically—this at least was Flaubert's
hope—meant to cease being oneself, to circulate freely
inside the larger creation. The *impersonnalité surhumaine*
which he advocated in his letters to Louise Colet was thus
not so much an esthetic dogma as a liberating exercise,
a form of ascesis in quest of a superior serenity. Flaubert's tragedy is that his mystic tendency only further
plunges him into an acute consciousness of heterogeneity.
The gap between phenomena refuses indeed to be filled.
The impossible mating of the Chimera and the Sphinx is
a fitting symbol of the essential cleavage between the
orders of experience. "You will not melt my granite!" says
the Sphinx. "You will not seize me . . . ," barks back the
green-eyed Chimera (p. 188). Their eternal divorce can
be interpreted, on a personal level, as the irreconcilable
exigencies of dream and of reality, whose tense coexistence
is behind much of Flaubert's urge to create fiction. Meta-
physically, their grotesque and futile efforts at intercourse
stress the impossibility of fusing the ever renewed accumulation of phenomena into a meaningful and cohesive
whole. Viewed in this light, *La Tentation de saint Antoine*
communicates in densely poetic terms the horror of unending discontinuity.

The very techniques exploited by Flaubert in this text
become tools of disjunction. A rapid succession of scenes
and dramatic moments, further intensified by surrealistic
effects, creates a permanent climate of disseverance. These
effects are responsible for what Paul Valéry disparagingly
described as a frustrating "diversity of moments and of

pieces."[20] But this is precisely the impression Flaubert desired to create. His vision throughout remains one of fragmented immediacy. Events and objects seem to flow rapidly into each other. But the impression of flow is deceptive. The "échafaudages dramatiques" to which Flaubert himself alludes,[21] often take the concrete form of a rapid succession of stage directions which lends much of the action the dizzying quality of quickly shifting tableaux. The long cataleptic Alexandrian vision at the beginning of Part II, thus substitutes for the flux of the saint's monologue a long series of dramatic "moments" which have the directness of photographic *instantanés*.

The techniques of profusion are of course Flaubert's most obvious device. His countless parades, cortèges, résumés, accumulations of gods and heresies, the very array of words and stylistic exuberance—all this creates the climate of a philosophical bazaar. The image of the fair is indeed implicit: the heretical Marcosians, with their golden rings and oily bodies, cry out to Antoine the mountebank's typical invitation: "Entre chez nous pour t'unir à l'Esprit! Entre chez nous pour boire l'immortalité!"[22]

But the most effective techniques of proliferation and fragmentation are those which suggest a somnambulist and oneiric state. The absence of transitions produces effects of dissociation. Thus Antoine, deep in his Alexandrian dream, finds himself "lost in a succession of apartments" (p. 24). The ambiance can perhaps best be described as resembling that of a surrealist film. Objects and beings undergo the most unexpected metamorphoses. The old palm tree near the edge of the cliff suddenly becomes the torso of a woman leaning over the precipice. Images

[20] Valéry, "La Tentation de (saint) Flaubert," in *Variété V*, pp. 199–207.
[21] Flaubert, *Corresp.*, II, 362.
[22] P. 59. The very genesis of *La Tentation de saint Antoine* brings to mind the atmosphere of a fair, for it was at the fair of Saint-Romain in Rouen that the boy Gustave saw a performance of the mystery of Saint Antoine.

succeed each other abruptly and with an uncanny acceleration ("Leur mouvement s'accélère. Elles défilent d'une façon vertigineuse" p. 15) until they finally melt into an indeterminable irreality. Nothing seems quite authentic—or, to use a Sartrean adjective, all appears *louche*. At one point, during the gastronomic temptation, the wines begin to "flow," the fish to "palpitate," while the soft pulp of the fruit moves toward Antoine like obscene lips. This unstable, mutable quality of objects, this illusive and unpredictable life of "things" creates indeed an almost visceral malaise. The cinematographic impressions are further strengthened by the frequent use of "fade-ins." We glide from Antoine's monologue into his dream, from the conscious into the subconscious, with the same ease with which the *cinéaste* transmutes one image into another.

The frantic pace and assimilation of images imply a telescoping of forms. *Défiler, accélérer, multiplier, fondre* are the key verbs in this process. The result is a parade of weird anatomies: alligators' heads on deer's legs, owls with snakes' tails, frogs as hairy as bears. But the characteristic fusion of shapes fails to uncover the cosmic secret. It is not an underlying unity or fundamental link that is here being suggested, but a basic discrepancy, an essential incompatibility of all phenomena. The dwarf who appears at the beginning of Part III is a child with gray hair, and his huge head is totally out of proportion with the rest of his body. As Jean-Pierre Richard justly observes, the monster who for Hugo grows from an overabundant generosity of nature, is for Flaubert a proof of the ineptness of all forms.[23] Nature, one might say, is here twisted into its own caricature. This theme of the antiphysis once again makes of Flaubert a literary brother to Baudelaire. Only Flaubert, unlike the author of *Les Fleurs du Mal*, wallows in the reign of the amorphous.

Formlessness becomes a fascination and a terror. The boundless consumption of forms fills Antoine with an-

---

[23] Richard, "La Création de la forme chez Flaubert," in *Littérature et sensation*, p. 169.

bound up with images of corruption, destruction and death.

This is not to underestimate the erotic charge of the book, which, even in its later versions, projects into word and rhythm the wildest yearnings of adolescence. The onanistic suggestions are often unmistakable—notably in the scenes of self-flagellation. Although Jean Seznec was able to show a literary or scholarly source for almost every sentence in the episode of the gods in the 1849 version, references to the "sève sucrée" and the "sperme gras" are clearly Flaubert's own.[26] His longing for almost super-human sexual ecstasies is transmuted artistically ("sub-limated," Theodor Reik would say)[27] into a figure such as the queen of Sheba, who promises that the possession of the tiniest portion of her body will fill the hermit with a pleasure "more vehement than the conquest of an em-pire" (pp. 36–37).

On closer inspection, however, it becomes clear that just as Lust and Death constitute the inescapable couple, so the notion of sexuality is intimately wedded to images of devastation. Apollonius evokes the ire of Astarte and the rigor of a Venus who "kills the flesh" (p. 309). The version of 1849 is studded with suggestions of this an-nihilating potential of sex. Lust longs to fall into a bottom-less pit of sensual delight, and to "lose herself" in this abyss. When, like a procuress, she offers to Antoine uni-versal contingents of available females, Ire—without any transition—proposes visions of blood dripping from human bodies and from ceilings. Frenetic indulgence in sensuality is seen at every point as conducive to the anesthetization and extermination of the flesh. The heretical Nicolaists put it succinctly: "to rid ourselves of the cupidities of the flesh, we plunge it into delights which exhaust it." Carnal desire is to be the instrument of a morbid and fatal sur-

[26] Seznec, Les Sources de l'Épisode des Dieux dans la Tentation de Saint Antoine, p. 137.
[27] Alfred Lombard suggests that, according to psychoanalysts, La Tentation is "the most complete example of the sublimation of sexuality through art" (Flaubert et Saint Antoine, p. 52).

feit. The death in question is of course primarily the death of the body. The basic wish is to see the body "perish through matter" (p. 270). The speech of the Nicolaists in the final version is shorter, but it still makes the same point: "Gorge your flesh with what it desires. Try to exterminate it by dint of debauches!" (p. 59).

This paradoxical hatred of the flesh assumes sadistic proportions in *La Tentation*. One of the earliest images conjured up by Antoine's imagination is a scene of lustful cruelty: the writhing body of a naked woman whipped to death in broad sunlight. What gives this episode added meaning is that he identifies the woman with Ammonaria, the fiancée he abandoned. The same image is evoked later in an equally disturbing scene: the act of self-flagellation ("Sifflez, lanières, mordez-moi, arrachez-moi!" p. 28) brings back the vivid image of the torture of Ammonaria. As he flogs himself and indulges in self-pollution, he imagines that he is tied to a column next to her, that he watches Ammonaria and is watched by her as their two bodies succumb amorously under the blows.

Elsewhere the descriptions of savage pleasures and of murderous impulses take the form of an orgiastic delirium. The "voices" alerting him to his homicidal vocation ("Tu les égorgeras, va, tu les égorgeras!" p. 15) might have been addressed to Saint Julien. The thirst for martyrdom seems to be allied with an unrelenting hatred of life, of which concupiscence is the deceptive symptom. This destructive urge and taste for the degradation of the flesh show up most flagrantly in the Alexandrian dream sequence. Antoine meets all his former enemies; he defiles and eviscerates them with the greatest zest. He tramples on infants and beats wounded men to death. He watches with intense pleasure the massacre of women whose blood spurts up to the ceiling and flows from decapitated corpses. The expression "blood-bath" quite literally applies: Antoine wades in puddles "knee-deep," relishes the smell and taste of blood and shivers with sensuality at the contact of the soggy clothes against his limbs. Flaubert here outdoes the goriest passages of *Salammbô*.

More conspicuously, however, than in any other novel of Flaubert, the sadistic motifs in *La Tentation* are in the service of a philosophical and almost religious pessimism. An unmistakable horror of the flesh and a chastising asceticism preside over Flaubert's thought. It is not surprising that he was from childhood on haunted by the image of the *saint*, and that at least two of his major works —not to mention many oblique treatments—are devoted to this figure and this theme.

It is easy enough, in all three versions of *La Tentation*, to point to an explicit abhorrence of the body. The Patricianists, in the 1849 version, approve of Antoine's fear of the flesh. "Like you, we escape from it, we mortify it, we abhor it" (p. 250). For the Montanists, the body is the hated dungeon of the soul: "Thus you must destroy your flesh," is their pressing advice (p. 273). The "Apostrophic" Venus—the Venus of the strong and pure heroes—is great, according to Apollonius, because she wards off passion and kills the flesh. And the attraction to the sex act is hardly distinguishable from a latent but pervasive revulsion. Copulation is seen very much as a drowning in the "chair molle" (p. 310). The climactic duet between Lust and Death in the final version sums up the intimate relation between lewdness and decay. No wonder the hermit is repeatedly tempted to abandon the "dirty inn" of his body, "filled with garbage," and to seek ultimate peace and purity in Nothingness (p. 87). And is there not the symbolic example of Atys, who castrates himself and is responsible for an entire epidemic of castration among his faithful?

It could be argued that this contempt for man's carnal reality and all these invitations to abolish the flesh are the advice of "heresies." To which one can only answer that this is precisely the specific Flaubertian heresy: the sacrilegious revolt against the very conditions of human existence. His correspondence contains repeated evidence of this insurgence. "Who has not felt the fatigue of his body! how heavy the flesh weighs! . . ." he writes to his mistress, to whom he enjoys communicating his most depressed moods. Or this statement, more revealing still: "There comes a moment when *one needs to make oneself suffer*, to hate one's flesh. . . ."[28] As for his frequent mental dwelling on images of putrifying corpses, this cannot be attributed to a mere literary vogue of "charnel house" writings; it does have a compulsive ring. "Poor Father Parain, I see him now in his shroud as though I had the coffin where he rests on my table, before my eyes. The idea of the maggots eating into his cheeks does not leave me."[29]

The macabre vision is here the obverse of the image of carnal excess. Both derive from a chronic need to explode the boundaries of the human. Negation of life, with Flaubert, most often paradoxically affirms itself through an aggressive insatiability. The suicidal impulse turns out to be a symptom of both self-deprecation and of pride. Antoine's puzzlement after the Gymnosophist sets himself aflame is significant. "Quelle haine de la vie il faut avoir! A moins que l'orgueil ne les pousse?" (p. 88). Significantly also, the monastic image remains throughout an ambiguous one. The "asprous solitude"[30] in which he enjoys secluding himself during his childhood in time becomes for him the saintlike apanage of the artist. His exacerbated sensuality in turn leads to a sense of shame and an almost religious desire to chastise and vilify the body. The monastic cell, as metaphor, suggests both the hothouse and the austere place of penance—a combination which was to become a typically decadent motif. But half a century before Huysmans and the fin-de-siècle writers, the most frenetic Romantics had discovered the deep truth and shock potential of this ambiguous image. One might even wonder whether Flaubert, as he set out to write about his tempted hermit, did not have faintly echoing through

[28] Flaubert, *Corresp.*, III, 77, 110.
[29] Flaubert, *Corresp.*, III, 340.   [30] Flaubert, *Corresp.*, I, 320.

his mind some particularly relevant lines of a curious poem by Pétrus Borel—a poem, incidentally, much appreciated by Baudelaire—which the "Lycanthrope" had published as a preliminary piece to his horror novel *Madame Putiphar*, and which specifically alludes to the saint.

Au cloître, écoute-moi, tu n'es pas plus idoine
Qu'au monde; crains ses airs de repos mensongers;
Crains les satyriasis affreux de saint Anthoine;
Crains les tentations, les remords, les dangers,
Les assauts de la chair et les chutes de l'âme.
Sous le vent du désert tes désirs flamberont;
La solitude étreint, torture, brise, enflamme;
Dans des maux inouïs tes sens retomberont.

The horrible "satyriasis," in the Flaubertian context, implies not only the self-destruction of the saint through a refusal of the world, but a metaphysical annihilation: excess of desire brings about a cosmic Götterdämmerung. In a letter to George Sand, Flaubert explains that he will show all the gods in a state of agony, that his book could be subtitled "Le Comble de l'insanité."[31]

A Poem of Death

"The heart of man is made for life," says deceptive Lust in the 1849 version (p. 435). Yet no matter how one interprets its various endings, *La Tentation* ultimately appears as a poem of destruction and death. The Flaubertian satyriasis is more self-damaging by far than insatiable venereal appetite can ever be. It is a global appetite doomed to turn on itself and become the self-devourer. This is Antoine's most heartfelt complaint leading to the overwhelming question: *à quoi bon?* "Like an arrow projected against a wall, desire always escapes, bounces back on you and pierces the soul" (p. 427). It is this fiasco of life that is proclaimed by the moribund and defeatist gods. "All is going to die," says Buddha. "All is dead," echoes

31 Flaubert, *Corresp.*, VI, 276.

Neptune (pp. 128, 153). The process of decay is infinitely repetitive. The images projected by desire multiply, accelerate, melt into each other, become indistinguishable and finally dissolve. This, once again, is the basic syndrome of *bovarysme*—and Flaubert's entire work is a series of variations on the theme of this malady. In *La Tentation,* the disease assumes metaphysical proportions; but it is basically the same as in the story of Emma or that of the Carthaginian virgin. Dreams of immensity and dreams of violence go hand in hand, as the goddess Diane finds out in her ultimate moments. And Antoine sums up this intolerable feeling of spiritual explosion: "Ma conscience éclate sous cette dilatation du néant!" (p. 176)

The only significant difference in the spiritual pathology of *La Tentation*—a difference which brings this work closer than any other to *Bouvard et Pécuchet*—is that the fundamental obsession centers not exclusively on experience but on knowledge. When the Devil, at the end of Part VI, suggests to Antoine that behind all experience and beyond all learning there is perhaps "nothing," he is merely putting into the simplest and most brutal terms a latent fear of our humanistic culture. This tragedy of modern humanism Flaubert felt perhaps more acutely than any of his contemporaries. Like the Gymnosophist, who proclaims his loathing for all knowledge, he suspects that to know everything is to understand nothing—which is the obverse of the other Flaubertian *idée fixe* that one knows nothing until one knows everything. The circle is more than vicious. The encyclopedic disease is lethal: all knowledge cancels itself out.

Images of despair are of course not uncommon in Flaubert's work. In the version of 1856, he had even conceived (it was one of the few innovations) a typically Pascalian image of man's prison-destiny: in a dungeon men are seen sitting in a "fierce and desperate attitude," holding knives in their hands and watching the continuous flow of sand as it gradually fills the entire tower (p. 588). This image of the human condition Flaubert omitted in the final version. But the suicidal obsession and the fascinated stare in the face of nothingness remain permanent realities. As early as in *Smarh*, Satan sings the joy of nonbeing and nihility. "O béatitude de la mort, quand viendras-tu donc?" In the 1849 version of *La Tentation*, the heresies curse mankind ("malédiction sur le monde! malédiction sur nous-mêmes!"), call for self-murder and string together dithyrambs in praise of ultimate dissolution (p. 280).

This suicidal joy remains one of the chief strands in the final version. The Circoncellios want to poison, burn and massacre in order to "hasten the end of the world" (p. 67). The Gymnosophist seeks not merely the chastising of his flesh, but the ecstatic absolute of "Anéantissement" (p. 87). The suicidal instinct, on one level, is of course the most pernicious temptation of pride. The Old Woman knows this as she flatters Antoine into "doing a thing which equals one with God" (p. 181). But the call to self-destruction cannot possibly be dismissed as a simple expression of an external temptation, to be rationalized in theological terms and fought through lucidity and prayers. A gust of self-suppression blows from one end of this work to the other, suggesting a collective yearning and a collective madness. The nightmare of universal emasculation is only one of the most obvious manifestations. Images of self-inflicted death stud the text: the leopard Phalmant rends its own belly, while the three-headed bear Senad tears its offspring to pieces and the bitch Cepus spills all its milk.

The death-wish is evidently a frequent theme with the Romantic writers. What distinguishes Flaubert's brand of pessimism is that in his private universe the very plethora of life becomes a principle of undoing, that abundance and vitality are here in the service of corruption. Others, like Hugo, welcomed the profusion of knowledge and experience as a healthy superabundance, and optimistically prophesied the progress of humanity. Flaubert sees only a choking saturation, overmeasure and superfluity. In part, this concern with excess and massive accumulation of phenomena must be related to a social and cultural diagnosis, to the denunciation of the sanguine arrogance of bourgeois society of which Flaubert felt himself simultaneously the critic and the accomplice. But to an even larger degree it does point to a form of self-denunciation, to the mythopoeic diagnosis of a private disease: the tragic combination of gigantic yearnings and a fundamental debility.

6

La Légende de saint Julien l'Hospitalier:

THE SIN OF EXISTING

> Je vis seul, très seul, de plus en plus seul.
> Lettre à Maxime Du Camp

The Mythical and the Private World

This streamlined tale, which Flaubert claims to have composed as a relaxing exercise, but which he himself termed "effervescent,"[1] is in fact, in its very craftsmanlike perfection, one of his most turbulent texts. Cruelty, spirituality, pathology—the most disturbing aspects of his temperament as well as the most paradoxical interplay of themes make of this reworking of a minor saint's legend one of Flaubert's most "personal" works. No text of Flaubert's appears on the surface more impassive and more liberated from any element that is not under the strictest esthetic control. The aloofness of an almost inhuman hero, the historical and mythical distance, the utilization of an already existing legend, the display of quaint erudition— all suggest a totally impersonal relation between the author and his literary material.

Yet *Saint Julien* could serve as a point of departure for a study of Flaubert's most intimate motifs. Above all, the pervasive theme of unwitting and yet deeply wished-for parricide assumes such a haunting and even nightmarish

---

[1] "Quant au *Coeur simple*, c'est aussi bonhomme que *Saint Julien* est effervescent . . ." Flaubert, *Corresp.*, VII, 320–321. Complete citations for all notes may be found in the Bibliography.

quality that it is difficult not to relate it in depth to Flaubert's own involved guilt feelings. And around this central obsession, a cluster of other themes casts a light which, in esthetic as well as in psychological importance, extends far beyond the miraculous and obscure existence of the saint. No literary subject is ever chosen altogether fortuitously. Flaubert himself might have thought that all he wished to do was to rival in words the images of a stained-glass window—a tempting enterprise, no doubt, for one who, like Flaubert, enjoyed the challenges of art. In fact, however, *Saint Julien* yields to the careful reader a rich repertory of the most revealing Flaubertian themes which are here interwoven in a particularly interesting manner: the fascination of the bestiary, the monastic urge, the image of the alienated saint, the temptation of despair, self-abnegation as a form of self-disgust ("Sa propre personne lui faisait tellement horreur . . ."), the dream of possible regeneration through copulation with Horror ("Julien s'étala dessus complètement . . ." III*). The very structure and rhythm of the tale, with its apparent lack of psychological determinism, sum up the climate of Flaubert's work. A crisis of the human will is at its center. The guilelessness of Julien, the ineluctability of his situations, which succeed each other in paratactic fashion, while stressing the mystery of the human potential, confirm a sense of impotence and surrender which characterize the over-all vision of Flaubert. The vocation of sainthood, much like the artist's vocation, is a retreat from oneself.

It was in the fall of 1875, during a leisurely stay in Brittany, that the idea of the tale crystallized in Flaubert's mind. A letter to Mme Roger des Genettes informs us about his frame of mind: he wants to verify whether he "can still write a sentence"; he assures his friend that the project amounts to nothing at all, that it is devoid of any

* Roman numerals following the quotations from the *Trois contes* refer to the sections of the respective tales.

importance.[2] A therapeutic exercise, one gathers! To be sure, Flaubert was in need of some distraction. The endless task of *Bouvard et Pécuchet*, the failure of his play *Le Candidat*, the death of his friend George Sand in 1876, made this a disheartening period in his life. But neither the idea of a literary "distraction," nor the later claim to compose a triptych covering three different historic periods (*Hérodias* and *Un Coeur simple* were to represent antiquity and the modern world) can be taken at face value. In fact, the genesis of *Saint Julien* goes back to about thirty years earlier when, in the spring of 1846, during an excursion to Caudebec-en-Caux in the company of Maxime Du Camp, Flaubert saw a little statue of the saint which unquestionably brought back to his mind the well-known stained-glass window of the Rouen cathedral. Moreover, it is very likely that, as early as 1846, he was already familiar with the work of E. H. Langlois entitled *Mémoire sur la peinture sur verre et quelques vitraux remarquables des églises de Rouen*, which gave an account as well as reproductions of this work.[3]

The literary sources of Flaubert's tale are well known; they have been discussed with much finesse by Marcel Schwob in *Spicilège*. The life of the saint as gathered by Jacques de Voragine in the *Légende Dorée*, and as reproduced in Vincent de Beauvais' *Speculum historiale*, constitutes the fundamental text. But influences other than those suggested by Schwob are possible. In 1825, a Scottish ballad, *Lord Kenneth et la Belle Ellinour*, in which a huntsman aiming at a swan kills his beloved, appeared in *Ballades, légendes et chants populaires*. A few years later, a

[2] Flaubert, *Corresp.*, VII, 267.

[3] A. W. Raitt, speculates that Flaubert might have become acquainted with the legend as early as 1835 during an excursion to Caudebec in the company of Langlois himself. If this is so, the genesis of the work goes back to Flaubert's fifteenth year, and the gestation lasted forty years! This would further stress the permanence and significance of *Saint Julien*'s themes. ("The Composition of Flaubert's *Saint Julien L'Hospitalier*," *French Studies*, October 1965, pp. 358–372.)

story on a related theme appeared in *La France littéraire*.[4] It is not unlikely that Flaubert was acquainted with both. At any rate, the hunting motif coupled with that of the murder of a loved one was certainly not alien to the Romantic imagination.

The mythical context of the legend is banal enough. Behind the story of hunting, suffering animals, and a sinner's existence which, through a mortification of the flesh, leads to sainthood, it is easy to recognize some archetypal themes: the human soul imprisoned in an animal, the oracle in the form of a nonhuman, the long expiation of a much-feared crime. The basic legend is unquestionably endowed with a strong poetic potential: the hunting motif and fairy-tale atmosphere, the image of the wide river and of the difficult crossing, the miraculous element and the strong dose of naïveté. Flaubert was no doubt drawn to this basic simplicity of a folk story which preserves and communicates a whole range of undefinable and somewhat mysterious affective values with the strength of an indisputable evidence. Flaubert adheres to the poetic spirit of the legend. He preserves and exploits the forest and the hunting scenes, the feeling of the miraculous and the sense of violence tamed by magic.

There is, however, much poetry that is distinctly his own. A temporal unreality achieved through the rapid succession of tableaux such as occurs commonly in dreams is one of the characteristic features of this tale. Movement is here most often the quick transition from one form of immobility to another. The very landscape seems transfixed ("Il vit reluire tout au loin un lac figé, qui ressemblait à du plomb" I), and the characters appear like plastic

---

[4] See Jean Giraud, "La Genèse d'un chef-d'oeuvre—'La Légende de Saint Julien L'Hospitalier,'" *Revue d'Histoire Littéraire de la France*, 1919, pp. 87–93; and René Jasinski, "Sur le 'Saint Julien L'Hospitalier' de Flaubert," *Revue d'Histoire de la Philosophie*, April 15, 1935, pp. 156–172. It must also be recalled that Flaubert's journey to the Near East provided him with vivid images of leprosy. See Sergio Cigada's well-documented essay "L'Episodio del Lebbroso in 'Saint Julien L'Hospitalier,'" *Aevum*, September-December 1957, pp. 465–491.

figures, like statues in slow motion. But the most masterful Flaubertian touches are those which communicate an
uncanny poetry of darkness and of silence. The rooms of
the palace are "filled with twilight." The shadows of the
trees cover the moss; and in the heart of the woods the
obscurity becomes "profound." As for the silence, it
amounts almost to an unheard music. In the white marble
palace, the silence is such that one can hear the rustle of
a scarf or the echo of a sigh.

Although Flaubert claimed to have recaptured the imag-
inative world of medieval legends and of iconography,
there are some differences which point to a total departure
from the spirit of the sources. I refer not only to the concern for structure, rhythm and symmetry, nor to the taste
for the somewhat artificial picturesque detail (archaic
forms, terms of venery, epic enumerations, lists of sonorous names of dogs and falcons), but to Julien's choice to
remain utterly alone in penitence. For according to the
folkloric tradition, his wife accompanies him on the hard
road toward salvation. Marcel Schwob very astutely comments that the Julien of the legend, submissive to his destiny, is a man who does not know guilt.[5] He is apparently
not in need of that solitude sought by the anguished soul.
And this is the significant difference—a difference which
makes of this work something of a fascinating, disturbing
and unwitting confession: Flaubert's Julien feels secretly
and irremediably *guilty*.

To insist almost exclusively on the technical features
of the tale—as so many critics have done—represents therefore a very limited reading of the text. Some go so far as
to banish any "meaning" whatsoever from *Saint Julien*.
René Descharmes, for instance, not only refuses to read
any psychology into the work, but categorically denies
that there is any significance to be derived from it.[6] Ac-

---

5 Schwob, "Saint Julien L'Hospitalier," in *Spicilège*, p. 79.
6 Descharmes, " 'Saint-Julien L'Hospitalier' et 'Pécopin,' " *Revue
Biblio-Iconographique*, 1905, pp. 1–7; 67–75. This view has of
course been challenged. Benjamin Bart, for instance, believes
that concern for symmetry and harmony of structure have led

cording to him—and this seems to be the prevailing view—
Saint Julien is nothing more than a fully satisfying *esthetic*
construction.

It is true that Flaubert himself, in his conversations as
well as in his letters, repeatedly denounced "moral" preoccupations in art as a sure source of boredom and in-
authenticity (though the didactic heresy was not always
absent from his literary enterprises: *Bouvard et Pécuchet*
is a most ambiguous work in this respect). But granted
that *Saint Julien* is pure of any such intention, it is obvious
that a work can be deeply meaningful, in personal as well
as in artistic and thematic terms, without any clearly formulated moral or conceptual preoccupations on the part
of the author. To a careful reader, aware moreover of the
many threads which bind this unassuming tale to the rest
of Flaubert's writing, *Saint Julien* is undeniably a most
rewarding text for close scrutiny. It offers some search-
ing insights into the author's own tormented psyche.

Family, Blood and Guilt

Perhaps the most significant departure from the sources
is Flaubert's insistence on Julien's family situation. Whereas traditional accounts—for instance that of Saint Antonin,
which proceeds immediately to the hunt—do not deal with
the world of his parents,[7] Flaubert devotes a relatively great
amount of space to the future saint's relations with his
father and mother, and to his "home"-atmosphere. "Father"
and "mother" are the very first words of his text. And the
opening paragraphs are exclusively devoted to the evocation of family values: order, peace and security. The family
castle is a solid establishment. Solidity is, as it were, the
central motif of these first pages. The four towers are
covered with plates of lead, the heavy walls are supported

Flaubert to a "moral structure" as well ("The Moral of Flaubert's
Saint Julien," *Romanic Review*, February 1947, pp. 23–33). The
equation of beauty and morality does not, however, account for any
personal or intentional meanings.

[7] See Marcel Schwob, "Saint Julien L'Hospitalier," in *Spicilège*.

by massive rocks. And with solidity goes self-sufficiency, opulence and a sense of protection. Several enclosures enfold this world on itself. The castle has its own bakery, wine presses, stables and granary. Nothing seems to be lacking in this well-provided, well-ordered, well-administered little universe. The shiny locks, the rich tapestries, the closets filled with linens, the cellars filled with wine, and the coffers filled with bags of silver symbolize a sense of property and of propriety which—if translated into "bourgeois" terms—is reminiscent of Flaubert's own prosperous, well-established, respected and respectable family. And yet this peace and order the young Julien feels somehow compelled to disrupt. The tale is first of all the account of a moral and psychological explosion.

The paternal house—or castle—is indeed a place of security; it is also one of enclosure. Walls protect, but they also imprison. This world of towers, hedges and enclosures is a private world, an inner world—but it is also a contained world from which one may need to burst out, even if the price be the very loss of the much-needed security. This ambivalence (one of the aspects of the dialectics of immurement and freedom) is further stressed by the dual and contradictory values represented by the father and the mother. The very prophecies concerning Julien's future seem mutually exclusive. The mother is told by the old hermit that Julien will become a saint; the father is promised by the old gypsy that his son will become a glorious warrior. That Julien, despite the apparent incompatibility, will in fact be both warrior and saint only stresses the fundamental tension between thought and action, between the life of the spirit and the life of material exigencies and worldly success. There is little doubt that in Flaubert's own private universe, the father—an energetic and successful physician—represented activity, responsibility and practical achievement, whereas his mother, soon to become a widow, stood for the monastic values of retirement, serenity, meditation and passivity.

This polarization of the parents is quite obvious in the tale. The mother, who is modest, serious and thoughtful, has organized her household "like the interior of a convent" (I). The father, on the other hand, appears in the triple rôle of warrior, initiator and judge. He is the arbiter of his vassals' quarrels, he advises the peasants (Flaubert's father was revered by the simple folk of Rouen), he teaches Julien the art of venery, presents him with a pack of dogs, and entertains his old war companions. Ironically, it is with the very sword which his own father gave him that Julien by accident almost kills him before even leaving the castle.

Surely the figure of this competent and materially minded, benevolent father, husband and justicer suffices to give some relevance to the Sartrean analysis of the relations of Gustave with the grave Dr. Flaubert, médecin-chef of the Hôtel-Dieu in Rouen. According to Sartre, the "terrible docteur" was a heavy presence: he dominated his son, he destroyed his spiritual longings toward faith, he was responsible for his monastic writer-vocation and even for his dose of femininity.[8] Even after allowing for much sophisticated exaggeration and dogmatic prejudice, Sartre's diagnosis of Flaubert's father-fixation and father-contempt comes much closer to the truth than the traditional view—for which Flaubert himself is in large part responsible—of an admiring son, filled with affection and with esteem for his meritorious father.[9] In reality, the philistine limita-

[8] Sartre, *Critique de la raison dialectique*, pp. 46–48.
[9] In understandable reaction to Sartre's excessive affirmations, Jean Bruneau maintains that Flaubert had a deep love for his father (*Les Débuts littéraires de Gustave Flaubert, 1831–1845*, p. 88, n. 40). But Bruneau's assertion, in an otherwise solid and cautious study, is based on rather weak evidence: a youthful statement in *Souvenirs, Notes et Pensées intimes* (*ibid.*, p. 279, n. 88) and the suggestion that Dr. Flaubert was not quite the philistine Maxime Du Camp made him out to be. The proof is thin. Bruneau, on the other hand, strangely neglects the implications of *Saint Julien*, which he considers exceptionally, a work of "pure imagination" (*ibid.*, p. 481). Moreover, there is very little in Flaubert's work that can possibly suggest love for his father. In *L'Éducation sentimentale* and in *Un Coeur simple* (the text richest in evocations of his own childhood) the father is totally absent.

tions of Dr. Flaubert were only too evident to the sensitive Gustave, and on such occasions as the family voyage to Italy, during Caroline's honeymoon, these limitations appeared almost as a caricature of the bourgeois. To be sure, when convenient, Flaubert derived considerable pride from his family's status in Rouen (at the time of his trial, for instance, he considered this status as a weighty argument in his favor); but it is clear also that he derived considerable satisfaction from indirect, and perhaps only partly conscious, debunking of his father's values and professional abilities. The clubfoot incident in *Madame Bovary* (it would seem that Flaubert read a treatise which mentions an unsuccessful treatment of a clubfoot by his very father[10]), and even more the relevant pages in *Bouvard et Pécuchet*, should be read in this light. It is also significant that the father and the mother, in *Saint Julien*, hide from each other the contradictory prophecies they have heard: the secret they do not want to share is symbolic of a fundamental disharmony.

The Oedipal situation in *Saint Julien* is bound up with the theme of escape and liberation. The young man, having discovered death, discovers also a basic rift and a latent chaos in the apparent order. He not only desires to elude his destiny, but feels positively ill at ease in an oppressive and confining family atmosphere. Symbolically, he now wants to hunt "loin du monde"—alone and far from everyone. Symbolically also, he is attracted to vast forests and interminable plains. He develops a taste for the absolute and appears to be absorbed by deep meditation. Most significant, even his mother's kisses are now met with reluctance ("il acceptait froidement son étreinte" I). Flaubert's tale is in part the account of a rebellion weakened by scruples and by infinite regrets. Nothing is more pitiful than Julien's ultimate nostalgia for family life. The hermit,

[10] See Jean Pommier, "Noms et prénoms dans 'Madame Bovary,'" *Mercure de France*, June 1949, pp. 244–264. The treatise in question is Vincent Duval's "Traité Pratique du pied-bot" (1839), which mentions a ten-year-old girl treated by Dr. Flaubert, and "enfermée dans des attelles de fer"—without any sign of improvement.

living alone near the big river, occasionally feels the yearning to plunge into the life of a community just to feel
human contact. And as he glimpses through ground-floor
windows old men holding infants on their knees, he feels
"choked with sobs" (III). Similarly Flaubert, the Croisset
hermit, occasionally visited the capital, only to seek refuge
once more in the house near the "big river." And nothing
is more pathetic—and also more relevant to Julien's situation—than Flaubert's confession to George Sand, written
only a short time before composing the tale: "I adore
children, and I was born to be an excellent daddy. . . . It
is one of the melancholies of my old age not to have a little
being to love and to caress."[11]

But more significant than these affinities between the
medieval and the nineteenth-century hermits is the deep-
rooted obsession with parricide which pervades the entire
tale. For parricide in *Saint Julien* is not merely a fact, it
is a permanent and haunting terror. Uncanny incidents
announce a fate that cannot be eluded: the sword which
Julien clumsily lets fall almost wounds his father; the
javelin which he aims at what he takes to be a stork almost
kills his mother; animals lead him to the place where
he will murder his parents. And the outraged and accus-
ing glance of these animals is like a parental reproach.
The huge stag he has mortally wounded looks at him like
a solemn "patriarch," or better still, like a "justicer." A
strong sense of guilt darkens the entire work, a guilt which
preëxists to the actual fact of the crime. For Julien, long
before his dreadful deed, is terrorized by his own potential,
by his inner temptation. "Si je le voulais, pourtant? . . ."
(I) he asks himself in anguish, aware of a personal demon
(the word "diable" is actually used) that propels him to
criminal action. And when the parricide is consummated,
Julien's memory assumes a nightmarish turn, as it constantly reënacts the deed which he both needed and hated

<hr>

[11] Flaubert, *Corresp.*, VIII, 209–210.

to commit: "chaque nuit, en rêve, son parricide recommençait" (III).

The association of the animals, his parents and the murder is particularly interesting. Animals and the hunt are of course an important element in the folk legend concerning Julien. But not only is there an extraordinary concentration of animals in Flaubert's tale, it is also quite obvious that he has tried more consciously to establish a correspondence between the beasts and the theme of parricide. The weird invulnerability of the animals in the surrealistic sequence that precedes the murder is symbolic of a conscience that refuses to be silenced. The beasts and the motif of bestiality are deeply bound up with the father and the mother images. (Does he not mistake his mother for an animal?) In one of the most curious sentences of *Saint Julien*, this relationship is explicitly stated: "il lui semblait que du meurtre des animaux dépendait le sort de ses parents" ("it seemed to him that his parents' fate depended on the murder of the animals" II). Finally, the impassioned killing of his parents, in bed and in a blind spell of sexual jealousy, adds further weight to this important theme.

The violence and indulgence in cruelty which characterize *Saint Julien* are another "personal" Flaubertian element. In this short work, as much if not more so than in *Salammbô*, Sainte-Beuve might have detected a "pointe d'imagination sadique." When Julien, as a boy, discovers the reality of death, he discovers at the same time his own destructive urges. The hunt becomes for him a mere pretext for murder and gratuitous savagery. But it is not a simple exercise in brutality. His surprise when he watches the bleeding mouse, his delight when his dogs break the rabbits' backs, the zest with which he lops off the rooster's feet, the joy with which he plunges his dagger into the goat, the skillful thoroughness with which he kills cranes with his whip—all this sanguineous enthusiasm points to an infantile sadism and to a savagely voluptuous imagination which links agony and guilt with the earliest manifestations of sex. Flaubert's vocabulary is here of the utmost interest. The convulsions of the pigeon Julien strangles fill him with a "volupté sauvage et tumultueuse." At the bird's ultimate spasm of life he almost swoons ("il se sentit défaillir"). Similarly, at the thought of real carnage, "il suffoqua de plaisir." His arrows produce "enfonçures" in the mass of the animals. Dreams and acts of slaughter soon assume orgiastic proportions. There is no end to his murderous appetite: "Julien did not tire of killing." After the massacre, he contemplates with an "oeil béant" the enormities he has committed (I). Then, as after an orgy, an "immense sadness" overcomes him. The taste for blood grows into a real addiction: his very notion of Paradise is a place where he sees himself surrounded by animals he can kill. The murder of his parents in his own bed is characteristically gory: splashes and "pools" of blood cover their white bodies, the bedsheet, the ground; they stain an ivory figure of Christ hanging in the alcove. This taste for physical horror comes to a climax in the final scene, when the leper with the running sores and nauseous breath penetrates into Julien's bed.

What immeasurably increases the interest of these themes of the hunt and of cruelty is that they are here clearly coupled with the theme of failure—not to say impotence. The heaviness of the atmosphere is oppressive, at times paralyzing. The "lac figé"—that immobilized, imprisoned body of water, almost Mallarmean in its sterile nature—is an objective correlative of an inner landscape that becomes increasingly static and demoralizing. Even the amazing energy that goes into killing becomes ineffectual in the face of a quantitative massiveness. The proliferation of phenomena is such that the human will and the human deed turn out to be derisory: "cela n'en finissait pas" (II). The hunt ultimately appears like a desperate and futile effort in a noxious dream.

The oneiric oppression and sense of frustration become the central motif in the second hunt, when invulnerable animals seem to mock and defy the ineffectual huntsman. But it is not so much the animals who are endowed with invulnerability, as it is Julien's own weapons which prove to be inoffensive. His arrows, aimed at the wild animals, land like gentle white butterflies. His lance, as it reaches the bull, bursts into fragments. Freudian exegetes and symbol hunters could hardly hope to find a more rewarding document.

What develops is a sense of entrapment. From the beginning of the tale, the paternal castle, with its enclosures and walls, suggests confinement and constriction. No real liberation occurs. The departure, the crime, the penance, and even the eventual sainthood—the elements of the basic folk story—do not free Julien from the obsession with immurement and ensnarement, so central also in *Madame Bovary*, and again in *Salammbô*, where an entire army is trapped. In *Saint Julien*, the animals who at the beginning were trapped by the protagonist (there is a parallel between the "cirque" and the "défilé de la Hache" in *Salammbô*), later, during the second hunt, form "a narrow circle" around the powerless huntsman. The cluttered forest, through which he has to cut his way, is similarly a confining element from which he feels the need to extricate himself. And the peering eyes of the animals staring at him are like an exteriorization of his own ensnaring conscience. A chronic and inescapable sense of guilt is indeed one of the most fundamental traits of the Flaubertian psychology: not a Christian guilt, but a deep-rooted sense of the *péché d'exister*, almost Sartrean in nature, and which explains perhaps why Sartre has been for so long fascinated and at the same time repelled by Flaubert.

It is easy to see by what logic the frenzy of destruction ultimately results in an urge to self-destruction. An oppressive sense of guilt leads to dreams of annihilation which, echoing similar dreams in other works of Flaubert, constitute a recurrent and major theme. Julien, the torturer, becomes the self-torturer. His own person inspires him with an invincible aversion. The temptation of suicide compels him to expose himself to countless perils. But salvation, he learns, cannot be achieved through the simple refusal to live. Saintly abnegation is for him the only death in this life—which is also a form of reconquest and repossession. Sainthood, in Flaubertian terms, is of course a concept which, together with monasticism, can easily be related to the artist's self-abnegation. "I live like a Carthusian friar"—"I live like a monk"—these expressions occur repeatedly in his correspondence, and they are always related to his dedication to the mystique of Art. The need to abhor his flesh is certainly not a religious reaction with Flaubert, but it is a manifestation of a deep-seated hate of life on the one hand (". . . moi je la déteste, la vie"[12]), and on the other a permanent spiritual quest. Flaubert, who did not strictly speaking write a "novel of the artist," is nonetheless an outstanding illustration of the modern writer's tendency to make of the artist—himself—the hero of his own creation. In the nineteenth century, Art becomes the subject of art, and Thought the subject of thought. The artist, even when he feels saved by Art, is caught in his own private drama, in the mirror-disease of his own mind.

Thus, despite the artistic "distance" the author establishes between himself and the subject of his tales, despite the apparent quest for a formal perfection, there is much in this short work that is extremely self-revealing. The theme of isolation is perhaps nowhere more bitter in Flaubert. Of all his characters, Julien is probably the most "alone." Emma at least had her lovers, Mathô has Spendius as a companion, and Frédéric has his childhood friend Deslauriers. Even Saint Antoine, the hermit, has the company of the loquacious Hilarion. In fact, the notion of the "couple" seems quite basic to the structure of many of Flaubert's novels, culminating in the caricatures of Bouvard

12 Flaubert, *Corresp.*, III, 398. Curiously, what follows is: "Je suis un catholique; j'ai au coeur quelque chose du suintement vert des cathédrales normandes. . . . "

and Pécuchet, who in turn seem to prefigure the pathetic couples of Samuel Beckett. Only Julien, and to some extent Félicité (who is also a manner of saint), are deprived of companionship. The weird silence which reigns throughout the story stresses the saint's alienation.

This aloneness is of course only one aspect of the work. A latent fear of life is another of Flaubert's basic themes. Did he not, at the age of twenty-five, advise a friend never to marry, never to have any children, to have as few sentimental attachments as possible so as to remain least vulnerable (". . . offre le moins de prise à l'ennemi"[13])? The enemy, of course, was life itself. This fear of life he later freely confessed. To George Sand he admitted that he had been a "coward" in his youth: "*j'ai eu peur* de la vie."[14] The statement, in Flaubert's case, must be taken quite literally. His fear is really a form of horror and revulsion: "Life is such a hideous thing that the only way to bear it is to avoid it."[15] This escapism explains in part Flaubert's ambiguous attitude toward "reality": a mixture of fascination and repugnance. For quite surely Flaubert was not merely trying to justify an esthetic aberration when he wrote to Laurent Pichat, the director of the *Revue de Paris*, which was publishing *Madame Bovary*, that the "ignoble reality" described in the novel made him sick, that he abhorred "la vie ordinaire."[16]

Flaubert's chronic attraction to unreality and "surreality," the recurrent motifs of metamorphosis and undoing, have no doubt much to do with this need for escape. The very structure of *Saint Julien* produces the effect of a succession of tableaux which rapidly glide by and fade into each other. Flaubert's conscious desire was evidently to reproduce, in literary terms, the rhythm and the atmosphere produced by a sequence of frescoes or a series of stained glass windows. But the technique goes in depth, and represents more than a literary exercise. The very articulations of the narrative ("Puis," "Cependant," "Bien-

[13] Flaubert, *Corresp.*, I, 200.   [14] Flaubert, *Corresp.*, VII, 122.
[15] Flaubert, *Corresp.*, IV, 182.   [16] Flaubert, *Corresp.*, IV, 125.

tôt"), the fading and melting of forms, the movement of dark shapes—all this suggests a constant alteration. The world of Flaubert is indeed a strange combination of sameness and undoing, of immobility and violence, of stasis and destruction. Are creation and destruction "sisters," as Marcel Schwob suggests? Certainly the very blending in one single character of a potential for annihilation and a potential for sainthood is highly revealing.

Finally, this very theme of sainthood is an important key to the understanding of Flaubert's work. Whether it is Saint Antoine, Saint Julien or the saintly provincial virgin who was to develop into the conception of Madame Bovary, the central figure remains that of a human being tormented by his own inherence, dreaming of an impossible escape and an unattainable absolute. It is this dissatisfaction and this longing, this condemnation to the self and this desire to transcend it which bring out in Flaubert's work this "aspiration vers l'infini" which, according to Baudelaire, is one of the most significant characteristics of Romanticism. There is little doubt that his obsession with the theme of sainthood marks, in its various disguises and avatars, a definite crisis of faith. Sartre makes Flaubert's father directly responsible for this crisis: ". . . this crushing father who did not cease, even once dead, to destroy God."[17] Sartre's blunt emphasis on the nefarious influence of one of the parents is thoroughly dogmatic and fails to take into account the role of the mother. But if indeed, as is very possible, the materialistic Doctor was an impediment to his son's idealistic aspirations—if indeed, to use Sartre's image, he partly succeeded in killing "God" in him—then the theme of parricide, related to the theme of sainthood, takes on a renewed meaning.

[17] Sartre, *Critique de la raison dialectique*, p. 46.

7

Un Coeur simple:

TENDERNESS AND IRONY

At first glance, *Un Coeur simple* seems equally removed from the turbulent world of *Saint Antoine* and the satire of *Madame Bovary* and *Bouvard et Pécuchet*. Flaubert himself, in sketching an outline of the story for Mme Roger des Genettes, insisted that it was in no way ironic, but rather "serious" and extremely "sad."[1] Admittedly, this account of the obscure life of a tender, devout, naïve peasant girl was to be different from anything he had written so far. Under the influence of his friend George Sand, who gently admonished him to devote himself to a literature of consolation rather than of desolation, Flaubert set out to "move and make cry" all tender-hearted readers, being—as he affirmed—tender-hearted himself. The story is simple enough. A country maid who spends her entire life in humble and dedicated domestic service loves successively a man who abandons her, the children of her mistress (the one dies, the other becomes a good-for-nothing), a nephew who dies in a distant land, an old man in the last stages of his illness, until she finally discovers a superior happiness with a parrot which she has stuffed after he also dies. This stuffed bird, the sole consolation in her own lonely death, becomes for her a mystic fetish. *Un Coeur simple* tells the pathetic story of a *servante au grand coeur*, a woman poor in spirit but immensely rich in her capacity to serve and love.

How "different," however, is the tone of this work?

[1] Flaubert, *Corresp.*, VII, 307. Complete citations for all notes may be found in the Bibliography.

One could stress any single mood or motif—pathos, irony, critique of stupidity, denunciation of the world's indifference to goodness, inadequacy of sainthood—only to discover that it appears with frequency elsewhere in Flaubert's writings. Even more characteristic are the key elements which relate this tale to the fundamental aspects of *bovarysme*: the need and ability to transfer dreams; the tendency to objectify longings by "attaching" dreams to external realities (whether Emma's lovers or Félicité's parrot); the indefatigable succession and repetition of images suggesting an unwillingness ever to resign oneself or to be cured from illusion by anything short of death; an elemental selfishness and solipsism (Félicité's confining deafness); and finally the recurrent notion of a "sensualité mystique" (V).

Overtly or implicitly, the subject of sainthood is at the heart of the *Trois contes*. In fact, it reappears insistently throughout Flaubert's work. While on his African journey, his head still filled with the anguish of Saint Antoine, Flaubert dreamed of several possible subjects, among which were the story of a woman who longs to be possessed by a god and that of a mystic Flemish virgin who lives and dies in a provincial town. The former, as we have seen, is at the origin of *Salammbô*. The latter became *Madame Bovary*. But it is clear that much of the primitive outline passed into *Un Coeur simple*, just as the episodic character of Catherine Leroux, who appears in all her peasant simplicity in the famous "comices" chapter of *Madame Bovary*, prefigures Félicité. Of this unity in his writings Flaubert himself was partially aware—though he tended to view it as a weakness rather than a virtue.[2]

Glancing at the external circumstances of Flaubert's life in the years 1875–1876, one can easily guess what ties bind this short story to his intimate sorrows. The predominant mood of tenderness and sadness corresponds to

[2] See the already quoted letter to Louis Bouilhet where he complains of the underlying kinship of his literary plans (Flaubert, *Corresp.*, II, 253–254).

a general state of depression from which he suffered ever since the Franco-Prussian war. His mother's death, in 1872, intensified the solitude he felt after the loss of his close friend Louis Bouilhet. Sainte-Beuve had also disappeared, and soon it was to be the turn of Théophile Gautier. The year of *Un Coeur simple*, 1876, was another year of mourning. News of the death of Louise Colet, his former mistress, brought back painful memories. Finally George Sand, the warm-hearted friend and confidante of his later years, she for whose sake *Un Coeur simple* was undertaken, died when the tale was only half finished, thus confirming an already pervasive sense of futility: "Il en est ainsi de tous nos rêves."[3] In him, and all about him, he felt decline, silence and desertion. The sense of gloom was further intensified when Flaubert generously sacrificed his personal fortune to save his niece's husband from bankruptcy. There was even some fear that he might have to sell his house in Croisset. Fortunately, it never quite came to that. But he did sell the family estate in Deauville, a deeply painful experience, not only because Deauville and nearby Trouville were fraught with memories (not the least of which was the encounter with Mme Schlésinger), but because in Flaubert's imagination the forced sale of property repeatedly symbolizes moral degradation, betrayal of the past and profanation. The anguish at the auction sale at the end of *L'Éducation sentimentale* was thus relived by Flaubert in his private life before it found a renewed echo in *Un Coeur simple* when Mme Aubain's furniture, after she dies, is appropriated or sold by her daughter-in-law, leaving the old house woefully empty and poor Félicité "ivre de tristesse" (IV).

The documentary trip which Flaubert made to Honfleur and Pont-l'Evêque in April, 1876, as he worked on *Un Coeur simple*, thus takes on added meaning. It is his own past he was out to recapture in this "bain de souvenirs."[4] The story of the faithful servant, symbol of allegiance and

[3] Flaubert, *Corresp.*, VIII, 65.
[4] Flaubert, *Corresp.*, VII, 296.

devoted memory, is moreover studded with evocative details. Many of the characters are clearly modeled on familiar figures from a now irretrievable past. Mme Aubain resembles an old cousin, Félicité a maid in the service of the Barbey family, Paul and Virginie play the games that Flaubert played with his own sister Caroline (now also dead), the marquis de Gremanville shows some similarities with a distant great-uncle. Even Loulou the parrot existed in real life: Captain Barbey had brought him back from one of his long trips overseas.

More poignant still to the author must have been the bittersweet pleasure of resurrecting privileged moments of another period. When Paul and Virginie, during the family expedition to the old farm, are amused by the enormous syringe they discover on the oak dresser, when they play with the pewter bowls, the wolf traps and the sheep shears, it is clear that it is the author himself who delightedly and sadly rummages through his own dear and now distant memories as he describes the old farmhouse with its "air of antiquity," its worm-eaten beams, its walls black with smoke and its window panes gray with dust (II). Even more elusive moments are relived in all their happy fragility: the sea, smooth as a mirror, glittering in the sunshine; the twittering of unseen sparrows; the immobility of those summer hours which every child has known. No work of Flaubert is richer in the poetry of intimate sensations. As the children hunt for shells, jellyfish and sea urchins, or as they take a nap in a darkened room while the relentless summer light shines in dazzling through the slats of the blinds, Flaubert revisits the *luoghi ameni* of his childhood.

Softness and sadness are the predominant mood: "tout semblait vivre dans une douceur profonde" (III). These simple words sum up the emotion of the two women—the mistress and the maid—as they survey (again on a summer day) the relics of Virginie: her dresses, her moth-eaten plush hat, her dolls, the washbasin she had used.

Summer occupies indeed a privileged position in *Un Coeur simple*. It is in August that Félicité has her first contact with a village dance and is brutally initiated to love; it is in July that her beloved Victor sails for Havana. Her own death occurs amidst "summer smells" and the buzzing of flies. Summer represents, as it were, the time of memory in *Un Coeur simple*. This is hardly surprising if one considers the genesis of the story and the evocation of the cherished *fantômes* of the vacations in Trouville.[5] The sanctity of even the most discordant memories is admirably suggested by an image Flaubert uses to describe Félicité's room. "This place, to which few people were ever admitted, looked simultaneously like a chapel and a bazaar" (IV). The fusion of miscellany and piety is, of course, habitual with Flaubert.

The meaning of the tale is in large part to be derived from this tone of tenderness and compassion. Any denial of the authenticity of this tone, on the assumption that goodness is here shown to be inept and that Flaubert could not possibly feel anything but contempt for as stupid a creature as Félicité, is most emphatically a misreading of the work. It is true that tenderness appears at first *negatively*, by a steady insistence on the victimized status of the "heroine." Félicité is not graced by nature, and she is exploited by her fellow human beings. For one hundred francs a year—so we learn in the second sentence of the story—she does all the cooking and the housework, the washing, the ironing and the sewing, not to mention various duties in the stable and in the barnyard. This theme of "exploitation" with which the story opens undergoes developments and variations. Thus Félicité is taken advantage of by a ruthless sister and her greedy family. But her innocence is such, her ignorance and saintlike naïveté prove to be so incorruptible, that nothing, neither betrayal nor loss, can embitter her.

Félicité is, however, more than a submissive victim.

[5] For a detailed study of Flaubert's fondest memories, see Gérard-Gailly's *Flaubert et "les Fantômes de Trouville."*

Her virtues are shown as positive—to begin with, her capacity to love, which remains unadulterated to the very end. In fact, this capacity seems to grow: "La bonté de son coeur se développa" (III). This congenital talent shows up as soon as she enters into the service of the Aubain family. The young children seem to her "made of some precious substance"; covering them with kisses becomes an almost compulsive activity (II). Her capacity for identifying scenes from life around her with scenes in the Gospels is paralleled by her tendency to identify herself with others and thus attain an almost miraculous self-abnegation. Watching Virginie during her first Communion, "it seemed to her that she herself was that child." Vicarious experience goes hand in hand here with utter generosity and lack of self-awareness. After Félicité saves the two children from a charging bull, it does not even occur to her that she may have been heroic. Nothing could be more appropriate than the image of vitality and bounty with which Flaubert closes the story of her life. Félicité's heartbeat grows slower and slower like a fountain running dry. The compassionate account of this simple woman at times comes close to hagiography. Thus Félicité takes care of the victims of cholera and later tends to a poor old man with a horrible tumor on his arm. Hers is the story of unsparing service, of a totally gratuitous and pathetically inefficacious tenderness.

"This time, they will no longer say that I am inhuman," Flaubert wrote to Mme Roger des Genettes.[6] Flaubert's protestation must be taken at face value. Félicité's innocence in a world she fails to understand, her touching and blissful stupidity, probably had a special meaning for Flaubert at the time he was slowly recovering from a period of despair. He needed this consolation and this self-administered lesson in humility. 1875–1876 was probably the gloomiest year in his life. Filled with self-pity,

6 Flaubert, *Corresp.*, VII, 331.

sapped by defeatism (he lost faith even in literature),[7] he created a figure of a humble servant, uncomplaining and capable of transcending her own suffering through love. Like that of Saint Julien, the story of Félicité had therapeutic value.

Yet the prerogatives of art and the virtuosity of the novelist pressed themselves to the forefront. When Flaubert writes of the day when the parrot Loulou enters into the house: "Ce jour-là, il lui advint un grand bonheur" (III)—it is not an expression of gratuitous irony at the expense of Félicité, but a stylistic device which guarantees the integrity of the character's point of view. In none of his works did Flaubert set out to accomplish a more difficult and at the same time a more typically Flaubertian feat. Only the most refined irony, in the esthetic sense, could have brought about a sophisticated insight into such a human being, and provided a fully articulate account of emotions that could not possibly have been articulated by as primitive a creature. On another level, the erosive flow of time is rendered by means of an evocative density which transmutes lived time into ironic time.

Flaubert's tour de force is that he presents as a central character an individual devoid of any gift of articulation, and yet makes us participate in her vision of things. The horizon of Félicité's private world steadily narrows. In her progressive deafness, only the parrot's voice reaches her. "The little circle of her ideas grew narrower and narrower." She no longer "communicates" with anybody, but lives in a "somnambulist torpor" (IV). Her cluttered room, in which she locks up her precious stuffed parrot, becomes the exact measure of her universe. It is Flaubert's supreme achievement to have penetrated into this unintelligent intimacy. Only an essentially ironic method could place the reader simultaneously inside and outside the character.

[7] While in Concarneau with the naturalist Georges Pouchet, he envies men of science: "Cela ne vous lâche pas son homme comme la littérature." (Flaubert, *Corresp.*, VII, 268.)

Hence the ambiguous nature of many sentences. When the long weeds bent over the river are compared to the hair of corpses floating in the river, the metaphor provides a fusion of Flaubert's poetry and of Félicité's wild grief (III). It is noteworthy, however, that for once Flaubert almost totally avoids the free indirect discourse, his habitual instrument of oblique intervention. He does not use it even to suggest the faint inner movements of Félicité's mind. The ironic texture is never permitted to subvert the directness and simplicity of her reactions.

Yet there are levels of irony in the tale which go beyond the requirements of artistic construction and dramatic point of view. The very names of the characters are not without an obvious ironic intention. Félicité, in objective terms, is hardly a "happy" creature. Nor is Mme Aubain particularly lucky, nor Théodore an outstanding example of a gift of the gods![8] M. Bourais' "sourire de cuistre" (III) when Félicité asks whether, in case of necessity, one can return from Havana by land, is not merely the smug smile of one who belongs to the vile race of the Homais, but almost a self-caricature. The author himself seems to relish Félicité's candor.

The satirical overtones of *Un Coeur simple* cannot be denied. That goodness should be embodied by an ignorant creature with a genius for confusing areas of experience may in itself be an indication of nothing more than an inveterate tendency on the part of Flaubert to wonder at the marvels of human stupidity. It is not at all sure that any intentional value can be ascribed to it. The parrot, however, is another matter. With his appearance in the tale, the author quite clearly transcends the anodyne ignorance of Félicité. Loulou, the parrot, repeats the clichés of human speech while delighted listeners indulge in further clichés on the subject of parrots. The impression is one of a closed circuit of inanity. Psittacism is a contagious disease—just as psittacosis; and it is, of course,

[8] See Paul Mankin's pertinent observations in "Additional Irony in 'Un Coeur simple,'" *The French Review*, February 1962, p. 411.

a further irony that Félicité dies of a bronchial pneumonia which can be one of the consequences of the so-called parrot fever. The symbol of the parrot is a real *trouvaille*, admirably suited to represent Flaubert's permanent fascination with the acute symptoms of mental vacuity. What lends the symbol additional pathos is that Flaubert himself as writer, though utilizing the cliché to denounce the cliché, feels constantly threatened by its all-invasive presence.[9]

But the satirical function of the parrot extends beyond human speech to the very level of belief and dogma. For Félicité not only falls in love with him ("he was almost a son, a lover . . ." IV), but ends up, after his death, by transforming his stuffed body into an icon, and she finally confuses him with the Holy Ghost. She gets into the habit of saying her prayers kneeling in front of Loulou, while the reflection of the sunlight in his glass eye sends her into ecstasies. The critique is obviously two-edged. Earlier in the story, Félicité is said to "understand nothing" concerning Catholic dogma, which casts considerable doubt both on her intelligence and on the intelligibility of the priests' message. When the deaf old servant later prays to a moth-eaten stuffed bird with a broken wing, the antireligious implications become even more obtrusive. Perhaps it is difficult to agree entirely with Ben Stoltzfus that *Un Coeur simple* is an "attack on organized religion and the church."[10] But certainly Loulou is Flaubert's symbol as much if not more so than Félicité's. And if Flaubert's satire is not aimed bluntly at the church or at organized religion, it is not only out of a taste and a dilection for ambiguities, but because his oblique attack, as elsewhere in his work, extends to the more general area of meaning.

The ironic modes in *Un Coeur simple* are thus traceable either to esthetic demands or to satirical velleities which

[9] Luc Dariosecq quite rightly relates Flaubert's desire for stylistic perfection to his "terreur du psittacisme" ("A propos de Loulou," *The French Review*, February 1958, pp. 322–324).

[10] Stoltzfus, "Point of view in 'Un Coeur simple,'" *The French Review*, October 1961, pp. 19–25.

tended to affirm themselves at the expense perhaps of the author's desire to create a compassionate tale. It cannot be said, however, that whatever cruelty does exist in this tale is directed primarily against the external world. Félicité is decidedly not Flaubert's victim! The cruelty, in an occult fashion, is largely self-directed. The author punishes himself for his own dreams. This perhaps is one of the basic differences between the vision of a Flaubert and that of a Stendhal. For whereas the author of the *Chartreuse* engages in a poetry of imaginary justification and compensation, granting his heroes attributes and victories of which he was always deprived, Flaubert endlessly ruminates over his losses and exposes his characters to frustration and erosion.[11] He thus seems to take an almost cruel pleasure in submitting Félicité to harassment and anguish. When she runs from Pont-l'Evêque to Honfleur to see her nephew off, he first has her take the wrong road and then has her arrive at the boat just as the gangway is pulled ashore. Similarly, she arrives at the convent in Honfleur when Virginie is already dead.

Perhaps the most gratuitously cruel incident occurs when Félicité, once again on the road to Honfleur, where she is carrying the dead parrot, is almost run down by a mail coach whose driver, angered by the deaf woman's lack of response to his warning shouts, raises his strong whip and gives her a lash from head to waist which knocks her down, wounded and unconscious. There was in fact no dramatic or thematic need for this detailed episode. Its cruelty is that much more revealing, especially if one connects it with another brutal "fall" on the highway: Flaubert's own seizure, in January 1844—over thirty years before he set out to write *Un Coeur simple*. The relation between the two episodes is unmistakable: the same winter scene, the same geographic locale, the same din and impression of being run over by galloping horses, the same

---

11 For a discussion of Stendhal's need for imaginary victories, see my chapter "Stendhal et son oeuvre: la victoire imaginaire," in *Stendhal et la voie oblique*, pp. 101–147.

discovery of blood as the two victims return to consciousness, the same pursuit of the journey to Honfleur.[12] But what concerns us is not the conscious or partially conscious autobiographical inspiration. It is the evidence of a self-directed pathos and cruelty.

This self-punishing descent into his past, however, is not an experience of horror. Flaubert feels pain, no doubt, but it is an elegiac, bittersweet pain as he conjures up a vanished reality into a dramatic presence. The mood is above all one of poetic grief. Never before in his work, or in his daily life, had Flaubert been so concerned with the distant memories of his childhood and adolescence. It is in that same year, 1876, just after he finished *Un Coeur simple*, that a former childhood friend, Gertrude Collier (now Mme Tennant), reappeared in his life. Flaubert was deeply moved, especially when Gertrude also went on a pilgrimage to Trouville. He wrote her: "Dear old Trouville! The best part of my youth was spent there . . . No tempest, my dear Gertrude, was able to erase these memories. Does the perspective of time enhance things? Was it really as beautiful, as nice?"[13] Now even the most unpleasant events are endowed with a luminous hue. Flaubert knew, of course, from past experience, certainly since writing *L'Éducation sentimentale*, that time can be both a gravedigger and a supreme alchemist.

The tale begins with an unmistakable temporal indication. "For half a century the women of Pont-l'Evêque envied Mme Aubain her maidservant Félicité." Also from the very start temporal suggestions are bound up with images of death, decay and semi-oblivion. Mme Aubain's husband died before the story begins. Her house is already filled with silent memories. The rooms smell a little musty, as the ground floor is on a level lower than the garden. There is a prevailing sensation of entombment. The furniture is of another period, and the drawing-room is always

[12] See the admirable and original treatment of this episode in Gérard-Gailly's *Flaubert et "les Fantômes de Trouville,"* pp. 205–206.
[13] Flaubert, *Corresp.*, VII, 378–379.

[243]

kept locked and full of furniture covered over with sheets. This atmosphere of mourning is graced by seventeenth-century etchings, "souvenirs of better days and vanished luxury" (I).

The omnipresence of Time is further brought out by the ageless face of Félicité and her unchanging costume, by the monotonous return of seasons and the steady hum of routine. "Tous les jeudis . . ."—"Chaque lundi matin . . ." —"Quand le temps était clair . . ."—"Un lundi . . .": the beginning of these paragraphs suggests an indeterminable dimension of time which assimilates and absorbs all events. Despite family losses, the world of *Un Coeur simple* is singularly eventless. Time is so overwhelmingly present that it is impermeable to occurrence. Not even history does here infringe on existence. Thus the July Revolution, in this provincial world, is marked only by the arrival of a new subprefect.

In fact, Flaubert's time, in *Un Coeur simple*, like Proust's reminiscences, involves a double perspective: time remembered, and the remembering of time. The evocation of a lost paradise turns into a mournful inventory of dispossession. Every morning, looking at her stuffed parrot, Félicité remembers "the old days." And indeed, her story is a succession of bereavements: her parents, Victor, Virginie, friends of Mme Aubain (Guyot, Liébard, Mme Lechaptois, Robelin, the old uncle Gremanville), Father Colmiche, Loulou, and finally Mme Aubain herself. It is at this level of retrospective grief that Flaubert's tale is most subjective and personally revealing. For he too, like Mme Aubain and Félicité, enjoyed staring at vestiges and relics. "What have you done with poor Mother's shawl and garden hat?" he asked his niece Caroline a few months after writing *Un Coeur simple*. "I looked for them in the drawer of the commode, but did not find them. For now and then I love to look at these objects again and to dream. With me, nothing is forgotten."[14]

The deepest level of irony thus corresponds to the re-

[14] Flaubert, *Corresp.*, VII, 367.

quirements of the narrative point of view, and combines satirical undertones with a stubborn delight in the pain of memory. Perhaps one could argue that the parrot, the embodiment of dreams, unintelligence and contempt, is the most complex single symbol in Flaubert's work. For he represents not merely Félicité's yearning and intellectual poverty, but the perversion of the Logos. This double treatment, at the level of character and at the level of concept, is made still more ironic by the implicit tension between the author and his material. For in the face both of Félicité's subjective confusion and of an objective "absence" and "silence," Flaubert remains tragically lucid and articulate.

If indeed Félicité is given to chronic confusion and a blurring of experiences culminating in the identification of her parrot and the Holy Ghost, this brings out an implicit drama of lucidity.[15] It is no doubt here, in this subjacent drama of awareness, that the real tension of the work is to be found. As is so often the case with Flaubert, the tragedy is essentially of an intellectual nature: the pain of facing a demythified reality. The old servant is relatively lucky: she lives a meaningless existence in a disconsolate world of which she herself is unable to make any critical assessment. For Félicité—and this is the supreme irony of an already ironic name—is truly fortunate. The suffering remains exclusively that of the omniscient and "impassive" author. Félicité cannot view her own fate; she does not even know that her story is one of pathos, tenderness, devotion and naïve moral beauty. The very description of such a character thus implies a great sense of distance and exclusion. The private world of Félicité remains locked in itself, innocent of corrosion by thought and doubt. And for this impossible innocence, Flaubert—especially in the year 1876—has an immense nostalgia.

[15] Anthony Thorlby sets forth the ingenious theory that realism is to Flaubert what the decrepit stuffed bird is to Félicité (*Gustave Flaubert and the Art of Realism*, p. 59). This is interesting and may well add another ironic dimension, but I find it difficult to agree completely. There seems to me no such gap between Flaubert's "lifelong yearning for real poetry" and the achievements of his so-called "realistic" art.

Hérodias

On servit des rognons de taureau, des loirs,
des rossignols, des hachis dans des feuilles de
pampre; et les prêtres discutaient sur la résurrection. Ammonius, élève de Philon le Platonicien,
les jugeait stupides, et le disait à des Grecs
qui se moquaient des oracles. Marcellus et Jacob
s'étaient joints. Le premier narrait au second le
bonheur qu'il avait ressenti sous le baptême de
Mithra, et Jacob l'engageait à suivre Jésus. Les
vins de palme et de tamaris, ceux de Safet et
de Byblos, coulaient des amphores dans les
cratères, des cratères dans les coupes, des coupes
dans les gosiers; on bavardait, les coeurs s'épan-
chaient. Iaçim, bien que Juif, ne cachait plus
son adoration des planètes. Un marchand d'Aphaka ébahissait des nomades, en détaillant les
merveilles du temple d'Hiérapolis; et ils de-
mandaient combien coûterait le pèlerinage.
D'autres tenaient à leur religion natale. Un Ger-
main presque aveugle chantait un hymne célé-
brant ce promontoire de la Scandinavie, où les
dieux apparaissent avec les rayons de leurs
figures; et des gens de Sichem ne mangèrent pas
de tourterelles, par déférence pour la colombe
Azima. (III)

(They served bull kidneys, dormice, nightingales, minced meat in vine leaves; and the priests
discussed the question of resurrection. Ammonius,
disciple of Philo the Platonist, thought them
stupid, and said so to some Greeks who were
making fun of oracles. Marcellus and Jakob had
met. The first was telling the second of the
happiness he had experienced on being baptized
into Mithras, and Jakob was urging him to follow Jesus. Palm and tamarisk wines, the wines
of Safet and Byblos, flowed from jars into bowls,
from bowls into cups, from cups into gullets;
there was much talking and all were in an ex-
pansive mood. Jacim, although a Jew, no longer
concealed his worship of the planets. A merchant
from Aphaka was dazzling the nomads by de-
tailing the wonders of the temple of Hierapolis,
and they were asking how much a pilgrimage
there would cost. Others held fast to the religion
of their birth. A German who was almost blind

sang a hymn of praise to that promontory of
Scandinavia where the gods appeared with their
radiant faces; and people from Sichem refused
to eat turtledoves, out of deference for the dove
Azima.)

This passage, so typical in its effects of variety, confusion and counterpoint, fulfills both a dramatic and a
thematic function preceding the climax in Section III of
Hérodias. Coming soon after the description of the lavish
banquet hall where the tetrarch Herod is entertaining
priests, Roman officers and notables of various faiths and
regions, it suggests the mounting frenzy of mind and body,
and sets the stage for Salome's dance and Saint John the
Baptist's decollation. The episode is based on accounts in
the gospels of Saint Matthew and Saint Mark, as well
as on a large iconography with which Flaubert was obviously familiar. The elaboration of details and the interpretation of psychological relationships and of events
are, however, Flaubert's own.

The story, in Flaubert's version, is set against a background of political tension. Herod, worried by the situation
at home and by military danger, anxiously awaits the
arrival of the Roman proconsul Vitellius and his legions—
though he is full of apprehension about them also. The
feast in celebration of his birthday is to have political as
well as diplomatic value. But when Vitellius and his decadent son Aulus arrive, it becomes increasingly clear that
Herod's worries are not exclusively political and military.
Symbolically locked up in a cistern like an underground
guilt, John the Baptist, known to the Jews as Iaokanann,
and reputed to be a resurrected Elias, continues to bellow
forth prophetic denunciations of the tetrarch's adultery
and incest, and to invoke eschatological punishment upon
the sinful Pharisees and Sadducees.

The gastronomic orgy and heated conversations thus
take place against a background of intrigue and fanaticism,
in a climate of latent guilt, suspicion, religious antagonisms
and racial hatreds. The appearance of rare dishes such as

bull kidneys and nightingales is preceded by agitated controversy on resurrection, and followed by explosions of bigotry and clear signs of a rebellious mood. Very skillfully Flaubert thus prepares the stage for Salome's dance. Almost without transitions, and with great naturalness, the political and religious turbulence is transmuted into sexual fever. The dance itself progresses from a mood of youthful expectation, to funereal despondency, to languid surrender, to brutal quest of satisfaction, and finally to a frenzy which mimes the female's lascivious ecstasy. This crescendo in turn builds up to the backstage execution of Iaokanann and to the lurid display, at the banquet table, of his decapitated head.

The beginning of the quoted paragraph reveals Flaubert's perennial fascination with eccentric feasts. His obsession with appetite and digestion comes to the fore in the figure of Aulus, who spends most of his time stuffing himself and vomiting. Aulus' capacity for gulping and guzzling is truly impressive. Once again, *goinfrerie* is the physical equivalent of a craving which betrays a fundamental lack of balance. Decadentism is here not merely a metaphor: Aulus, "this flower from the mud of Capri" (II), has participated in the debauches of Tiberius' imperial court, and was later to gain the favor of Caligula, Claudius and Nero. It would be a mistake, however, to attribute such decadent motifs to a simple desire to *épater le bourgeois*. The taste for truculence and exotic flight of fancy Flaubert carried deeply and permanently in himself. This, more so than any similarity of sources and setting, explains why he was so concerned with the danger of imitating *Salammbô*. He knew that the same fondness for the *gueulade* animated his Biblical tale. ". . . ça se présente sous les apparences d'un fort gueuloir . . ." he writes to Turgenev; and to Maupassant a few days later: "ça se gueule."[1]

The banquet, in addition to representing one of the set elements of the legend, is thus far from gratuitous. The

[1] Flaubert, *Corresp.*, VII, 369, 377. Complete citations for all notes may be found in the Bibliography.

personal and dramatic values of the episode are obvious. But its thematic function should not be overlooked. For this prelude to violence and death takes the form of a false communion. The guests partake of the same meats and wines, but nothing breaks down the barriers between them. Carnality is thus once again linked to the theme of incommunicability. On numerous other occasions the sharing of food, in Flaubert's novels, brings out a sense of distance and divorce. Emma Bovary feels most exasperated and lonely at mealtimes; the entire bitterness of her conjugal life seems served to her on her plate. Similarly, though in a different register, the dinner at the Café Anglais, in *L'Éducation sentimentale*, stresses the gap between Frédéric's desire and Rosanette's whorish perfidy. And after the supper he offers in his new apartment, the saddened young man feels as though a "large ditch filled with darkness" separates him from his friends (II, 2). An almost deathlike sterility is often associated, in Flaubert's work, with moments seemingly given over to sensuous provocation or satisfaction. Salome appropriately dances to the "funereal sound" of pipes. Death, of course, reigns in the very landscape of *Hérodias*. The hot wind seems to carry the stench of the accursed cities of Sodom and Gomorrah, buried under the heavy waters of the Red Sea. As for the mountains Herod surveys from the top of his citadel in Machaerus, they appear like tiers of huge petrified waves.

The opening sentence of the quoted paragraph is of further interest because of a characteristic construction repeated three times in the same passage. Its two parts are divided by a semicolon and by the conjunction *et*, which Flaubert here preferred to the more obvious temporal conjunctions *pendant que* or *tandis que*. The result is a total absence of subordination, and a leveling or equalization of all experience. The author subversively refuses to establish any hierarchy among the elements of the description or the events. Eating dormice and nightingales thus appears exactly as important, or unimportant, as discussing the question of resurrection. This juxtaposition of dissimilar elements is among Flaubert's favorite instruments of irony and intervention, one which he has inherited from the eighteenth-century ironists, in particular from Voltaire, whom he admired immensely. The paratactic *et* of course also helps establish an atmosphere of confusion, and suggests the din in the banquet hall; it does serve a function here not of consecutiveness but of simultaneity. Above all, it tends to discredit the manner and subject of the priests' discussion.

This equalization of values, leading to a pervasive relativism, is brought out even more sharply in the following sentence. A disciple of Philo the Platonist expresses his opinions about the stupidity of the priests to some Greeks, who in turn make known their contempt for oracles. The multiplicity of points of view is intensified by the fact that Philo was born a Jew (he represents Alexandrine Judaism) and that the Greeks, on the other hand, have become skeptical about their own traditions. This parallel and antithetic construction is carried on as we learn that Marcellus tells Jakob of the beauty of Mithraic initiation, while Jakob urges him to become a follower of Jesus. The syncretic tendencies of the conversations are neutralized by the fact that nobody seems really to listen. We witness a frantic bazaar of ideas, as Flaubert succeeds simultaneously in evoking the clash of beliefs and in establishing a climate of absurdity. Interest in the distant past and especially in the history of religions usually corresponds in him to his most pessimistic moods.

As the paragraph progresses, there is a crescendo of confusion and meaninglessness. The wines do not add to the lucidity of the guests. Flaubert insists on the variety and the flow of wines (from jars to bowls, from bowls to cups, from cups to gullets), and this variety and flow provoke and symbolize the nature of the conversation. Ebriety corresponds to ideological intemperance, to muddled talking and thinking. "Iaçim, bien que Juif, ne cachait plus son adoration des planètes." The sentence is loaded with the irony dear to the Encyclopedists. The "bien que Juif" stresses religious relativism; the adverb "plus" points simultaneously to the usual prudence of Iaçim and to the effects of alcohol. At the same time, religious beliefs are reduced to the level of personal preferences and passing fads, as erratic and eccentric as human temperaments under the effect of excessive libation.

Even more humorously degrading is the next sentence. A merchant flabbergasts the nomads by describing the marvels of the temple in Aphaka. *Merveilles* has an appropriate double sense: religion is here entrusted to the rhetoric of traveling salesmen. Religious pilgrimages are talked about as though they were visits to special fairs that should not be missed. Once again the sentence is divided by a semicolon followed by the conjunction *et,* thus establishing an ironic equality between the first part, in which the temple is extolled, and the second part, in which the listeners and putative converts inquire about the cost of the journey. A not so faint suggestion of charlatanism creeps into the account. Spirituality is replaced by pedestrian material concerns.

The last part of the paragraph completes the relativistic subversion. Flaubert utilizes the biblical historical moment to stress not revelation, but the absence of a unique Truth. "D'autres tenaient à leur religion natale." At first sight, the sentence seems to emphasize spiritual allegiance. But the very word "others" implies precisely that no experience is universal; it is a reminder of the fragmentary nature of experience. The allegiance is, moreover, of a very limited kind. The word "native" is brought into a critical, and potentially derogatory, association with the word "religion." The entire Voltairean heritage is felt in this sentence.

The climax occurs when the mystic song of a German praising the Northern gods is opposed antithetically to the superstitious refusal of the people of Sichem to eat turtledoves. Once again the semicolon followed by the conjunction *et* is the instrument of oblique irony. The evoked

THE NOVELS OF FLAUBERT

vision of divine figures appearing in all their radiance is brought into perfidious juxtaposition with some meaningless tribal taboo. The end of the sentence might have come straight out of the *Lettres persanes* or *Candide*. The sentence is doubly insidious, for the dove Azima is unmistakably an allusion to the Holy Ghost.

The paragraph which has been under discussion is an excellent example of Flaubert's passionate impartiality. For his apparent impassiveness is not to be taken as a sign of aloofness, but rather as the very method whereby he imposes his personal vision. It would be as wrong, however, to consider this style a proof of the author's archeological distance as it would to interpret such a passage as a blunt attack on religion. The critique goes deeper. Values, beliefs, truths, experiences—all these are thrust here, as elsewhere in Flaubert's work, into a hopeless juxtaposition. Coexistence brings about neither ultimate peace nor resolute war, but a latent frustration from which there is no cure. It makes of living and believing a chronic "impossibility." From contradictions arise neither a purifying conflict nor a definitive debate, but dizziness and surrender. Torn between incompatible imperatives, worn-out Herod gives up Iaokanann's head.

Although there is nothing in Flaubert's correspondence to indicate that he was interested in the mystic possibilities of the story (he claimed to be fascinated by the political and psychological elements), the tale suggests a nostalgia for that precisely which seems to be *absent*. If Flaubert can be said to "associate" with any of the characters in *Hérodias*, it is surely with the life-weary tetrarch. He was indeed very taken with this personage. "La vacherie d'Hérode pour Hérodias m'excite." And again: "What tempts me here is the official expression of Herod (who was a true prefect)."[2] But it is clear that the fascination, at least as it developed during the process of writing, had more to do with his sadness and his lethal fatigue. All

2 Flaubert, *Corresp.*, VII, 296, 309.

hope seems to escape from the fortress of Machaerus as the three men carry Iaokanann's heavy head toward Galilee. The end of *Hérodias*, appropriately ambiguous, reminds us that the spiritual theme is never absent in the *Trois contes*.

As usual, Flaubert reveals far more of himself than would at first be suspected. Personal memories are transmuted into a special form of poetry: the legend or historical fact "overdetermines" preëxisting experiences or velleities. This is especially obvious in the case of Salome's dance. The performance of Hérodias' daughter is indeed at the heart of the tale; it is that focal point in the genesis toward which all attitudes and events seem to converge. But its intimate significance is that it rehearses, after an interval of twenty-five years, the dances of the Near Eastern prostitutes Flaubert and his friend Bouilhet had witnessed in the house of the courtesan Kuchiouk Hanem during their journey through Egypt. It is clear that the dance of Salome was for Flaubert the culminating point of his tale. "I am sick with fear at the thought of Salome's dance. I'm afraid to spoil it," he writes to his niece Caroline.[3] The *Notes de voyages* of 1850 contained details which, from the point of view of 1876, present an undeniable proleptic interest. Aziza's motionless face as she dances with her neck sliding back and forth on her vertebrae ("terrifying effect of decapitation")[4] prefigures the expressionless face of Salome (". . . et son visage demeurait immobile" III). The performance of Kuchiouk Hanem, who during her dance gradually lowers the head until she reaches with her teeth a cup of coffee on the ground, prefigures Salome's feat of leaning over so low, with her legs spread apart, that her chin touches the floor. But far more interesting still is Flaubert's remark, in his 1850 travel notes, that while lying beside Kuchiouk, with his fingers passed through her necklace, he was reminded of

3 Flaubert, *Corresp.*, VIII, 14.
4 See Francis Steegmuller, *Flaubert and Madame Bovary*, p. 211.

Judith and Holofernes.[5] It is significant that from the outset the experience of the Near Eastern dance is associated with a biblical image, and more specifically with the decapitation of a man by a woman's will, in an atmosphere heavy with sexuality. The entire memory is further charged with a special melancholy, as Flaubert wonders whether Kuchiouk Hanem will think of him more than of the many others who have been there. The exercise of the senses leaves behind an acrid taste—an experience that was to become familiar in the fictional work of Flaubert.

Nothing is thus more deceptive than the apparent dryness and impartiality of the tone in *Hérodias*. The colors of the "Orient" and the tensions of the human drama are suggested in condensed, muscular, almost elliptic sentences. These sentences are often remarkable for their impeccable sobriety, which only stresses the latent violence of the atmosphere.

> Il fouilla d'un regard aigu toutes les routes. Elles étaient vides. Des aigles volaient au-dessus de sa tête; les soldats, le long du rempart, dormaient contre les murs; rien ne bougeait dans le château. (I)

It is truly a historian's style, exploiting in particular the resources of the indirect discourse:

> Vitellius demanda pourquoi tant de monde. Antipas en dit la cause: le festin de son anniversaire . . . (II)

At times the condensation is almost baffling:

> Les Sadducéens feignirent un grand émoi;—le lendemain, la sacrificature leur fut rendue;—Antipas étalait du désespoir; Vitellius demeurait impassible. (III)

or even more so in the following paragraph, which could come straight from the pen of the tersest memorialist:

> L'exaltation du peuple grandit. Ils s'abandonnèrent à des projets d'indépendance. On rappelait la gloire

[5] *Notes de voyages*, I, 160.

d'Israël. Tous les conquérants avaient été châtiés: Antigone, Crassus, Varus. . . . (III)

The lapidary quality of sentences such as these is clearly the result of a conscious effort. Shortly before writing *Hérodias*, Flaubert confided to George Sand his boundless admiration for the rhythmical achievements of Montesquieu's prose. He cited the following as an example: "Les vices d'Alexandre étaient extrêmes comme ses vertus. Il était terrible dans sa colère. Elle le rendait cruel."[6] The pattern is obvious: one could adduce endless examples of Flaubertian sentences modeled along these lines, in apparent contradiction to his turbulent lyricism.

This interplay of a chiseled prose and an eruptive physical and psychological setting, though it underscores the occult ferment and prepares the paroxystic effect, does bring about some needless obscurity. In his desire to streamline his tale, Flaubert was determined to avoid lengthy explanations. He tried to leave out what he himself, in a letter to Maupassant, calls the "explications indispensables." No wonder that Taine, despite his admiration, reproached Flaubert for some needless obscurities.[7] A number of passages indeed require elucidations: the genealogy of Herodias, the identity of the two Vitelliuses, the reasons for the Roman general's dislike of Herod are not made translucent to the unprepared reader. The verbal denseness, characteristic of Flaubert's art, is brought in *Hérodias* almost to the danger point. It has been said that Flaubert would tear down a forest in order to construct a matchbox. The documentation, even for his shortest works, is impressive and eclectic. The efficacy of his prose is in large part dependent on this wasteful and at the same time astringent economy. "It seems to me that French prose can achieve a beauty inconceivable so far," he writes to his

[6] Flaubert, *Corresp.*, VII, 282.
[7] Flaubert, *Corresp.*, VII, 353. The letter by Taine is quoted in the Conard edition of *Trois contes* (Flaubert, *Oeuvres complètes, op. cit.*), pp. 226–228.

friend Turgenev.[8] This obsessive struggle with the demon of language shows no sign of relenting. Neither *Madame Bovary*, nor *Salammbô*, nor *L'Éducation sentimentale*, nor even *La Tentation de saint Antoine* has satisfied his dream. He continues to yearn for that impossible beauty. He continues to search for that "bon motif," as he puts it, which will be just right for his "voice."[9] The artist's personal struggle remains to the very end at the center of his work.

Finally, the immobility of the moral and physical setting can be as deceptive as the apparent neutrality of the style. Stasis is in part the result of a repeated substitution of description for narration. As Geneviève Bollème puts it, with Flaubert "description is narrative."[10] It does seem to cancel the event. Moreover, in *Hérodias*—just as in *Salammbô*—Flaubert insists on the plastic and terrifying fixity of landscape and architecture, and toys with geometric patterns. The very first sentence describes a rocklike formation in the shape of a geometric figure:

> La citadelle de Machaerous se dressait à l'orient de la mer Morte, sur un pic de basalte ayant la forme d'un cône.

The geometric imagery is further developed as Flaubert describes the houses at the "base" of the rock, surrounded by the "circle" of a wall, and the wall of the fortress with its numerous "angles." Nor is this imagery reserved for military installations. The region of Engedi draws a black line ("barre noire") across the landscape; Hebron rises in the shape of a "dome"; and, dominating Jerusalem, appears the huge "cube"-shaped tower of Antonia. But this choreography of forms which seem immobilized (much like the hills which appear like petrified waves) conveys the impression of an eruptive terrain. Silence, in *Hérodias*, is oppressive; it announces the cry of terror or agony. And

---

[8] Flaubert, *Lettres inédites à Tourgueneff*, p. 106.
[9] To Louise Colet he writes: " . . . peut-être trouverai-je un jour un bon *motif*, un air complètement dans ma voix, ni au-dessus ni au-dessous" (Flaubert, *Corresp.*, III, 143).
[10] Bollème, *La Leçon de Flaubert*, p. 195.

it is significant that the most "silent" paragraph in the entire tale—the one that describes the empty roads, the sleeping soldiers and the ominous tranquillity in the castle —immediately precedes the outburst of the cavernous voice of Iaokanann rising as from the bowels of the earth. This disquieting irruption is symbolic of Flaubert's relation to his artistic material. From behind the apparently unperturbed surface and wall of controlled craftsmanship, a pressing, at times anguished voice can be heard. It belongs to one who is also a manner of prophet.

Bouvard et Pécuchet:

THE TRAGICOMEDY
OF INTELLECT

Penser c'est le moyen de souffrir.
Flaubert

The Inventory of Failure

The curious, and almost subversive prestige which this unfinished novel enjoys in our time reveals more perhaps about the intellectual frustrations and inadequacies of our own period than about the work itself. The artistic merits of *Bouvard et Pécuchet* are indeed difficult to assess, difficult even to discuss. The shortcomings of the book are self-evident. In many ways, it could be considered a monumental failure. Yet this strange enterprise which is precisely an encyclopedic inventory of failure, diagnosing, among other things, the very breakdown of Culture, is prophetic not only of subsequent developments in Western society, but also of the kind of literature ultimately represented by the arid and clownish bitterness of a Samuel Beckett or the laughter of the absurd of a Eugène Ionesco.

The very incompleteness of the novel strangely appeals to recent generations that have grown to prefer the problematic and shifting nature of a sketch to the finished and somewhat immobilized tableau. The *becoming* of art and thought often excites us more than their *being*. Among the clearly modern features of *Bouvard et Pécuchet* there is in the first place the drama of literature itself: through his characters the author seems to reënact his own efforts. Thought here becomes the subject of thought. The very writing of the book can be said to be its subject. With *Bouvard et Pécuchet*, we are witnessing not only the unequivocal emergence of the modern novel of ideas (did not Flaubert consciously aim at what he calls the "comique d'idées"?)[1], but also the decline of the conventional *roman d'analyse*. The two phenomena are obviously related. The gradual disappearance of the "personage" in fiction corresponds to a tragic questioning of humanistic values, as well as to a questioning of literature itself. Flaubert's last novel points to the subversive and explosive nature of much of contemporary literature. An impasse seems to have been reached. "Modernity begins with the search for an impossible literature," observes Roland Barthes.[2] Flaubert himself was fully conscious of the revolutionary role of his writing—at least that was his hope! His *Dictionnaire des idées reçues* in particular, so intimately bound up with the genesis of *Bouvard et Pécuchet*, was to be an ironic and stunning enterprise of demolition ("j'y attaquerais tout")[3] in order to achieve a fearful *tabula rasa*. "En finir une fois pour toutes . . ."—to finish with it once and for all: the expression reveals more than a fleeting bad mood. All of Flaubert's literary efforts, despite his concern for rhythm and form, tend toward a dislocation and breakdown of the traditional patterns.

But what is the meaning of this work? Is it a facetious critique of two inept individuals, a sad commentary on false values, or a more general diagnosis of our sick civilization? Nothing is in fact more elusive than the spirit which animates this strangely repelling and alluring text.

The plot is simple enough. Two lonely, middle-aged copyists—the one a sanguine widower, the other a hypochondriac bachelor—strike up a friendship. An unexpected inheritance permits them to retire to the country and to indulge in a life of leisure. They devote themselves at first

---

[1] Flaubert, *Corresp.*, VIII, 26 ("Je crois qu'on n'a pas encore tenté le comique d'idées"). Complete citations for all notes may be found in the Bibliography.
[2] Barthes, *Le Degré zéro de l'écriture*, p. 58.
[3] Flaubert, *Corresp.*, III, 66–67.

to the simple and harmless pleasures of gardening, but soon become more ambitious and, driven on by a frenzy of experimentation, expose themselves to a series of costly and humiliating fiascoes in agriculture and arboriculture. As their encyclopedic curiosity grows, they invade other areas of knowledge (anatomy, hygiene, medicine, geology, archeology) with the same pitiful results. Finally, their appetite for knowledge and experience propels them, always with naïve self-confidence and supreme lack of method, to explore the more abstract subjects of history, literature, esthetics, philosophy and religion. Thus they survey all areas of knowledge, hopelessly confused by these debauches of nomenclatures, categories and contradictory opinions. At the end, tired, dejected and financially ruined, the two quixotic clerks abandon their fruitless search for truth. They will no longer think or speculate, but instead, like aging Candides, they will tend their private little garden, and spend the rest of their lives simply "copying" as before.

The plot itself remains equivocal. Is this a caricature of two mediocre individuals (Flaubert first thought of calling the novel *Les Deux Cloportes*—the two woodlice—and referred to his main characters as "mes deux idiots"),[4] or does the author undertake a systematic debunking of something far more enormous and pernicious than the palpable stupidity of his two puppets? The ambiguity of the novel is in part due to the fact that these are not mutually exclusive propositions. The genesis of the work confirms this fundamental equivocation. "Le Garçon," that mythical and mirthful Rabelaisian figure invented by young Gustave and his friends, was at the same time a lusty incarnation of nineteenth-century "bourgeois" stupidity and a mocking denouncer of that very stupidity. As for the *Dictionnaire des idées reçues*, that lifelong compilation of clichés which was to nourish several of Flaubert's novels, and which culminated in the orgy of platitudes that constitute the sub-

---

4 Flaubert, *Lettres inédites à Tourgueneff*, p. 142.

stance of *Bouvard et Pécuchet*, it was planned, so to speak, as a work of mystification. Flaubert at one time thought of publishing his *Dictionnaire* with a preface so contrived that the reader would not know whether he was made fun of or not ("que le lecteur ne sache pas si on se fout de lui, oui ou non").[5] Again, a couple of years later, he referred to the *Dictionnaire* as an ironic *apologia* of human turpitude, filled from beginning to end with quotations and proofs "which would prove the exact opposite."[6]

Flaubert's friends were seriously worried by the obstinacy with which he pursued what he himself called "this hellish book."[7] Taine, to whom Flaubert had read from the unfinished manuscript, wrote an alarmed letter to Turgenev, expressing his dismay concerning this story of two "maniacal snails."[8] The research undertaken for this book is truly appalling. Flaubert consulted some fifteen hundred volumes, taking assiduous notes! The taste for erudition—a permanent trait of Flaubert—takes on disturbing proportions toward the end of his life, and contributes to the impression that fiction has here reached an impasse. Flaubert was not unaware of the danger. Not only did his readings, especially the endless cortège of philosophical absurdities, throw him into a depressed state of "sombreur," but he was the first to proclaim the utter madness of his undertaking. "Il faut être fou pour avoir entrepris une pareille tâche."[9]

Yet it would be most misleading to interpret this mad undertaking as a sort of superior joke, a "blague supérieure" by means of which, as Flaubert himself explains, the author assumes a God-like objectivity and indifference vis-à-vis the phenomenon he describes.[10] Once again, the apparent objectivity hides a very personal involvement of the author. For not only was Flaubert attracted to erudition

5 Flaubert, *Corresp.*, II, 238.   6 Flaubert, *Corresp.*, III, 66.
7 Flaubert, *Corresp.*, VIII, 126, ("mon abominable bouquin").
8 Letter quoted by René Dumesnil in the edition of the Société Les Belles Lettres, I, pp. lxxxix–xci.
9 Flaubert, *Corresp.*, VIII, 178, 283.
10 Flaubert, *Corresp.*, III, 37.

for its own sake and urged on by the desire to know ("Il faudrait tout connaître"), but he was convinced that all truly great literature is encyclopedic in nature: Homer and Rabelais, he observes, are "encyclopedias of their time."[11]

The defects and limitations of *Bouvard et Pécuchet* are flagrant. The characters are treated mechanically, there is hardly any development, and the novel tends altogether to be too much of a demonstration. Sometimes the author provides almost pure schemata. Often the debunking is accomplished by a mere résumé of undigested notes. Although this technique admirably conveys the innutritious quality of much pseudo-science and pseudo-philosophy, the reader experiences the uncomfortable feeling of having reached, and even crossed, the frontiers of literature. The incompetent exploration of overspecialized fields, with their respective jargons, creates a double sense of comedy (the absurdity of the two experimenters as well as the absurdity of any hermetic or fetishistic language), but it also brings about a sense of clutter and obstruction.[12]

Even the comic devices are tedious and strained. Occasionally Flaubert achieves truly Molièresque effects. When, in the Philosophy chapter, Bouvard almost strikes the servant for the inedible meal he has prepared, Pécuchet's admonition ("You are too much immersed in matter!") is worthy of *Les Femmes savantes*. Mostly, however, his comedy is devoid of such flashes. It is rather the typically slow and heavy humor of the middle of the nineteenth century which also inspired caricaturists such as Monnier and Daumier. Redundance, duplication, parrotism are the very substance of comedy here. Circularity is the most common pattern. And circularity is of course an excellent technique for discrediting an enterprise: one is bound to return—just a little more tired and less enthusiastic than

---

[11] Flaubert, *Corresp.*, IV, 52.

[12] Claudia Neuenschwander-Naef rightly speaks of the "Unbewohnbarkeit des Stils"—the "unlivable" nature of this particular style. (*Vorstellungswelt und Realität in Flauberts "Bouvard et Pécuchet,"* p. 38.)

before—to the very place from which one has set out. The entire novel is thus a "return" following a pointless odyssey.

The Religion chapter clearly reveals this cycle, which carries the protagonists from curiosity to a faint nostalgia, to a will to believe, to disillusion, and ultimately to a liberation through disgust. At first, Bouvard and Pécuchet are elated by the beauty of the Gospels. A sense of peace is much needed by them, after philosophical "anguish," in the preceding chapter, almost drove them to suicide. Soon, however, the prophetic texts of the Old Testament introduce a note of harshness and terror. The next phase, in the Flaubertian cycle, leads inevitably to excess and imbalance. Pécuchet, ever in search of absolutes, insists on the importance of dogma and of devotional practices. He sets out to repress his sensual dreams, punishes himself for his lewd thoughts, figures out penitences and mortifications of the flesh, and ends up with a ludicrous attempt at flagellation. Soon the chapter veers toward vulgarity: a pilgrimage brings out the more sordid side of the commercialization of religion. Finally, after unsuccessful attempts at developing a mystic vision by following published "methods," the chapter degenerates into the grotesque when Pécuchet, to the scandal of the local bourgeois, asseverates his intention of converting to Buddhism. To be sure, these pages reveal a passionate bias on the part of Flaubert. Research for this chapter had a particularly irritating effect on him: "C'est inouï d'imbecillité."[13] But it is nonetheless extremely typical of a cyclical development which carries the protagonists through increasingly preposterous experiences back to a point of departure. *Bouvard et Pécuchet* thus marks, in its very rhythm, a repeated betrayal of a recurring hope. The very monotony of the novel's structure reveals a profound sadness and, behind the heavy comic façade and repetitive jests, a profound discouragement.

[13] Flaubert, *Corresp.*, VIII, 184.

This disconsolate book remains ambivalent in a quixotic manner. Hope and bitter sadness are woven into each other from the very outset, and end up by resembling each other. It is without a doubt Flaubert's most desperate and most moving work. This despair has deep roots. For though Flaubert, after the events of 1870–1871, wanted to "vomit" his bile all over his contemporaries,[14] his acute state of despondency, assuming almost militant forms, cannot be attributed solely to the events of the war and of the Commune. Flaubert's is not merely a peevish, splenetic misanthropy, but a permanent indignation in the face of the immitigable scandal of existence. *Bouvard et Pécuchet*, in terms of its gestation, is a lifelong enterprise, reflecting lifelong attitudes and preoccupations. In this sense, it is— together with *La Tentation de saint Antoine*—the most personal work of Flaubert.

A system of polarities, which dialectically are never resolved, is maintained throughout the novel. The dream of the absolute becomes the madness of the absolute: Pécuchet has visions of "mountains of fruits," of "floods of flowers" and "avalanches of vegetables" (Chapter 2). But all reveries end in an irreclaimable fiasco. The vanity and tragedy of all ambition are thus at the heart of the book. All is destined to "go to pieces" in their hands. They want much, but tire easily—"Leur tête s'élargissait"; but two sentences later: "Les minéraux ne tardèrent pas à les fatiguer" (3). Similarly, the need for truths and Truth clashes with the constant discovery of the relative. The taste for history leads to a thirst for "truth for its own sake" (4). Hence the mad and maddening attempt to attain knowledge through inventories which grow into statistical and encyclopedic monstrosities as indigestible as the prodigious and utterly inedible cabbage that prospers in Pécuchet's garden.

The lack of certitude soon throws them into the opposite mania: the obsession with the relative and the tran-

14 Flaubert, *Corresp.*, VI, 460.

sitory. In observing the clouds, during their studies in meteorology, they try to distinguish the nimbus from the cirrus, and the stratus from the cumulus. But the shapes of the clouds change so fast that they do not succeed in classifying them. Almost perversely, they begin to derive satisfaction from fugacity, inconsistencies, contradictions and irreconcilable opposites. The book at times becomes an exercise in jarring effects, an orgy of the heteroclite. Their garden turns into something which is not merely in atrocious taste, but truly "frightening": the yellow Chinese pagoda, the Venetian bridge, the lightning-struck tree, the Etruscan tomb—all these props, much like the jarring architectural elements in the Alhambra in *L'Éducation sentimentale*, are a study in incongruence. The absence of harmony is not a simple comic feature: it points to a tragic inadequacy to cope with the multiform. "Où est la règle, alors?" ("Where then is the rule?" 2), sighs the more pessimistic Pécuchet.

The book thus stresses simultaneously an unending quest (always a new interrogation opens up a new inquiry) and an eternal dissatisfaction which once again makes the two copyists yearn for new experiences. Only it would be a mistake to believe that the novel describes a progression. Here too the movement is cyclical, and in typical Flaubertian manner this issueless motion suggests fixity and death.

Human Nature or Civilization?

No work of Flaubert seems indeed to propose a more doleful and disconsolate view of man. In *Bouvard et Pécuchet*, Flaubert's pessimism becomes incurable. For he blames neither environment nor society, but man's own fundamentally vitiated nature. His anti-Rousseauistic position, which brings him close to the vision of a Baudelaire (though he does not, of course, share Baudelaire's metaphysics), comes out most clearly in the chapter on education. Bouvard and Pécuchet, having decided to adopt and bring up the two children of a criminal, experience their bitterest fiasco as they experiment with the various pedagogical methods. In Victor and Victorine, the two stubborn, greedy and ungrateful brats, they face deep-rooted, congenital evil in its most elemental and unredeemable form. Referring no doubt to this episode, which occupies a major portion of chapter 10, Flaubert wrote to Maupassant: "I want to show that education, no matter of what kind, doesn't mean much, and that nature does all or almost all."[15] If indeed, as has been stated, *Bouvard et Pécuchet* is an anti-educational novel, a *"Bildungsroman* in reverse,"[16] this must not be understood merely as a criticism of the teaching methods adopted, or of the mental level of the two middle-aged clerks, but as a mournful commentary on man's inherent debility and meanness. The Education chapter thus transposes the education theme of the entire novel onto a philosophical level. And the atrocious description of the boiling alive of a cat by Victor and Victorine (Flaubert to be sure relished writing this horrible passage), must be read in the same spirit as Baudelaire's more sophisticated but equally cruel condemnation of children in "Le Gâteau" and at the end of "Les Veuves."

This somber image of man's inherence assumes, of course, social and political forms. The participants and nonparticipants in the events of 1848 are—if at all possible —more base, more stupid, more false than the petty and perfidious humanity described in *L'Éducation sentimentale*. Fear and cruelty seem to be the main distinctions of this "revolutionary" period. "Quels idiots! quelle bassesse!" (6) The indignation of Bouvard and Pécuchet reaches a peak when they hear about political repressions, and when they actually witness the heartless manner with which the local priest tyrannizes the underprivileged and idealistically republican *instituteur*. As for the events of 1851, they only further bring out the ferocious and servile nature of humanity. The typically "total" Flaubertian hatred (he

15 Flaubert, *Corresp.*, VIII, 353.
16 Harry Levin, *The Gates of Horn*, p. 298.

despises simultaneously the bourgeois, the worker, the priest, the politician, the rich and the poor) must be understood in the light of a nonpartisan, moral denunciation of human nature. Any attempt at analyzing Flaubert's views in terms of class allegiance or class consciousness is bound to be limiting. A more fundamental misanthropy underlies and animates his work.

It is evidently possible to read *Bouvard et Pécuchet* as a devastating critique of half-knowledge and a denunciation of the absence of intellectual discipline. "Pécuchet en accusa leur méthode" (8). The blame echoes Frédéric's lament in the final chapter of *L'Éducation sentimentale*: "C'est peut-être le défaut de ligne droite." Bouvard and Pécuchet, as individuals, are indeed remarkably clumsy and ungifted. Even in his activities as gardener, Pécuchet does about everything wrong. With the impatience typical of those who have neither the ability nor the desire to master a subject, he and his friend move from one enterprise to another, just as, after acquiring the artificial corpse, they jump without any patience or system from one organ to another. The fact that books determine and also demolish their various vocations is of course pungently comical. But this "bookish" approach to experience is also symptomatic of a more general disease of a civilization which increasingly experiences knowledge and even desire through various forms of intermediary.[17] Modern journalism and advertisement—spreaders of *idées reçues*—are not merely notorious perpetrators of bluff, corruption and counterfeit; they are above all the most flagrant agents of intercession in a culture that relies more and more heavily on moral and affective awareness by proxy.

Such a diagnosis, as well as the implicit protest against the very conditions of our culture, appears to contradict Flaubert's anti-Rousseauistic stand. But Flaubert's pessimism does precisely allow for no hiatus between the ills

[17] René Girard has discussed this phenomenon with finesse and imagination in *Mensonge romantique et vérité romanesque*. According to Girard, after Flaubert "spontaneous desire" plays a minor role in literature.

of civilization and the scandal of human nature. The Commune and the Prussian invasion of France confirmed him in his conviction that man was responsible for the calamities he suffered, that he was bent on self-destruction. The much vaunted modern science ironically served only to underscore, accelerate and intensify the horror of the modern world. Flaubert's correspondence, after 1870, is studded with bitter and prophetic remarks. He expresses his horror at these Prussian army officers who are *docteurs ès lettres,* know Sanskrit, steal clocks, guzzle champagne and commit mass murders. The notion of a decline and death of civilization (a "fin du monde") takes an increasingly firm hold over his imagination. "Can one believe in progress and civilization with all that goes on? What is the use of science, since this nation of scientists commits abominations worthy of the Huns . . .?"[18] He despises his epoch, not only for its Philistinism and vulgarity, but for inspiring him with the hateful thoughts of a "XIIth century brute." The notion of a decivilizing trend is quite explicit: "Quelle reculade!"[19]

Bouvard and Pécuchet, after dabbling in geology, are also gloomy as they meditate on "the end of the world." In one of the more clumsily comic scenes of the book, Flaubert has Bouvard run in terror at the thought of an imminent cataclysm. The mixture of author's gusto and character's panic is almost a caricature of Flaubert's own paradoxical feelings. For there is no doubt: Flaubert relished the thought of decadence. He was proud of his own "Barbarian" traits, and conceived of himself as a citizen of the Bas-Empire. This personal myth echoes no doubt some of the most cherished attitudes of the literati in the second half of the nineteenth century. But Flaubert, the bourgeois, was also haunted by fears which, after 1870, became realities and inspired his prophetic vein. He was convinced that the modern world was only beginning to learn the true meaning of the word "hate." He had visions of

18 Flaubert, *Corresp.,* VI, 183–185.
19 Flaubert, *Corresp.,* VI, 204.

"monstrous conflicts" in which several million people would be exterminated in one battle; he predicted "racial wars" that would pit against each other entire continents. "The entire East against Europe, the old against the new world! Why not?"[20]

The events of the Franco-Prussian War, of the Commune, of the defeat and of the enemy occupation served, however, only as a catalyst for Flaubert's anger. The diagnosis of the modern disease, of the crisis of our culture, was made by him much earlier. It was based not so much on political, as on intellectual and philosophical symptoms. The origins of the affliction, or at least the first epidemic signs, went back to the so-called Age of Enlightenment. The virus of Encyclopedism—for that would be an appropriate name for this peculiar pathology—had spread to the entire occidental civilization. Flaubert, in denouncing omnivorous and undiscriminating ingurgitation of facts, is touching in depth one of the vexing aberrations of our time: on the one hand, the boundless curiosity unleashed by the Renaissance; and on the other (a bitter price to pay!) a paralyzing relativism leading to frustration and despair. In 1846, at the age of twenty-five, Flaubert set out to write a burlesque tragedy called *Jenner ou la Découverte de la Vaccine*. This versified buffoonery had clear Faustian undertones. Agénor also found nothingness in his search for complete knowledge.

> Vainement j'ai cherché dans les soins et l'étude
> A me faire un destin libre d'inquiétude. . . .

Agénor's "studious courage" discovers only the "néant." Similarly Bouvard and Pécuchet, by reading too much, by cataloguing information, discover not truth but contradiction and confusion. An eternal postponement of opinion is the result of this mania for encyclopedic inventories.

Jean-Paul Sartre, in our time, has pursued this denunciation of the encyclopedic disease. In *La Nausée* in par-

[20] Flaubert, *Corresp.*, VI, 137–138.

ticular, and more specifically in the figure of the Self-Taught Man, that spiritual child of Bouvard and Pécuchet, he has carried on the Flaubertian critique. The Self-Taught Man stubbornly pursues his education by reading all the books in the Public Library in alphabetical order. Within his brain, the weirdest tribes—the Samoyeds, the Nyam-Nyams, the Fuegians—celebrate the strangest rites: they eat their fathers, copulate at random, dance to mad rhythms, castrate themselves, have monstrous animals tattooed on their backs. The Self-Taught Man becomes the very caricature of an optimistic humanism according to which the highest achievement of man is encyclopedic knowledge. But this encyclopedic obsession can become a form of escapism. The belief that wisdom comes through a sum total of data, that all one needs is to add another and still another odd fact—this intellectual tourism can be a pernicious denial of life. For such a relativism and concern for cataloguing ultimately lead to an abdication of man's responsibility to create values here and now.

Hugh Kenner, who has written incisive pages on the theme of cultural feedback in Flaubert, explains that dictionaries and encyclopedias are produced "by a feat of organizing, not a feat of understanding."[21] This is unquestionably true in the perspective of *Bouvard et Pécuchet*, where facts are shown merely to coexist, but are never brought into a meaningful or hierarchical relation to each other. This absence of meaning involves, in Flaubert's mind, a more general crisis of culture. The generations that had witnessed the events of 1870 and of the belated Industrial Revolution in France could not avoid defining their intellectual positions in relation to the growing prestige of science. In considering Flaubert's tragic misgivings, we must remember that his is not a lonely voice. Paul Bourget's *Le Disciple,* a frontal attack on positivism and scientism, appeared in 1889; and a few years later in 1895, Ferdinand Brunetière published his resounding essay

[21] Kenner, *Flaubert, Joyce and Beckett—The Stoic Comedians*, p. 2.

on the bankruptcy of science.[22] No study in depth of the fin-de-siècle intellectual anxiety, with its accompanying syndrome of decadentism, can afford to neglect that aspect of Flaubert's work which in *Bouvard et Pécuchet* finds its most comical and most desolate expression.

Indignation and Intervention: The Author's Voice

All, however, is not denunciation and gloom. There is also something authentically touching about this book. The two friends, like Beckett's two tramps, symbolize the eternal couple. Their temperaments complement each other. Pécuchet is thin, hypochondriac, doctrinaire and intransigent; Bouvard is stout, sanguine, materialistic and tolerant. The latter relishes coarse jests, the former displays an almost feminine *pudeur*. When they meet on the Boulevard Bourdon, in the summer heat, it is for them love at first sight, the classical *coup de foudre*. As they later reflect on their friendship, they are almost moved to tears. They discover that they are constitutionally made for a union such as theirs: they have the "bump" of friendship. And despite occasional sulking and misunderstandings (no more serious than lovers' quarrels), their shared experiences and mishaps only bring them closer to each other.

This notion of the friendship couple is one of the permanent traits of Flaubert's imagination. It occurs in many of his novels, and corresponds unquestionably to a deep need. One may even wonder whether the Bouvard-Pécuchet combination does not correspond to a semiconscious and somewhat sentimental caricature of his own relations with his old friend Louis Bouilhet. They too were associated in countless projects and knew how to console each other when depressed by failure: ". . . mon seul confident, mon seul ami, mon seul déversoir . . .," writes Flaubert to Bouilhet.[23] Few men have needed and experi-

---

[22] "Après une visite au Vatican," *Revue des Deux Mondes*, January 1, 1895, pp. 97–118.

[23] When Louis Bouilhet almost gives in to utter discouragement, Flaubert writes to him these moving words: "Allons, mon pauvre vieux, mon roquentin, mon seul confident, mon seul ami, mon seul

enced friendship as intensely as Flaubert. Few have so consistently projected their adolescent fervor into middle age. The curious mixture of pathos and ridicule in the book stems in part from this chronological incongruity. Pécuchet and his friend Bouvard remain eternal adolescents. They not only want to learn what they are not prepared to understand (or what cannot be understood), they want to learn at an age when others have long ago smugly settled into an unquestioned intellectual comfort. They are thus at the same time touchingly inept and incompetently heroic.

This inevitably raises the entire problem of the author's impersonality, esthetic distance and identification. For it is impossible not to sense the oblique interventions of the author. The author's presence makes itself felt through subtle forms of intrusion; and it is here—in certain stylistic devices—that Flaubert excels. The utterly "dry" presentation of Swedenborg's visions, by reporting these on the level of pure fact, reduces them to a series of absurdities. At times it is an apparently innocent subordinate clause which carries, very tenuously, the whole weight of the Flaubertian attack. Listing the faculties of the soul as they are described by textbooks on philosophy: "On en compte trois, pas davantage!" (8). This "pas davantage," half observation and half exclamation, is characteristic of a certain type of debunking intervention. Frequently, the subversion is achieved by means of a perfidious indirect discourse. The priest, for instance, claims that science is useless for it teaches nothing. "But he did know that the world has been created for us; he did know that the archangels are above the angels; he did know that the human body will be resurrected . . ." (9). Flaubert's most efficacious weapon, however, is a fake naïveté inherited directly from the militant ironic tradition of the eighteenth century. Viewed in this light, the many schematic résumés which clutter the text are not at all a sign of literary in-

---

déversoir, reprends courage, aime-nous mieux que cela." (Flaubert, *Corresp.*, IV, 96.)

digestion, but represent a circuitous method for discrediting. The word here carries its own condemnation. The apparently colorless synopsis, the factual *abrégé*, the deliberately dry abstract, function in this novel much as the *style indirect libre* functions in *Madame Bovary* and *L'Éducation sentimentale*: the technique allows the author to be simultaneously inside and outside the object he describes. The technique of the digest could in fact be considered as the free indirect discourse carried to a logical extreme. It is a supremely refined and elusive instrument of ironic intervention.

Flaubert was aware of the dangers of the game. The false remoteness implied a paradoxical form of intimacy. "Bouvard and Pécuchet fill me to such a point that I have become them. Their stupidity is mine, and I'm dying of it." And to his friend Turgenev he writes: "At times, it seems to me that I am becoming idiotic."[24] The fear that in the process of writing this epic of mediocrity his "deux idiots" might have proved to be contagious has been shared by many a critic. The truth may well imply a reversal of this proposition. It is probably not so much Flaubert who becomes his two caricatures, as they who represent a good deal—and more than appears at first sight—of their author. No one indeed seems to have taken the trouble to list all they do and feel that clearly brings to mind Flaubert's own feelings, attitudes and propensities. The complete catalogue would be lengthy. Like his characters, Flaubert enjoys repeating the same joke twenty times a day, for more than three weeks—and even longer. He too undertakes documentary expeditions, he too settles in Normandy, he too bothers his friends to send him books from Paris. The vulgar bric-à-brac in the clerks' house, their addiction to bibelots, have their counterpart in Flaubert's affectionate collecting of odd objects in his room in Croisset. Their declamatory period when they discover the beauties of dramatic literature evokes Flaubert's own private sessions in his "gueu-

[24] Flaubert, *Corresp.*, VII, 237; Flaubert, *Lettres inédites à Tourgueneff*, p. 83.

loir." Even their melancholy has a peculiarly Flaubertian hue. Their poetic landscape of ennui not only recalls the mental landscape in *Madame Bovary*, but is in harmony with many a page of the *Correspondance*.

A closer scrutiny may even suggest a semiconscious parody of self. It is not by coincidence that the genealogical tree of the Croixmare family entirely covers the back of one of the doors in Chavignolles: it happens to be the name of Flaubert's own maternal grandmother. Similarly, when Bouvard, with his round face and bald patch, gives himself a head à la Béranger, this is quite clearly an allusion to a personal anecdote which for Flaubert was a source of endless mirth: one day he overheard a young girl point out the resemblance between him and the very poet he despised.[25] These are of course marginal private jokes, at best designed to be understood by the initiated. But there are analogies involving a more biting humor. Pécuchet and Bouvard "crown" themselves artists, take pride in provoking contempt or hostility, and patiently, stubbornly wait for inspiration. The description of their "literary" working habits and of their desperate attempts to generate ideas inevitably suggests a caricature of Flaubert's own sedentary concentration and artistic self-torture, including the subterfuges of daydreams.

The chapter on literature reveals indeed the ambivalence of the caricature. A strange amalgamation occurs as the work on the novel progresses. The two puppets display an increasing family resemblance with their author. They develop an independence of mind which makes them dislike what the reading public approves, and relish what others reject. Not only their tastes and even more so their aversions bring them into close harmony with Flaubert, but the very quality of their sadness bestows upon them a distinction of mind that is given only to the Flaubertian "happy few." The world's indifference to Art—or its utili-

25 The anecdote was told by Edmond Laporte to René Dumesnil. See the latter's note in his edition of *Bouvard et Pécuchet*, Société Les Belles Lettres, 1945, II, 337–338.

tarian use of Art in search of intellectual comfort—shows up their essential alienation. They learn or intuit that mankind will always resent the loftiest creations of the spirit. "On n'aime pas la littérature." This sad discovery, at the end of the crucial chapter 5, clearly suggests that the tragedy of the novel is in large part to be attributed to the irresolvable frustrations in a society fundamentally hostile to art and knowledge.

Fools and Heroes: The Tragedy of Thought

The caricature is thus doubly ambiguous. On the one hand, the two *bonshommes* develop a critical spirit and grow in stature; on the other, the caricature itself leads to an indirect condemnation of our society and to an implicit glorification of the absent intellectual virtues. It is in the chapter on Literature that Bouvard and Pécuchet begin truly to "suffer," together with Flaubert, from their contact with human stupidity. Concurrently, there is also, in this pivotal chapter 5, a significant increase of author's interventions suggesting, so to speak stylistically, a fusion of points of view. But it is above all the chapter on Philosophy which marks the copyists' intellectual emancipation. Bouvard, for instance, expresses his doubts concerning the laws of causality in the sharpest terms. Both friends observe with painful logic how the various systems discredit one another. Yet although they are sickened by the platitudes they read, they take pride in their metaphysical excursions. "Philosophy elevated them in their own estimation." Ultimately, they almost appear as martyrs of intellect. They develop the "pitiable faculty" of observing stupidity and no longer tolerating it (8). Trifling things read or overheard sadden them, and they feel the heaviness of the whole world weigh down on them.

There can be no doubt that Flaubert wanted his two characters to develop a self-torturing independence of judgment. "Through sheer mutual contact they develop themselves . . .," he writes in one of his first scenarios.[26] It is further clear that Flaubert related this potential development to a propensity for anguish. "They have this in common that they have congenitally a certain anxiety, a certain agitation."[27] Learning and suffering are indeed bound up from the outset. Bouvard's and Pécuchet's intellectual development is explicitly stated as early as the first pages of chapter 1. As soon as they begin to inquire and read, "their intelligence developed itself." Pain is of course the immediate reward. "Having more ideas, they also knew more suffering." Even their estrangement from the community—the perennial self-exile of the thinker—is comically but unequivocally established at the beginning of the first chapter. Their colleagues become unbearable to them.

As for the ambiguity of the specific caricature of intellect, it has its roots in a long tradition. For such laughter is the recurrent symptom of an uneasiness, the symptom of the tragic gap between what Alfred de Vigny called the *homme esprit* and the *homme matière*. Caliban is responsible for the pariah-status of the thinker. But the ostracized intellectual only increases his own pain: he punishes himself for the hostility he provokes. That, no doubt, is the underlying reason why *Bouvard et Pécuchet* proposes simultaneously a critique of society and a caricature of the two adventurers into the realm of ideas. Intellect, in self-defense and out of self-consciousness, here apes its very enemies. The two copying-clerks, once they have achieved a measure of intellectual superiority,

---

[26] "Par le seul fait de leur contact, ils se développent. . . . " Quoted by René Dumesnil in his "Introduction" to *Bouvard et Pécuchet*, Société Les Belles Lettres, I, xlix. One of the scenarios contains the following revealing remark: "Ils peuvent . . . après une étude, formuler leur opinion (=la mienne) par des desiderata sous forme d'axiomes." (Quoted by Maurice Nadeau, "Sur 'Bouvard et Pécuchet,' " *Les Lettres Nouvelles*, May-June 1965, pp. 67–87.

[27] This sentence from Flaubert's first outline is quoted by René Dumesnil in his "Introduction" to *Bouvard et Pécuchet*, Société Les Belles Lettres, I, liii.

become aware that their superiority offends the community.[28]

"Tout bon raisonnement offense," said Stendhal, thus tersely explaining why ever since antiquity (see Socrates' remarks in *Theatetus*) the philosopher is the jest of the common herd. The divorce between the *vulgus* and the cleric has saddened many a mind. "The populace loves ignorance," Vigny asserted with bitterness in *Le Journal d'un poète*. All through Western history, one can find traces of this conflict, of this deep suspicion. Renan, in *L'Avenir de la science*, observed with gloom that thinkers would always irritate the people who might be willing to forgive the wealth of the nobleman but never intellectual superiority. To trace the continuity and development of the caricature of intellect in European literature would lead to a study in depth of some of the basic tensions in our civilization. Such a study would have to go back as far as Pindar, who, while singing of athletic victories, repeatedly proclaimed the inferiority of learning to action, and who mocked that "mortal breed full of futility" which hunts for impossibilities on the "wings of ineffectual hopes."

It may indeed appear strange to equate Pécuchet and Bouvard with intellectual heroism. But this is what one must ultimately do. Lionel Trilling, who considers the novel Flaubert's spiritual testament, is right in reminding us that, after all, they do "live by the mind," and stand for intelligence.[29] There is unquestionably something "sacrificial" (the theme of sainthood runs through Flaubert's entire work) in their final return to the double copying desk. The paradox is no more startling than the one of Don Quixote—a figure who fascinated Flaubert almost more than any other, and who had inflamed his imagination in his childhood. For the sad knight is pathetic and grandiose, and Cervantes' novel is all at once a parody of an artificial

---

[28] "L'évidence de leur supériorité blessait." The problem of the caricature of intellect is raised repeatedly in my study, *The Intellectual Hero.*

[29] Trilling, "Flaubert's Last Testament," *Partisan Review*, November-December 1953, pp. 605–630.

tradition and a lyrical affirmation of some of its most Romantic values.

Flaubert's repeated glorification of the intelligentsia— Sartre would call it his mystical allegiance to an imaginary freemasonry of artists and thinkers[30]—confirms such an interpretation. "We, and we alone, that is the literati (*les lettrés*) are the people, or better still the tradition of Humanity."[31] The realm of ideas is indeed the only true fatherland to which Flaubert feels committed. This priority of ideas sometimes worried the novelist in him. At the time he was writing *Madame Bovary*, he observed that "the facts are lacking"—meaning thereby that there was little action. But immediately he added: "I claim that *ideas* are facts. . . ."[32] It is not an exaggeration to say that Flaubert fully understood that ideas could be transmuted into dramatic forces. Despite *Madame Bovary* and *L'Éducation sentimentale,* at the center of which still stands a hero or heroine, Flaubert's entire work moves away from the novel of analysis toward the novel of ideas. The brothers Goncourt prophesied that the novel of the future would concern itself more with "what happens in the brain of humanity" than in the heart.[33] They were not alone in this claim for the preeminence of intellect as the authentic tragic hero of our time. Other voices proclaimed much the same, and not only in France. Leonid Andreev, whose novel *Mysl* reveals the tragic immurement of thought by thought, was soon to assert even less equivocally the heroic stature of intellect and its preeminence as a literary subject. This new "hero" is clearly emerging in Flaubert's work. *Bouvard et Pécuchet* establishes—transposing it onto the universalizing level of caricature—the relationship of suffering and intelligence.

"Et, ayant plus d'idées, ils eurent plus de souffrances." This piteous, thoroughly sympathetic observation in chap-

---

30 See the "Introduction" to Baudelaire's *Écrits intimes,* in *Oeuvres complètes.*
31 Flaubert, *Corresp.,* V, 300.   32 Flaubert, *Corresp.,* II, 351.
33 Goncourt, *Journal,* July 16, 1856.

ter 1, the echo of which lingers and becomes more meaningful as the novel progresses, sounds like a derisive corollary of Pascal's famous dictum on the dignity of thought: "Pensée fait la grandeur de l'homme." Impotence and greatness are here intimately bound up. The two friends reenact, in a burlesque mode, the drama of human reason condemned, as Pascal put it, neither to know nor to ignore. This basic duplicity weighs on man like a curse. But it is also this very duplicity which elevates him over the beasts. Bouvard and Pécuchet stand high above their placidly ruminating, bovine neighbors. But they stand alone.

This aloneness is the appanage of the intellectual hero. It is not merely the global feeling of solitude and ennui which accompanies a philosophical despair ("a quoi bon?" they ask in chapter 7), but a separation from the "others," the price they pay for their superiority and for their "difference." Ultimately, they derive satisfaction from the very gap that separates them from the community, while at the same time they concoct utopian projects which would transform the very society in which they feel alienated. In *Bouvard et Pécuchet,* Flaubert seems almost to have written a parable of the modern intellectual. Their persecution goes hand in hand with an irrepressible vocation for subversion. They easily become suspect to the community. Their opinions have an alarming effect. They give utterance to odd ideas on education. They are known to maintain "abominable paradoxes" and "immoral propositions" which, in the opinion of the community, "sapped the foundation" of everything (8). And in the concluding portion of Volume I, of which only the outline exists, the two utopian copying-clerks were to give a public lecture asking for the suppression of the religious and military budget, and calling for the emancipation of women. Evil tongues accuse them of proposing the establishment in Chavignolles of a bordello! No wonder they are arrested for having made attempts on religion and on order, for having roused people to revolt.

An unbounded sadness overcomes the two friends. They feel oppressed by "the heaviness of all the Earth." But it is neither the world's stupidity nor their isolation which produces their most characteristic dejection. Far more distressing is the irremediable gulf which now separates them from their own former innocence. "Something irrevocable had happened" (8). The irrevocable event is the development of their curiosity and intelligence. "Leur tête s'élargissait" (3). Intelligence has exiled them from happiness. The bucolic, idyllic notes of the beginning soon give way to an increasing sense of hopelessness.

Ultimately this sense of futility and despair has its origin in knowledge itself. Man's eternal desire is doomed to eternal frustration. A Faustian anguish invades the two retired copying-clerks. Thought tortures them. Bouvard gloomily notes the inadequacies of materialistic philosophies; Pécuchet is left profoundly disappointed by his adventures into the realm of spiritualism. Both are corroded by doubt, and dream of annihilation. "Oh! le doute! le doute! j'aimerais mieux le néant" (8). The parallel with Goethe's *Faust* is not gratuitous. Faust also knew "that we can know nothing." He, too, knew that whatever knowledge we can achieve is at best not the knowledge we need.

Was man nicht weiss, das eben brauchte man,
Und was man weiss, kann man nicht brauchen.

Flaubert's two unheroic heroes are at times not only disgusted, but literally afraid of further studies. "Ils n'étudiaient plus dans la peur des déceptions" (7). Faust also is nauseated ("Mir ekelt lange vor allem Wissen") at the mere thought of further inquiry into knowledge.

This particular despair is once more related—as it is repeatedly in the novels of Flaubert—to the inability of desire to cope with the proliferation of phenomena. Life is an indigestion, Flaubert once complained to his mistress Louise Colet.[34] Too many love-dreams, too many religions,

34 Flaubert, *Corresp.*, II, 47.

too many fields of knowledge, too many truths . . . Flaubert's protagonists—whether Emma Bovary, Salammbô, Saint Antoine or the two quixotic clerks—are all the victims of a boundless quest. But this flirtation with the limitless is perhaps after all man's only claim to grandeur. The true ambiguity and meaning of *Bouvard et Pécuchet* must probably be assessed in such a "Faustian" perspective. For only someone profoundly suspicious of ideas, but also passionately attracted to them, could have written such an unlikely book. Much of the Romantic and post-Romantic vision is summed up by these Faustian dialectics. The voice of the Devil, the corrosive voice of doubt and pessimism, proclaims that the Dreamer or Thinker (the "Kerl, der spekuliert") is the fool. But another voice, no less insistent, somehow manages to affirm that the pursuit of "Vernunft" and "Wissenschaft"—even in the parody-form of two mediocre clerks' fruitless odyssey—remains man's highest virtue.

❦ 10 ❧

Epilogue

L'ineptie consiste à vouloir conclure.
Flaubert

Few novelists lend themselves better to a study of themes
and techniques; few indeed have placed their techniques
so steadily in the service of themes. Flaubert's patient
weaving of images into elaborate patterns testifies to the
supreme importance of larger motifs in his work. The
stylistic prowess of the craftsman and artificer is rarely
gratuitous. Whether it be the contrapuntal handling of
tenses, the exploitation of the resources of free indirect
discourse, or the artful marshalling of a massive yet supple
prose, the results usually transcend the immediate effect.
Style and form convey some of Flaubert's most haunting
moods: immersion into an oppressive world of unassimilated phenomena; exposure to the mental landscapes of
indefinite flow and destructive immobility; a stubborn
yearning for precisely that which language cannot formulate. Gloom and weariness here nourish a latent idealism.
Flaubert's pessimism feeds his poetic vision.

Neither heroes nor plots determine the meaning of Flaubert's fiction. Among the truly modern features of his
work there is not only the steady perception of the event-
lessness of events, and the ability to transmute triviality
into a destiny, but the example of a novelistic construction
in which the very characters and even the author's point of
view are subservient to thematic developments. This underlying coherence and fertilization of subject by form—to
use Henry James' expression—was possible, however, only
because of the tenacity of Flaubert's obsessions.

For Flaubert is a haunted writer. His so-called clinical and realistic approach, in works such as *Madame Bovary* and *L'Éducation sentimentale*, is intimately connected—not as a banal reaction, but as a tragic poetry of frustration and incipient idealism—to the agitated dreams which make up the substance of *La Tentation de saint Antoine* and, in a grotesque mode, of *Bouvard et Pécuchet*. Flaubert's achievement as a literary artist, and his relevance in historical terms, is largely due to a subtly intuited parallelism between his private obsessions and the social and intellectual tensions of his period. The apolitical Flaubert is thus simultaneously a diagnostician and a committed bard. So also, the critic of Romanticism is at the same time one of its most impressive victims and most glorious heirs.

The compulsive capacity to feed on dreams characterizes the young Gustave. It still is at the heart of the mature writer's work and of his stubborn dedication to art. These dreams assume many shapes: exotic longings, nostalgia for the historic past, mental appetite for superhuman sexual ecstasies, craving for total experience and total knowledge. Imaginary orgies are with him not so much a vicarious indulgence in the senses as a spiritual ebullience and a thirst for the absolute. Idealism and spirituality at times wear the mask of sacrilege, or disguise themselves behind the subterfuges of profanation. Transfer of dreams and self-inflicted cruelty bring him close, occasionally, to the tragic vision of a Proust. Even taste for violence and outright sadism are with him not outbursts of sensationalism, but signs of exasperation in the face of an unattainable ideal. Thus Mâtho, confronted with an impregnable reality, conceives of "terrible and extravagant things."

Dreams that nourish are for him also dreams that undo. Flaubert, much like Baudelaire, is a specialist in self-tortures. His blasphemies against the very conditions of life do not console him of a sense of loss that precedes the event. Frédéric is tired and defeated before having lived—one might say from fear that lived life cannot possibly measure up to his elated view of it. Flaubert's self-punishment often takes the form of a disguised descent into his own past, illustrating the deep and creative ties between memory and imagination. Through his relentless, and apparently unmerciful, treatment of his characters, he thus denounces, persecutes and strangely exalts himself.

Entrapment and failure are his basic terrors. Repeated images of confinement and obstruction alternate with images of horrendous proliferations with which neither the senses nor the intellect can cope. But more devastating still is the omnipresent sense of metaphysical ennui, the obverse of his spiritual longings, whose destructive yawn and paralyzing irony are as intense as Baudelaire's *monstre délicat* dreaming of sanguinous scaffolds. Pervading all of Flaubert's texts, there is a guilt of existing, a hatred of the flesh (and of the spirit too) which find their culmination in the acrid and strident pages of what perhaps stands out as his most revealing book, *La Tentation de saint Antoine*. The asceticism of the saint, much as the asceticism of the author, is not of a resigned and peacefully contemplative nature. It is a tormented and tormenting solitude, a tenacious and almost vengeful exercise in self-maceration.

The theme of sainthood, so central to Flaubert's vision, must thus not be limited to the hackneyed notion of an artist-monk's vocation. The image of the saint corresponds to a persistent algolagnia, to a desire to suffer and mortify himself of which the hermit's "temptations" are the clearest symptoms. The concept of "temptation" is indeed a key to Flaubert, and Valéry's ironic title—"La Tentation de (saint) Flaubert"—is profoundly true. Assailed by insatiable desires, Flaubert knows the whole range of allurements, just as the saint experiences all the avatars of the Tempter. The chain of lethal enticements extends from gross carnality to intellectual relativism, and ultimately to the quest of the absolute. The very eremitism of the saint and of the artist turns out to be a dangerous mental aphrodisiac. The love of claustration becomes a fear of solipsism and perdition.

Desire and death are thus firmly allied in Flaubert's imagination. Abundance, fecundity and multiplication of life are in fact constantly viewed as principles of ruin and decay. Disintegration and dissolution are central themes around which Flaubert develops manifold variations: the processes of time and of aging, the fatigue of living, the death of each instant, the circularity of events, deadly constriction and stasis. But the most characteristic manifestations of undoing are those which, in Flaubert's mind, are linked to the fascination with polymorphism. His obsession with unmanageable heterogeneity and with the gap between all phenomena is responsible for a latent sense of terror. His protagonists thus evolve in an atmosphere of nonassimilated reality, caught in the oppressive routine of a repetitive discontinuity. Saint Antoine's exposure to monsters reveals a concern for the cleavage between the orders of experience. Flaubert and his hero-saint long to discover the underlying link. But the mating of the Chimera and the Sphinx remains an eternal impossibility.

Private obsessions are at the heart of the Flaubertian creation. After early experiments such as *Mémoires d'un fou* and *Novembre,* Flaubert may have eschewed overt or literal autobiography. Yet in a deeper sense, one cannot ignore the autobiographical nature of much of his writing. He has not only repeatedly transposed and transmuted personal memories, piously recapturing, in *L'Éducation sentimentale* and in *Un Coeur simple* for instance, his most precious love-dreams and his fondest childhood recollections; even more significantly, he has given literary life to the most intimate motifs and hidden symbols, largely unaware perhaps of the self-revealing nature of protagonists such as Saint Julien and Saint Antoine.

This subconscious, symbolic autobiography deals with a spiritual reality rather than with material facts. It dramatizes a metaphysical malaise and, through attraction to excess, stresses the awareness of incommunicability or—more ironically—of false communion. Flaubert's pessimism is not the product of a petty, peevish disposition; it is an expression of indignation in the face of a reality so cluttered that it leaves no room for meaning.

The anguished craving for significance is the obverse of the famous symptom of *bovarysme*: the desire to see oneself other than as one is. This search for meaning is the positive aspect of the disease. Flaubert's pessimism thus proves to be of an idealistic nature, and results in the unremitting opposition of art to life. Flaubert's basic anti-Rousseauistic stand makes him a spiritual heir to Sade and a brother to Baudelaire. He would unquestionably subscribe to the latter's "Éloge du maquillage" which proposes the view that virtue and beauty are "unnatural," that they are the arduous products of art and artifice. The pessimism of Flaubert quite logically leads to a cult of Art, to the extolling of Art's redemptive power. The very fear of polymorphism paradoxically implies a glorification of Form. It is in this sense that one could say that, although no novel of Flaubert is literally speaking a "novel of the artist," the true hero of all literary creation, according to Flaubert, can be only the author himself.

"Indignation alone keeps me going," he confided to Edmond de Goncourt.[1] This need and talent for sustained anger is not merely private or metaphysical. Flaubert's exasperation extends to collective issues. Wrath is a chief component of his social diagnoses. Much—perhaps too much—has been made of Flaubert's resentment of bourgeois vices and foibles. If he is, in the words of Barbey d'Aurevilly, "a locomotive of hatred,"[2] if he sees himself as the "bourgeoisophobus" par excellence, this cannot be interpreted narrowly as an exasperation against the materialism of an Homais. What Flaubert denounces is the climate of an entire community which pathetically and criminally betrayed every ideal during its aborted Revolution. Roque, the bloodthirsty and merciless murderer of the

---

[1] Goncourt, *Journal*, X, 123. Complete citations for all notes may be found in the Bibliography.
[2] Barbey d'Aurevilly, "Gustave Flaubert," in *Le Roman contemporain*, p. 134.

imprisoned insurrectionist, is in this respect far more representative than Homais.

In fact, Flaubert's concern is not so much with a given society as with a civilization sick with hate and false values. Or rather, it is with the very conditions of a culture, caught between the uncompromising claims of science and religion, suffering from surfeit, constipation, sterile relativism and a general collapse of values. François Mauriac felt that Flaubert was the victim of an anti-Christian period which had slandered human nature.[3] Flaubert might not have cared to put it in theological terms; but certainly his denunciations of emptiness, false idols and sacrilegious denial of beauty are of a tragic and prophetic nature.

The tragic spirit is here directly dependent on intellectual awareness. Flaubert's taste for erudition serves as a constant reminder that the real drama is played out at the level of ideas. We may not agree with Edmund Wilson that Flaubert was "one of the great minds of his time."[4] In subtlety as well as in systematic thinking others outclass him. He has neither the intuition of a Stendhal nor the capacity for abstractions of a Balzac. And yet his work, more profoundly than theirs, explores the suffering of the mind as it struggles with its own dreams and with the snares of reality. If Flaubert is fascinated with what he calls the "comique d'idées," it is because he knows that ideas are dramatic forces. Faustian motifs occur in his earliest literary exercises and culminate in the final version of the *Tentation de saint Antoine* and in the posthumous *Bouvard et Pécuchet*. No French novelist of the nineteenth century has more movingly evoked the erosive potential of thought. Balzac's mad geniuses embody in a more spectacular way the principle of self-destruction inherent in all intellectual effort. But theirs is the disease of genius; their suicide, insanity and martyrdom are justified by a demonic greatness, by a Promethean pride in creation and in defeat.

3 Mauriac, *Trois Grands Hommes devant Dieu*, p. 91.
4 Wilson, "Flaubert's Politics," in *The Triple Thinkers*, p. 103.

Flaubert's work proposes no such Promethean consolation. His tragic sense is suffused with the gloom of the very absence of tragedy. His artistic achievement is in large part due to the exploitation of a genre which, because of its temporal and psychological possibilities, lends itself to the poetic evocation of the hum of life and of the tasteless taste of existence. But this poetry is deeply moving. Even the world of banality takes on a pathetic meaning; it is against this background that Flaubert's lyricism affirms itself. And it is not only a question of the survival of poetry within a trite and even sordid framework. If clichés fill Flaubert's work, if erosion rather than climax and catastrophe is its most characteristic mode, this is because the "untragic" tragedy stems not from a sense of crisis but from a climate of dissatisfaction and fundamental frustration. The sadness and the beauty of loss are at the heart of Flaubert's literary creation. Better than any contemporary, Flaubert was spiritually equipped to understand the noble melancholy of Renan's "Prière sur l'Acropole": "Tout n'est ici-bas que symbole et que songe. Les dieux passent comme les hommes. . . ."

Flaubert proudly viewed himself as the last of the troubadours. He sensed that he was one of the late, but most imposing manifestations of the literary phenomenon known as Romanticism. He called himself a "débris d'un monde disparu," a "vieux fossile du romantisme."[5] And *La Tentation de saint Antoine*, a book he carried in his mind for over thirty years, is a true summa of Romantic themes and tensions. But if he is, in a sense, a splendid crepuscular figure, he also stands at the threshold of modern literature, as a direct link between Romanticism and our own visions of reality. The oppressive heterogeneity of phenomena, the fragmented immediacy of experience, the constant fading or alteration of forms, the disappearance of the conventional polarity of object and subject—all these were to become central assumptions as well as tragic motifs in twen-

[5] Flaubert, *Lettres inédites à Tourgueneff*, p. 29.

tieth-century writing. Similarly, Flaubert's awareness of Time as a qualitative, elastic and subjective principle of erosion, but also as a regenerative and liberating force, ushers in modern experiments in fiction. Long before Proust, Flaubert intuited that Time was a destructive, but also alchemical agent, marking the death of each instant, and yet redeeming that death through memory and the imagination. The double ending of *L'Éducation sentimentale*, despite its apparent hopelessness and cynicism, thus effectively reclaims a whole life of defeats and lost opportunities.

Finally, it is the modern crisis of language that Flaubert diagnoses and translates into a subject for literature. Language with him becomes its own denouncer. He is aware not merely of the inadequateness of language in coping with our dreams, but of the basic rift between the sacred "word" of the literary artist and the words of social and political intercourse perpetually subject to imprecision, inflation and corruption. The breakdown of language under the degrading impact of journalism, advertisement and political slogans parallels the breakdown of a culture over-inflated with unassimilated data. Both ultimately lead to the incoherence of a Lucky in Beckett's *Waiting for Godot*— a play which, in its debunking and distorting way, reënacts the drama of intellectual and moral bankruptcy depicted in *Bouvard et Pécuchet*.

Despite his chronic grumblings and utterances of despair, Flaubert loved nothing better, however, than the challenges and even the impossibilities of his art. "If there were no difficulties, where would be the fun?" he confided to Turgenev.[6] His approach is basically that of the experimenter who, every time, enjoys the new problem he forces himself to solve against all possible odds. The notion of art as a defiant experimentation is of course eminently "modern."[7]

[6] Flaubert, *Lettres inédites à Tourgueneff*, p. 118.
[7] Harry Levin puts it very well: "His self-conscious 'need for metamorphoses,' for exhausting subjects, experimenting with forms, and outdoing himself along with his predecessors, may well mark the

And it would be tempting to conclude on such a note. One might rejoice in Flaubert's contemporary relevance, invoke the *roman nouveau* or Malraux's notion of the "personnage significatif," toy with the idea that Flaubert created the first nonfigurative fiction, list the avant-garde writers he anticipated, speculate on the cinematographic qualities of his vision or on his ontological approach. Such games might, however, kindle Flaubert's ire in the Elysian fields where he no doubt walks *in luogo aperto, luminoso e alto,* and continues to be filled with lusty indignation. For has he not warned his future critics? *"L'ineptie consiste à vouloir conclure."*[8]

---

effectual beginning of what we now call modernism in literature" (*The Gates of Horn*, p. 272).
[8] Flaubert, *Corresp.*, II, 239.

Bibliography

The body of Flaubert criticism is immense; to list all the studies consulted would be a pointless display. The following bibliography is limited strictly to the works cited in the text. Dates refer to the editions which I have consulted.

Auerbach, Erich. *Mimesis*. New York: Doubleday Anchor Books, 1957.

Bachelard, Gaston. *La Poétique de l'espace*. Paris: Presses Universitaires de France, 1957.

Balzac, Honoré de. "Des Artistes," *La Silhouette*, February 25, March 11, April 22, 1830. Reprinted in *Oeuvres complètes*. Paris: Conard, 1912–1940, vol. XXXVIII.

———. *Histoire des Treize*. Paris: Lévy, 1872. In *Oeuvres complètes, op.cit.*, vol. XXII.

———. *Louis Lambert*. Bibliothèque de la Pléiade, vol. X. Paris: Gallimard, 1950.

Banville, Théodore de. *Critiques*. Paris: Charpentier, 1917.

———. *Les Stalactites*. Paris: Didier, 1942.

Barbey d'Aurevilly, J. "Gustave Flaubert." In *Le Roman contemporain*. Paris: Lemerre, 1902.

Bart, Benjamin. *Flaubert's Landscape Descriptions*. Ann Arbor: University of Michigan Press, 1956.

———. "The Moral of Flaubert's *Saint Julien*," *Romanic Review*, February 1947, pp. 23–33.

Barthes, Roland. *Le Degré zéro de l'écriture*. Paris: Éditions du Seuil, 1953.

Baudelaire, Charles. *Correspondance générale*. Paris: Conard, 1947.

———. *Oeuvres complètes*. Bibliothèque de la Pléiade, Paris: Gallimard, 1961.

Benedetto, Luigi Foscolo. *Le Origini di "Salammbô": Studio sul realismo storico*. Firenze: Bemporad e Figlio, 1920.

Bertrand, Louis. *Gustave Flaubert: avec fragments inédits*. Paris: Mercure de France, 1912.

THE NOVELS OF FLAUBERT

Bollème, Geneviève. *La Leçon de Flaubert.* Paris: Julliard, 1964.

Borel, Pétrus. *Champavert: les contes immoraux.* Paris: Éditions Montbrun, 1947.

———. *Madame Putiphar.* Paris: Willem, 1877.

Bourget, Paul. *Le Disciple.* Paris: Nelson, 1911.

———. "Gustave Flaubert." In *Essais de psychologie contemporaine.* Paris: Plon, 1924.

Brombert, Victor. *The Intellectual Hero: Studies in the French Novel, 1880–1955.* Philadelphia and New York: Lippincott, 1961.

———. *Stendhal et la voie oblique.* Paris: Presses Universitaires de France, 1954.

———. "Victor Hugo, la prison et l'espace," *Revue des Sciences Humaines,* January-March 1965, pp. 59–79.

Bruneau, Jean. *Les Débuts littéraires de Gustave Flaubert, 1831–1845.* Paris: Colin, 1962.

Brunetière, Ferdinand. "Après une visite au Vatican," *Revue des Deux Mondes,* January 1, 1895, pp. 97–118.

———. *Le Roman naturaliste.* Paris: Calmann-Lévy, 1892.

Cigada, Sergio. "L'Episodio del Lebbroso in 'Saint Julien L'Hospitalier' di Flaubert," *Aevum,* September-December 1957, pp. 465–491.

Cuvillier-Fleury, Alfred Auguste. "La Satire dans le roman," *Journal des Débats,* December 14, 1869.

Dariosecq, Luc. "A Propos de Loulou," *The French Review,* February 1958, pp. 322–324.

Demorest, D. L. *L'Expression figurée et symbolique dans l'oeuvre de Gustave Flaubert.* Paris: Les Presses modernes, 1931.

Descharmes, René. " 'Saint-Julien L'Hospitalier' et 'Pécopin,' " *Revue Biblio-Iconographique,* 1905, pp. 1–7, 67–75.

Du Camp, Maxime. *Souvenirs littéraires.* Paris: Hachette, 1882–1883. 2 vols.

Durry, Marie-Jeanne. *Flaubert et ses projets inédits.* Paris: Nizet, 1950.

Faguet, Émile. *Flaubert*. Paris: Hachette, 1906.

Fairlie, Alison. *Flaubert: Madame Bovary*. London: Arnold, 1962.

Fischer, E. W. "La Spirale," *La Table Ronde*, April 1958, pp. 96–124.

Flaubert, Gustave. *Bouvard et Pécuchet*. Paris: Société Les Belles Lettres, 1945. 2 vols.

———. *Correspondance*. Paris: Conard, 1926–1933. 9 vols.; and *Supplément*. Paris: Conard, 1954. 4 vols.

———. "Lettres inédites de Flaubert à Sainte-Beuve," presented by B. F. Bart, *Revue d'Histoire Littéraire de la France*, July-September 1964, pp. 427–435.

———. *Lettres inédites à Tourgueneff*. Monaco: Éditions du Rocher, 1946.

———. *Madame Bovary—Nouvelle version précédée des scénarios inédits*, ed. Jean Pommier and Gabrielle Leleu. Paris: Corti, 1949.

———. *Notes de voyages*. 2 vols. In *Oeuvres complètes*, *op.cit.*

———. *Oeuvres complètes*. Paris: Conard, 1910. 18 vols.

———. *Oeuvres de jeunesse inédites*. Paris: Conard, 1910. 3 vols.

———. *Par les Champs et par les grèves*. Paris: Charpentier, 1924.

———. "La Spirale," ed. E. W. Fischer, *La Table Ronde*, April 1958, pp. 96–98.

François, Alexis. "Flaubert, Maxime Du Camp et la Révolution de 1848," *Revue d'Histoire Littéraire de la France*, 1938, pp. 183–204.

Friedrich, Hugo. *Die Klassiker des französischen Romans*. Leipzig: Bibliographisches Institut, 1939.

Froehner, Wilhelm, "Le Roman archéologique en France. G. Flaubert," *Revue Contemporaine*, December 31, 1862; February 15, 1863.

Gaultier, Jules de. *Le Bovarysme. La Psychologie dans l'oeuvre de Flaubert*. Paris: Cerf, 1892.

Gautier, Théophile. *Emaux et camées*. Paris: Didier, 1852.

———. *Les Jeunes-France*. Paris: Charpentier, 1875.

Gautier, Théophile. "Salammbô," In *L'Orient*. Paris: Charpentier et Fasquelle, 1902. 2 vols.

Gérard-Gailly, Émile. *Flaubert et "Les Fantômes de Trouville."* Paris: La Renaissance du Livre, 1930.

Gide, André. *Journal*. Bibliothèque de la Pléiade. Paris: Gallimard, 1939.

Girard, René. *Mensonge romantique et vérité romanesque*. Paris: Grasset, 1961.

Giraud, Jean. "La Genèse d'un chef-d'oeuvre—'La Légende de Saint Julien L'Hospitalier,'" *Revue d'Histoire Littéraire de la France*, 1919, pp. 87–93.

Giraud, Raymond. *The Unheroic Hero in the Novels of Stendhal, Balzac and Flaubert*. New Brunswick, N.J.: Rutgers University Press, 1957.

——. ed. *Flaubert: A Collection of Critical Essays*. Englewood Cliffs, N.J.: Prentice-Hall, 1964.

Goncourt, Edmond and Jules de. *Journal*. Monaco: Éditions de L'Imprimerie Nationale de Monaco, 1956–1958. 22 vols.

Gothot-Mersch, Claudine. *La Genèse de Madame Bovary*. Paris: Corti, 1966.

Gourmont, Rémy de. *Le Problème du style*. Paris: Mercure de France, 1907.

Grappin, Henri. "Le Mysticisme poétique et l'imagination de Gustave Flaubert," *La Revue de Paris*, December 1 and 15, 1912, pp. 609–629, 849–870.

Guisan, Gilbert. "Flaubert et la Révolution de 1848," *Revue d'Histoire Littéraire de la France*, 1958, pp. 183–204.

Huysmans, Joris Karl. *A Rebours*. Paris: Charpentier, 1884.

James, Henry. "Gustave Flaubert." In *Notes on Novelists*. New York: Scribner, 1914.

Jasinski, René. "Sur le 'Saint Julien L'Hospitalier' de Flaubert," *Revue d'Histoire de la Philosophie*, April 15, 1935, pp. 156–172.

Kenner, Hugh. *Flaubert, Joyce and Beckett—The Stoic Comedians*. Boston: Beacon Press, 1962.

Lapp, John C. "Art and Hallucination in Flaubert," *French Studies*, October 1956, pp. 322–334.

Leleu, Gabrielle, with Pommier, Jean. "Du nouveau sur 'Madame Bovary,'" *Revue d'Histoire Littéraire de la France*, July-September 1947, pp. 210–244.

Lemaître, Jules. "Gustave Flaubert." In *Les Contemporains*, 8ème série. Paris: Société Française d'Imprimerie et de Librairie, 1918.

Le Poittevin, Alfred. *Une Promenade de Bélial et oeuvres inédites*. Paris: Les Presses Françaises, 1924.

Levin, Harry. *The Gates of Horn: A Study of Five French Realists*. New York: Oxford University Press, 1963.

Lips, Marguerite. *Le Style indirect libre*. Paris: Payot, 1926.

Lombard, Alfred. *Flaubert et Saint Antoine*. Paris: Attinger, 1934.

Lubbock, Percy. *The Craft of Fiction*. New York: Cape and Smith, 1929.

Lukács, Georg. *The Historical Novel*. London: Merlin Press, 1962.

Madeleine, Jacques. "Les Differents 'États' de 'La Tentation de Saint Antoine,'" *Revue d'Histoire Littéraire de la France*, 1908, pp. 620–641.

Mankin, Paul. "Additional Irony in 'Un Coeur simple,'" *The French Review*, February 1962, p. 411.

Martino, Pierre. *Parnasse et Symbolisme*. Paris: Colin, 1947.

Maupassant, Guy de. Study on Flaubert for the edition of Flaubert's works edited by Quentin. Reprinted in the Conard edition of *Madame Bovary* (Flaubert, *Oeuvres complètes, op.cit.*).

Mauriac, François. *Trois grands hommes devant Dieu*. Paris: Hartmann, 1947.

Mazel, Henri. "Les Trois Tentations de Saint Antoine," *Mercure de France*, December 15, 1921, pp. 626–643.

Mein, Margaret. "Flaubert, a Precursor of Proust," *French Studies*, July 1963, pp. 218–237.

Murry, John Middleton. *Countries of the Mind*. New York and London: Oxford University Press, 1931.

Nadeau, Maurice. "Sur 'Bouvard et Pécuchet,'" *Les Lettres Nouvelles*, May-June 1965, pp. 67–87.

Neuenschwander-Naef, Claudia. *Vorstellungswelt und Realität in Flauberts "Bouvard et Pécuchet."* Winterthur: 1959.

Pommier, Jean. "Noms et prénoms dans 'Madame Bovary,' " *Mercure de France*, June 1949, pp. 244–264.

———. with Leleu, Gabrielle. *See* Leleu, Gabrielle.

Poulet, Georges. "Flaubert." In *Les Métamorphoses du cercle*. Paris: Plon, 1961.

———. "Timelessness and Romanticism," *Journal of the History of Ideas*, 1954, pp. 3–22.

———. *Studies in Human Time.* Baltimore: Johns Hopkins Press, 1956.

Proust, Marcel. "A Propos du style de Flaubert." In *Chroniques*. Paris: Éditions de la Nouvelle Revue Française, 1927.

Raitt, A. W. "The Composition of Flaubert's *Saint Julien L'Hospitalier*," *French Studies*, October 1965, pp. 358–372.

Renan, Ernest. *L'Avenir de la Science.* Paris: Calmann-Lévy, 1890.

———. *Prière sur l'Acropole*, ed. Vinaver and Webster. Manchester: Manchester University Press, 1934.

Richard, Jean-Pierre. "La Création de la forme chez Flaubert." In *Littérature et sensation*. Paris: Éditions du Seuil, 1954.

Rousset, Jean. "*Madame Bovary* ou 'le livre sur rien.' " In *Forme et signification*. Paris: Corti, 1962.

Sainte-Beuve, Charles-Augustin. *Causeries du lundi.* Paris: Garnier, 1853–1862, vol. XIII.

———. "Salammbô." In *Nouveaux lundis.* Paris: Lévy, 1865, vol. IV.

Sarraute, Nathalie. "Flaubert le précurseur," *Preuves*, February 1965, pp. 3–11.

Sartre, Jean-Paul. "La Conscience de classe chez Flaubert," *Les Temps Modernes*, May, June 1966, pp. 1,921–1,951; 2,113–2,153.

———. *Critique de la raison dialectique.* Paris: Gallimard, 1960.

———. "Flaubert: du poète à l'artiste," *Les Temps Modernes,* August 1966, pp. 197–253.

———. "Introduction." In *Écrits intimes de Baudelaire.* Paris: Éditions du Point du Jour, 1946.

———. *La Nausée.* Paris: Gallimard, 1938.

———. *Situations.* Paris: Gallimard, 1947–1965.

Schérer, Edmond. Review article of *L'Éducation sentimentale* in *Le Temps,* December 7, 1869.

Schwob, Marcel. "Saint Julien L'Hospitalier." In *Spicilège.* Paris: Au Sans Pareil, 1920.

Seznec, Jean. *Nouvelles Études sur la Tentation de Saint Antoine.* London: Warburg Institute, University of London, 1949.

———. *Les Sources de l'Épisode des Dieux dans la Tentation de Saint Antoine.* Paris: Vrin, 1940.

Spencer, Philip. *Flaubert.* London: Faber and Faber, 1952.

Spinoza, Benedict de. *The Chief Works of Benedict de Spinoza.* London: Bell, 1887. 2 vols.

Steegmuller, Francis. *Flaubert and Madame Bovary.* New York: Viking Press, 1939.

Stoltzfus, Ben. "Point of View in 'Un Coeur simple,'" *The French Review,* October 1961, pp. 19–25.

Taillandier, Saint-René. Review article of *L'Éducation sentimentale, Revue des Deux Mondes,* December 15, 1869.

Tate, Allan. "Techniques of Fiction." In *Collected Essays.* Denver: Swallow, 1959.

Thibaudet, Albert. *Gustave Flaubert.* Paris: Gallimard, 1935.

Thorlby, Anthony. *Gustave Flaubert and the Art of Realism.* New Haven: Yale University Press, 1957.

Trilling, Lionel. "Flaubert's Last Testament," *Partisan Review,* November-December 1953, pp. 605–630.

Turnell, Martin. *The Novel in France.* New York: New Directions, 1951.

Ullmann, Stephen. "Reported Speech and Internal Monologue in Flaubert." In *Style in the French Novel.* Cambridge; At the University Press, 1957.

Valéry, Paul. "La Tentation de (saint) Flaubert." In *Variété V*. Paris: Gallimard, 1944.

Wellek, René. "The Concept of Realism in Literary Scholarship." In *Concepts of Criticism*. New Haven: Yale University Press, 1963.

———. "The Concept of Romanticism in Literary History." In *Concepts of Criticism, op.cit.*

Wilson, Edmond. "The Ambiguity of Henry James." In *The Triple Thinkers*. New York: Harcourt, Brace, 1938.

———. "Flaubert's Politics." In *The Triple Thinkers, op.cit.*

Zola, Émile. "Gustave Flaubert." In *Les Romanciers naturalistes*. Paris: Charpentier, 1890.

Index